MW00607907

MISSION PRESIDENT OR SPY?

DESERET
BOOK

RSC
BYU

MISSION PRESIDENT OR SPY?

The True Story of Wallace F. Toronto, the Czech Mission, and World War II

Mary Jane Woodger

On the cover and interior: Photos of Wallace F. Toronto and family. Courtesy of Daniel Toronto.

Published by the Religious Studies Center, Brigham Young University, Provo, Utah, in cooperation with Deseret Book Company, Salt Lake City.
Visit us at rsc.byu.edu.

Printed in the United States of America by Sheridan Books, Inc.

DESERET BOOK is a registered trademark of Deseret Book Company.
Visit us at DeseretBook.com.

Cover and interior design by Carmen Durland Cole.

ISBN: 978-1-9443-9466-0

Names: Woodger, Mary Jane, author.
Title: Mission president or spy? : the true story of Wallace F. Toronto, the Czech Mission, and World War II / Mary Jane Woodger.
Description: Provo, Utah : Religious Studies Center, Brigham Young University in cooperation with Deseret Book Company, Salt Lake City, [2019] | Includes bibliographical references.
Identifiers: LCCN 2018025574 | ISBN 9781944394660
Subjects: LCSH: Toronto, Wallace Felt. | Mormon missionaries--United States--Biography. | Church of Jesus Christ of Latter-day Saints--Missions--Czechoslovakia--History--20th century. | Mormon Church--Missions--Czechoslovakia--History--20th century. | Czechoslovakia--Church history--20th century. | LCGFT: Biographies.
Classification: LCC BX8695.T67 W66 2019 | DDC 289.3092 [B] --dc23 LC record available at https://lccn.loc.gov/2018025574

CONTENTS

vii Preface

x Events Surrounding the Life of Wallace F. Toronto

1 1. "He Should Stand at the Head of His Race"

11 2. "Character and Grit, . . . Determination and Fortitude"

17 3. "Immersing Himself in Bohemian Life"

29 4. "The Mission Princess"

41 5. "How Can Our Brethren Become More Zealous?"

57 6. Making the Czech People "Mormon Conscious"

69 7. "What a Power We Could Have"

81 8. "How Long Can Peace Last?"

91 9. "Back to the Uncertainty of Czechoslovakia"

109 10. "This Boiling Cauldron of Political Madness"

127 11. "Put the Pieces Back Together"

151 12. "The Little Spy"

167 13. "Satan's Workers"

191 14. "Leader of a Spy Ring"

209 15. "Communism Espouses Religious Freedom!"

217 16. "The Toronto Mission"

225 Index

235 About the Author

PREFACE

Wallace "Wally" Felt Toronto became a pioneering missionary leader for The Church of Jesus Christ of Latter-day Saints among the Slavic people. Serving three missions among the Czechs, he continued as their mission president in absentia for another twenty-five years. He holds the longest term as a mission president: thirty-two years. Born December 9, 1907, in Salt Lake City, Utah, Wally was originally called to serve in the German Mission, but less than a year into his mission he received a transfer, where he joined the first elders to open the Czechoslovak Mission.

At the young age of twenty-seven, just two years after marrying, Wally was called to preside over the Czech Mission. Under his leadership, new cities were opened, conversions continued, and branches of the Church were organized. The Nazi occupation of Czech lands in 1938 and 1939 led to the evacuation of all missionaries including President Toronto and brought the dissolution of the Czech mission during World War II.

After a seven-year hiatus, and much to Toronto's surprise, he and his family were called once again to preside over the mission. With a larger missionary force, the Church expanded even after the February 1948 Communist coup. With the Communist restrictions growing, the young mission president came under more and more scrutiny. By 1950, Wally was considered one of the top wanted spies by the Communists, and both he and his wife were under twenty-four-hour surveillance. In the end, all Czech missionaries were expelled, the registration of the Church was canceled, and faithful Saints were now left without the opportunity even to hold branch meetings.

After returning home, through cryptic letters, Wally kept in touch with the Saints in Czechoslovakia for the next eighteen years serving as the Czech mission president in absentia. In 1964, President David O. McKay assigned the Torontos to visit the Czech Saints as tourists, and the next year the prophet asked Wally to return alone to meet with the ministry officials. He did so but was arrested following his interview on television during a huge national sports festival. Wally's request for Church recognition was rejected by the Czech government, and he was deported at the German border. Wallace Toronto would remain president of the Czech Mission until his death from cancer on January 10, 1968, in Salt Lake City.

As I began to write this biography, I knew from the enormous amount of data I had collected I could write several volumes about this man's life and still never fully tell the whole story. Such a portrait may be frustrating to those who would like a more critical treatise, but the full life of Wallace F. Toronto cannot possibly be told in these limited pages. It is my hope that Wally's courage and great ability to love others, which he became known for, will carry from these pages into the hearts of the readers.

Acknowledgments

Any published book is collaboration of effort. I express heartfelt appreciation to Alexander L. Baugh, Thomas A. Wayment, Joany Pinegar, Devan Jensen, Brent Nordgren, Carmen Durland Cole, Emily Strong, Megan Judd, and administrators at the Religious Studies Center at Brigham Young University for research support, design, and editing. I would also like to thank the staff at the Church History Library for their service. I wish to express special thanks to Daniel Toronto for supplying journals and other documents from his grandfather's papers that added Wally's own voice to this volume. I am also indebted to the entire Toronto family, including Marion Toronto Miller, Judith Toronto Richards, Ed and Norma Morrell, Bob Toronto, David Toronto, and Scott Miller, for sharing their father and grandfather with me and to the many former Czechoslovakian missionaries that provided firsthand knowledge of their former mission president.

I am very thankful for Kalli K Searle, my student assistant, who interviewed former Toronto missionaries and took care of the huge task of typing material included in this manuscript. She has been one of the most cheerful, dependable, and intelligent of assistants to bless my office. Most especially, I express deepest appreciation to student editor Allison Noelle Wiser, who grew to love Wally in the same way that I did and who applied her talents to the polishing of this volume.

Events Surrounding the Life of Wallace F. Toronto

September 20, 1848	Guiseppe Taranto arrives in the Salt Lake Valley.
June 14, 1905	Albert Toronto and Etta Felt are married.
December 9, 1907	Wally is born in Salt Lake City, Utah.
October 1928	Begins service as missionary in the German Mission.
June 1929	One of the first elders is transferred to open the Czechoslovak Mission.
September 15, 1933	Wally marries Martha Sharp in the Salt Lake City Temple.
1936–39	Wally serves as president of the Czechoslovak Mission of The Church of Jesus Christ of Latter-day Saints.
September 1938	Evacuates Czechoslovakia with family and missionaries to Switzerland.
November 1938	Calls local leaders to take charge of branches until the missionaries can return.
December 1938	Returns to Czechoslovakia with family and missionaries.
March 15, 1939	Nazis occupy Czechoslovakia.
July 1939	Four missionaries arrested by the Gestapo, held in prison for forty-four days.
August 1939	Wally evacuates again with family and missionaries before outbreak of World War II.
September 1, 1939	World War II begins; Wally calls Josef Roubíček to preside as mission president in his absence.
June 1940	Wally graduates with an MA in sociology from the University of Utah.
1942–45	Works as director of Red Cross for Utah.
1946–68	Reopens the Czechoslovak Mission, serving as president.
February 1948	Communist coup in Czechoslovakia; government begins controlling all businesses, industries, churches, and schools.
March 1, 1950	Martha and children leave Czechoslovakia.

March 1950	Last of LDS missionaries are expelled by Communists.
March 30, 1950	Wally leaves Czechoslovakia and heads to Basel, Switzerland.
April 6, 1950	Governmental decree terminates the legal entity of the Church in Czechoslovakia.
May 1950	Wally returns home to Salt Lake City.
1950–64	Serves on the general board of the Young Men's Mutual Improvement Association.
1951–68	Heads the Anti-Cancer Society in Utah.
1963	Travels to Northern Europe and Germany with the general board of the Mutual Improvement Association to hold a series of conventions.
December 1964	President McKay assigns Torontos to visit the Czech Saints as tourists.
January 1965	Wally returns with Martha to Czechoslovakia to aid and counsel Church members.
July 1965	Wally returns for the last time to Czechoslovakia to visit government authorities and attempt to reestablish the mission.
1966–67	Serves as president of the Utah School Boards Association.
January 10, 1968	Dies in Salt Lake City at age sixty.
November 14, 1985	The Church of Jesus Christ of Latter-day Saints begins formally requesting official recognition in Czechoslovakia.
October–December 1989	"Velvet Revolution" of 1989; Vaclav Havel becomes president of free Czechoslovakia.
February 21, 1990	The Church of Jesus Christ of Latter-day Saints is officially recognized by the Czech government.
January 1, 1993	"Velvet Divorce" of clashing governments; Slovakia declares independence from the Czech Republic.

1 "HE SHOULD STAND AT THE HEAD OF HIS RACE"

Nothing in the birth of Wallace "Wally" F. Toronto in Salt Lake City on December 9, 1907, suggested he would have any connection with Czechoslovakia nor achieve any greatness. His birth was a normal one in the obscurity of the Rocky Mountains. The only inkling that he would become great, and had a destiny to fulfill, came from two generations earlier because of his grandfather Giuseppe Efisio Taranto.

Giuseppe Taranto, the son of Francesco Taranto and Angela Fazio, was born on June 25, 1816, in Cagliari on the island of Sardinia. Sometime in his early twenties, he joined the Mediterranean Merchant Service, which was a commercial shipping company that often took him to foreign ports around the world. At one point, he found himself in New Orleans and decided to stay and work there for a while on American ships. He frequently sailed to other states on the coast such as Massachusetts and New York.[1] He worked hard and saved his money,

1. James A. Toronto, "Giuseppe Efisio Taranto: Odyssey from Sicily to Salt Lake City," in *Pioneers in Every Land*, ed. Bruce A. Van Orden, D. Brent Smith, and Everett Smith Jr. (Salt Lake City: Bookcraft, 1997), 126–27.

rather than spend it "on wine and women" as other sailors did, so he could send it back to his family in Italy.[2] During one journey to New York City, he began to fear that someone might steal his money once he got there.[3]

That night, he had a dream where a man approached him and told him to give his money to "Mormon Brigham." He told him that if he did so, he would be blessed for it. Once the ship anchored at the harbor, Giuseppe went to work finding "Mormon Brigham," but nobody he asked seemed to know anything about him.[4] Though he went on with his life the same as usual, the dream would stay with him and prepare Giuseppe and later his grandson's participation in not only a religion but an entire way of life.

From New York, Giuseppe went to Boston, where he started working for an Italian shipping firm, earning enough to purchase a small boat of his own and start his own business. "He made a living by buying fruits and vegetables from the wholesale vendors in Boston and then selling them to the large ships at anchor in the harbor."[5]

In Boston, Giuseppe first learned of some Mormon missionaries preaching about "the gospel as restored through Joseph Smith only a few years before." When Giuseppe heard the truth, he embraced it, and in 1843, at the age of twenty-seven, he was baptized by Elder George B. Wallace, becoming "the first native Italian and also the first Roman Catholic to join The Church of Jesus Christ of Latter-day Saints." The missionaries counseled him to join with the Saints in Nauvoo as soon as possible. But he was doing so well financially that he decided instead to continue increasing his profits to send back to his "poverty-stricken family in Sicily."

---

2. Samuel W. Taylor, *Nightfall at Nauvoo* (New York City: Avon Books, 1971), 356.
3. Toronto, "Giuseppe Efisio Taranto," 127.
4. John R. Young, *Memoirs of John R. Young* (Salt Lake City: Deseret News, 1920), 47.
5. Toronto, "Giuseppe Efisio Taranto," 127; see also Alan F. Toronto, Maria T. Moody, and James A. Toronto, comps., *Joseph Toronto (Giuseppe Efisio Taranto)* (Salt Lake City: Toronto Family Organization, 1983), 7.

Giuseppe remained in Boston for about another year and a half, coping with the new language and culture. In an effort to fit in a little more, he anglicized his name to Joseph Toronto. The spelling change in his surname resulted from his illiteracy. Like most Sicilians of his age (or any foreigner for that matter), he could not read or write his natural dialect and had someone else write his name down for him, spelling it the way it sounded in English. Hence, the new name stuck for the following generations.

One irony of Joseph's life was that though he was a highly skilled seaman and had spent most of his life in ships on the water, he did not know how to swim. He might have stayed in Boston for much longer had he not experienced a nearly fatal accident in the spring of 1845. One day, while transporting a load of fruits and vegetables in the Boston Harbor, his boat collided with a larger ship and capsized. He lost most of his cargo and almost his life from drowning. The event marked a traumatic and terrifying turning point in his life, for because of the accident he decided to heed the counsel of the elders and go to Nauvoo, Illinois. Subsequently, he sold his small vessel and his business and headed west.

By the time Joseph Toronto immigrated to Nauvoo, the capstone of the Nauvoo Temple had just been put into place. As work inside the temple progressed, persecution and the Saints' lack of financial means to provide food and clothing for the workmen slowed the work. Some men working on the temple were even barefoot and shirtless. "When the situation became critical, President Brigham Young instructed those in charge of the temple funds to deal out all the remaining provisions with the promise that the Lord would give them more."[6] On Sunday, July 6, 1845, he announced that the "work on the temple would have to cease." The tithing funds were depleted. Even though he had appealed to Saints who were traveling from overseas to sacrifice some of their money "to finish the Lord's house," their contributions had not produced as much as the prophet had hoped for. "Work on the temple

6. Toronto, Moody, and Toronto, *Joseph Toronto*, 8.

would have to stop, with the Mormons endangering their salvation thereby"[7] (see D&C 124:31–33).

Joseph Toronto, who was present in the congregation, was deeply moved by the words of the prophet and "determined to do whatever he could to help move the work along." The very next afternoon, President Young met with him in his office and recorded in his diary the events that transpired. "Brother Joseph Toronto handed to me $2,500 in gold and said he wanted to give himself and all he had to the upbuilding of the church and kingdom of God; he said he should henceforth look to me for protection and counsel. I laid the money at the feet of the bishops."[8] William Clayton recorded that $2,599.75 was the exact sum that Joseph gave to the Church—all in gold that was wrapped in old rags and tin boxes.[9] As Joseph donated his hard-earned life savings to the temple, Brigham Young blessed him that "he should stand at the head of his race and that neither he nor his family should ever want for bread."[10] That promise would extend through the next two generations, eventually even down to Wallace Toronto, his grandson.

When Joseph had first arrived in Nauvoo, some Saints were prejudiced against him because he was the only Italian they had ever met. His olive skin, jet-black hair, and dark eyes yielded condescending remarks from a vast number of Saints, who were predominately Northern European. Joseph never exhibited any knowledge that he was not accepted. Instead, he would flash a genuine smile to everyone he met. "He was [as] friendly as a puppy dog. He loved to bear his testimony . . . and didn't seem to notice that as the spirit came upon him and he became emotional about the gospel, his accent became thicker and thicker, until the Saints ducked their heads with tongue in cheek to repress smiles." Those feelings of bias, however, dispelled completely

7. Taylor, *Nightfall at Nauvoo*, 356.

8. Toronto, "Giuseppe Efisio Taranto," 129.

9. William Clayton, "Nauvoo Diaries and Personal Writings," Nauvoo, July 8, 1945, http://www.boap.org/LDS/Early-Saints/clayton-diaries.

10. Toronto, Moody, and Toronto, *Joseph Toronto*, 8.

when the Saints witnessed Joseph's act of financial generosity and sacrifice. One Latter-day Saint in particular, Dr. John M. Bernhisel, had been deeply prejudiced against the young Italian convert. But he was present at Joseph's meeting with President Young and watched as Joseph "fumbled under his shirt [to draw] forth [his] money belt." As he opened it and spilled the gold on the table, immediately "Bernhisel felt sheepish at his superior attitude toward a man because of his olive complexion and strange accent."[11]

After Joseph's donation, a strong relationship grew between him and the prophet. Joseph "became a permanent member of the [Young] family." And, once he arrived in Salt Lake City, he began working for President Young.[12] However, this employment was short-lived when on April 29, 1849, President Young informed Joseph of his desire to send him "to his native country . . . to start the work of gathering from the nation." During general conference that next October, President Heber C. Kimball called Lorenzo Snow and Joseph Toronto to serve a mission in Italy. On this mission, Joseph was able to visit his home in Palermo and share the gospel with his family. By the time he returned to Salt Lake City in August 1851, he had even baptized several members of his own family.[13]

The prophet continued to provide for Joseph once he got back to Utah and was even instrumental in finding him a wife. As Joseph was beginning to establish a homestead, President Young called him into his office one day and announced, "There is a nice Welsh convert named Eleanor Jones, and I think that you should marry her." Following the prophet's counsel as always, Joseph married Eleanor in the fall of 1853, and Zina D. Young provided a beautiful reception for them at the Lion House.[14]

---

11. Taylor, *Nightfall at Nauvoo*, 356.
12. Young, *Memoirs of John R. Young*, 47; and James Toronto, "Joseph Toronto" *Pioneer* 62, no. 1 (2014): 15.
13. Toronto, "Joseph Toronto," 15–16.
14. Toronto, Moody, and Toronto, *Joseph Toronto*, 16.

After almost twenty years of marriage, the Torontos hired a young Swedish convert named "Anna Catharina Johansson to live with them and help care for the family." When Eleanor and Anna became very close, Eleanor suggested that Joseph take Anna as a second wife because she had no family of her own to support her. "Reluctantly, and only after much persuasion from Eleanor" and an endorsement from the prophet, Joseph finally agreed. On January 22, 1872, he took Anna's hand in marriage at the Endowment House. At the time, he was fifty-six years old, and she was thirty. From that union would come Albert Toronto, the father of Wallace F. Toronto. Albert was born on February 4, 1878, in Salt Lake City. Just five years later, Joseph Toronto would pass away.[15]

Albert Toronto

As a young adult, Albert Toronto attended the University of Deseret, graduating with a major in business. Following his father's example, he served a mission in Germany from 1899 to 1902. Early in his mission, he experienced the blessing of the gift of tongues. He had barely arrived in his mission area, having not yet learned German, when he and his companion began tracting. For some reason, his companion had to leave him for a moment. While his companion was gone, Albert struck up a discussion with a German stranger. Albert was amazed to see that the stranger understood what he was saying, and he understood the man's German just as well. As the two conversed, Albert began to teach him about the gospel. When his companion returned, he suddenly found that he could no longer speak or understand German. The companion then continued teaching the man where Albert had left off. This man eventually joined the Church. Thereafter, Albert

15. Toronto, Moody, and Toronto, *Joseph Toronto*, 17.

picked up the German language quickly.[16] Albert's propensity for languages would be passed down to his son also.

When Albert returned from his mission, he found employment at Barton's Clothing Store in Salt Lake City as a cashier. Through his experiences there, he learned how to maintain a neat and attractive appearance, which was especially beneficial to his social life. In 1902 he attended a party with his sister. The siblings did not stay very long, but they made sure that they met everyone there before they left—including one Etta Felt. When Etta returned home from the party that night, she told her mother that she had found a young man she wanted "to marry someday, if he would have her. 'I've never heard you say anything like that before,' her Mother said. 'I've never met anyone like him before,' Etta answered."[17]

Etta Felt

Etta was born in Salt Lake City on February 21, 1883, to Joseph Henry and Alma Elizabeth Mineer Felt. Her schooling started when she was eight years old. Just five years later, when she was only thirteen, she graduated from the eighth grade. Most of her classmates "claimed she was the teacher's pet," but she declared that she had received her "class promotions" because she worked so hard. After graduation, she went to work at a cracker factory, receiving $3.50 a week. At age fourteen, she got a job at a telephone company, gaining a small improvement in wages: fifteen dollars a month. At the time, the minimum age to be hired by the phone company was fifteen, and Etta was a bit too young. Nevertheless, the chief operator liked her and decided to test her to see if she could do the job. One of the tests required that the applicant's arms be "long enough to reach to the outer edges of the switch board." Luckily, Etta's arms passed the test. She was also

16. Joseph Y. Toronto, Maria T. Moody, James A. Toronto, comps., *The Story of Albert and Etta Toronto* (Albert Toronto Family Organization, February 21, 1983), 1, 5.

17. Toronto, Moody, and Toronto, *Story of Albert and Etta Toronto*, 1, 15.

fairly tall and looked older than her age. As such, the operator said, "Maybe if you put your hair on top of your head like the older girls and lengthen your skirts, you can pass for 15." She did as she was instructed and was hired.[18]

In 1903, Etta was called to serve on her stake Sunday School board. When she attended her first board meeting, who should appear but the young man she had met at the party two years earlier, Albert Toronto. After the board meeting ended, Albert asked her if he could walk Etta home, and from that time forward, the two were inseparable. John R. Winder officiated their marriage on June 14, 1905. The couple then moved to Portland, Oregon, where Albert sold insurance and Etta worked in the Utah booth at the World's Fair. After three months of an extended honeymoon in Oregon, they returned to Salt Lake City and moved in with Albert's mother in the Toronto home on A Street. It was not uncommon at that time for newlyweds to live with their parents because it was an "old country" tradition.[19]

For many years, Etta cotaught an institute class with another teacher, Lowell Bennion. The University Ward had many students attending and there would sometimes be as many as forty or fifty students in the class. For Etta, it felt like a great challenge to provide the students with lessons that would benefit them. She must have succeeded for years later, many of her former students returned to tell her of the good influence she had been in their lives.[20]

While Etta devoted much of her time to teaching institute, her husband worked to support his family. At one time, "[Albert] bought into National House Cleaning, a janitorial business for cleaning homes; but it proved too much for both him and Etta, so he gave it up." Afterward, they ended up moving in with Etta's mother in her small home on Seventh East, where Etta assisted her mother in sewing burial clothes. Albert was able to help support Etta's brothers, Joe and Lamont, on

18. Toronto, Moody, and Toronto, *Story of Albert and Etta Toronto*, 14, 68.
19. Toronto, Moody, and Toronto, *Story of Albert and Etta Toronto*, 15, 32.
20. Toronto, Moody, and Toronto, *Story of Albert and Etta Toronto*, 16.

Karlstejn, dedication site for Czechoslovakia, July 24, 1929. Courtesy of Mary Jane Woodger.

their missions. Albert and Etta never wanted for food and were always able to support themselves.[21]

When Brigham Young prophesied that Joseph Toronto "should stand at the head of his race and that neither he nor his family should ever want for bread," that promise seemed to extend to his son and then his grandson Wally, and, more importantly, he would stand at the head of *another* race: the Czechoslovakian Latter-day Saints.[22]

21. Toronto, Moody, and Toronto, *Story of Albert and Etta Toronto*, 2.

22. Toronto, Moody, and Toronto, *Joseph Toronto*, 8.

2 "CHARACTER AND GRIT, . . . DETERMINATION AND FORTITUDE"

Ruth Toronto, a beautiful, black-haired baby girl, was born to Albert and Etta on September 1, 1906. They lost her to spinal meningitis at just six months of age, a great tragedy of their early married life. But because of such a sorrowful experience, Albert and Etta were extra grateful and delighted when they welcomed their second child, Wallace Felt Toronto (Wally), into their lives on December 9, 1907.[1] Albert and Etta eventually added seven more children to their family, five boys and two girls: Joseph, born on June 1, 1909; Robert, on April 28, 1911; Lamont, on February 21, 1914; Paul, on December 25, 1917; Helen, on January 19, 1920; Alan, on January 4, 1923; and Norma on June 29, 1926.

Wally enjoyed a typical childhood during the second decade of the twentieth century. One of his favorite activities included going to the movies and watching William S. Hart and Douglas Fairbanks on the big screen. He loved swimming at the Deseret Gym, where

1. Albert Toronto Family Organization, *Story of Albert and Etta Toronto*, 15.

he also learned about woodworking. He frequently went to the gym for "men and boys" nights. All the participants had to go "September Morn style," which involved going through a long process before getting in the water. They first took a shower and immediately got into a hot steam bath so that they could break a sweat and lay on a palette in the steam room. Finally, they could dive into the pool. Wally took swimming lessons at the gym from Charles Welch, who also became his swimming coach in high school. Church, of course, was always a part of the week's activities as well. His father, Albert, served in bishoprics for more than twenty-two years as Wally grew up. Wally often resisted going to church. His faithful mother would wisely respond, "You don't have to go to church, but remember, we would like you to go—we would be happy if you would go."[2] And for the most part, Wally went.[3]

In 1915, when Wally was eight years old, the Torontos acquired a new home on 239 Douglas Street. Wally found there were many nearby conveniences to their new house. A small store was situated just across the alley in the backyard of the home, which was helpful when they needed to get things quickly and easily. Both the chapel and the university were only two blocks away. Every day, the older children walked to the old LDS High School one mile toward the center of town.[4]

Growing up, Wally enjoyed many of the same things as the other children his age. He was fascinated by trains and he watched them come, go, and switch tracks. He also loved eating peanut butter sandwiches at picnics with his cousins in the park. Also like other children, Wally had experiences that were not as enjoyable. Dr. Schofield, the

2. Many primary source materials are used, and these sources regularly have misspellings and unusual punctuation. In an attempt to preserve the integrity and authenticity of these journals and other primary source documents, the original spellings and punctuation are preserved except for typos. Because of the frequency at which these errors occur, *sic* appears infrequently unless needed for clarity.

3. Albert Toronto Family Organization, *Story of Albert and Etta Toronto*, 8–9.

4. Albert Toronto Family Organization, *Story of Albert and Etta Toronto*, 2, 16.

family doctor, often went to the Toronto house in person with plenty of different kinds of medicine to ease whatever illness someone might have. He even performed a tonsillectomy on Wally on the kitchen table.[5]

Wally's mother was a spiritual person who worked well with her husband, supporting him in his businesses, Church callings, and everything else that he did. Nevertheless, Etta was the disciplinarian of the family, not Albert. As in any typical family, there were times when the children would fuss and argue with each other. Albert's response would always be something like, "Stop that. Get quiet or go outside and play." Etta's reaction, on the other hand, was a different story. For instance, once when she discovered that her boys were repeating some foul stories, she washed their mouths out with strong soap and water to make them "pure" again. She told them that her little practice symbolized how "that which comes out of our mouths must be pure and clean." But while Etta was good at keeping her children in line, she made sure to let her fun side shine just as easily. She frequently sat down to play with her children and suggested games they loved, like "Cardinal Puff Puff" or "50 cents" or "crossing the plains." She also taught them fun songs like "Do Your Ears Hang Low?"[6]

The two parents did not always agree with each other on how to discipline their children. When they did disagree, Etta's attitude was unique. She felt it was good for Albert to know that she was upset with him on occasion. At times, he did not meet her expectations; for instance, he sometimes forgot an anniversary or to call her when he was going to be "exceedingly late" getting home. While she thought disagreement once in a while "was good for him," he could not stand the thought of her being at odds with him.[7]

On Sundays, Etta always prepared a roast, mashed potatoes, and a chocolate cake or lemon pie. During the years that Albert was in the bishopric, Wally remembered his father bringing extra people home

5. Albert Toronto Family Organization, *Story of Albert and Etta Toronto*, 16.

6. Albert Toronto Family Organization, *Story of Albert and Etta Toronto*, 20, 22.

7. Albert Toronto Family Organization, *Story of Albert and Etta Toronto*, 10.

often, such as visitors to sacrament meeting or new college students, to eat Sunday dinner with the family. The Toronto family was already fairly large, so the food that had been prepared was not always sufficient to satisfy additional guests as well. The Torontos worked out a system of signals and codes to alert family members to be on their guard. Whenever Etta whispered "F. H. B.," they knew it meant "family, hold back." Their servings, then, were politely small while the guests could have larger helpings. But even at "F. H. B." meals, it seemed to Wally that there was always enough food to go around.[8]

The codes were not restricted to mealtime. After dinner, the children often marched off to the front room, leaving Etta to clean up all by herself. But all it took was a look on her face expressing deep disappointment that indicated, "You don't care." The children shamefully received the nonverbal message and returned to the kitchen to clean up. Even then, they made the chore fun by creating a relay race with the dirty dishes. They first ran from the dining room, through the pantry, and back to the kitchen. Then they washed and dried the dishes. Then the real fun began. They tossed the dishes across the room to one another until every dish sat in its proper place. Despite the elaborate relay system, they surprisingly dropped and broke very few dishes.[9]

As a child in the 1910s, Wally witnessed the dawning of the electric age. The Toronto kitchen would eventually boast one of the first electric automatic dishwashers ever to be sold. But it was not made very well. After too much use, the mechanism wore out. It was not a complete loss, however; the children got to return to their exciting dish-cleaning relay race. The dishwasher remained in place even though it did not work. Because it was part of the sink and drain board, the Torontos never took it out. Apart from the short-lived dishwasher, Etta also experienced the wonder of going from a wood range to an electric one. She was thoroughly pleased by how quickly the stove

---

8. Albert Toronto Family Organization, *Story of Albert and Etta Toronto*, 36.
9. Albert Toronto Family Organization, *Story of Albert and Etta Toronto*, 23.

heated up and by how much cleaner her kitchen stayed because the smoke no longer clung to the walls.[10]

For the Torontos, one of the most special times of the year was Christmas. Although they did not always have a lot of presents to open, they were all delighted in what they received, oohing and aahing at each gift, even if it was simply "a tiny little red and white striped sock, filled with pennies or nickels." On occasion, some of their Felt cousins visited the Toronto home on Christmas day, bringing gifts of their own that were more fun and expensive than those the Toronto children had received. Nonetheless, the Felt cousins often wished that their Christmas morning had been as much fun as the one at the Toronto house, even though their cousins had received less.[11]

As Wally matured, he became the "leader of the pack" amongst his cousins, siblings, and the neighborhood kids.[12] Wally was a very well-proportioned teenager who stood out among other swimmers on the high school swim team. He had a great capacity for swallowing air and could stay underwater for quite a while. He once entered a Boy Scout swimming contest at the Deseret Gym. When he dove off the bank, everybody cheered on to see if he could endure the length of the gym pool. He did not make it to the end, but the way he hung on for so long impressed the onlookers. Those watching "could tell there was character and grit and determination [and] fortitude. And it had an influence . . . on all the . . . 13 and 14-year-old youngsters" watching him. Wally was "a great example, . . . the right example." The sense of responsibility and perseverance he developed during high school stayed with him throughout his life. He was elected student body president of the high school in 1927 and president of the senior class.[13]

10. Albert Toronto Family Organization, *Story of Albert and Etta Toronto*, 35.

11. Albert Toronto Family Organization, *Story of Albert and Etta Toronto*, 18, 35.

12. Carma Toronto, interview by Daniel Toronto, February 26, 2004, Salt Lake City, transcription in author's possession, 2–3.

13. Albert Toronto Family Organization, *Story of Albert and Etta Toronto*, 64, 65.

Wally was a tease. He was full of fun and always had a prank up his sleeve. He and his brothers loved playing tricks on anyone and everyone. They once went back and forth down the street where they lived and streamed a roll of toilet paper across the road. As the cars drove by, the drivers had no choice but to drive through the toilet paper. Another prank Wally once did as a teenager was using electricity to shock chickens. They also enjoyed pranking the family livestock. Wally, perhaps more than once, tied a clothing line wire across two poles. He then hooked up a battery to the wire using jumper cables, hoping the chickens would perch on it. The boys sat and waited in anticipation to see what would happen. Wally wanted only to scare the bird, but instead, as an unsuspecting chicken moved to perch there, it was electrocuted.[14]

One story became legendary in the neighborhood. Close to the Toronto home, the trolley tracks meandered along South Temple and rounded up a hill between South Temple and the top of Second South. Wally had the bright idea of spreading suet grease along the tracks on the hill. He and his "followers" hid out of sight and waited until a trolley came their way, watching as it rounded the corner. All of a sudden, the train got stuck on the grease, leaving the poor conductor confused as he tried to figure out what was wrong.[15]

Wally—a future mission president—greased tracks, electrocuted hens, and frustrated many a driver using toilet paper. Amidst all of his tricks, though, he emerged as a leader who could get others to follow him. In the next decade, he would guide an entire nation of converts.[16]

14. Judy Richards, interview by David Toronto, Salt Lake City, transcription in possession of David Toronto, 1.
15. Carma Toronto interview, February 26, 2004, 3.
16. Carma Toronto interview, February 26, 2004, 3.

3 "IMMERSING HIMSELF IN BOHEMIAN LIFE"

In the 1920s, serving as a full-time missionary was an exception for young LDS men, not a rule. One had to be asked to serve a mission by his priesthood leaders. Unlike today, a young Latter-day Saint did not just decide to go; rather, others made the decision. In the summer of 1928, Wallace F. Toronto received a letter from Box B (the address of the First Presidency of The Church of Jesus Christ of Latter-day Saints) calling him to serve in the German-Austrian Mission. And so, Wally, in the great tradition of his grandfather, Joseph, and his father, Albert, accepted the call to serve as a missionary.

Typical of many missionaries, Wally left a girlfriend at home. Her name was Dolores. The two had been dating for some time before Wally received his call. They agreed to write each other often once he entered the mission field in Germany. Saying goodbye was not easy.

Wally arrived in October of 1928, at the mission headquarters in Dresden.[1] Like his father, he found that

---

1. Joseph Young Toronto, *Forever and Ever: The Life History of Joseph Young Toronto*, ed. Shannon Toronto (Provo, UT: Brigham Young University Press, 1996), 47.

<< Wallace F. Toronto, 1928. Courtesy of Church History Library.

the German language came easily. Later, Wally wrote in third person about the first year of his mission experience in his master's thesis: "In October of 1928 he located in Germany, and there during almost a year's stay attempted to learn the German language and to acquaint himself with the social customs and behavior of the people. This proved to be a most enjoyable and profitable year for it gave him an insight into the life and culture of a people, who, prior to this time, were known to him largely by name only. He enjoyed their hospitality and goodness and insofar as he was capable became one of them. He learned to love the common folk and admired them for their sincerity."[2]

Wally soon grew accustomed to the different aspects of missionary life, including distributing missionary pamphlets (tracting), giving speeches, studying, visiting members and investigators of the Church, learning to live with a companion, and dealing with homesickness. In one of his journal entries from four months into his mission, he provided a small glimpse into the daily life of a missionary. "Visited a number of favorable prospects and invited them to attend our meeting. We were called upon today to administer to two sick kiddies. I think they have whooping cough. The parents are not members of the church. It was the first time for both Bill and I. I did the anointing. The Priesthood is a wonderful gift. Had a fine spirit in our meeting."[3]

After Wally had acquainted himself with the German people for a year, he was transferred, not from one town to another town, but from one nation to another.[4] The catalyst was a request to President Heber J. Grant by Františka Vesela Brodilová, who was born in 1881 in southern Bohemia. When her mother died, eighteen-year-old Františka

2. Wallace F. Toronto, "Some Socio-psychological Aspects of the Czecho-Slovakian Crisis of 1938–39" (master's thesis, University of Utah, 1940), 6.

3. Toronto, Wallace F., journal, February 5, 1929, 44, Church History Library, (hereafter Toronto, journal).

4. Ed and Norma Morrell, interview by Mary Jane Woodger, May 8, 2013, Provo, UT, transcript in author's possession, 3.

moved to Vienna, Austria, to live with an older sister. There, Františka married Frantisek Brodil in 1904. In 1913, she learned of the restored gospel and was baptized in the Danube River. In 1919, due to World War I and other situations, the family moved to Prague. Shortly thereafter, her husband passed away.

In Prague, she had no contact with the Church. Despite Františka's diligent efforts and prayers to bring the gospel to Czechoslovakia, years passed without Latter-day Saint missionaries entering Czechoslovakia.

After more than a decade of praying for missionaries to come to her country, "Františka felt impressed to write to the First Presidency. . . . To [her] great joy, her letter to President Heber J. Grant got immediate results."[5] In that same year, Wallace F. Toronto was called on his mission to Germany. Under President Grant's direction, Edward P. Kimball, president of the German-Austrian Mission, was asked to choose his strongest missionaries and send them to Czechoslovakia in June of 1929. Among them was Arthur Gaeth. Elder Gaeth had attended "the Priesthood Centennial of the German-Austrian Mission in May 1929." While there, John A. Widtsoe, president of the European Mission, said he wanted to call Arthur on a special mission. Arthur felt inspired that he would be going to Czechoslovakia because his mother, a Czech, had a promise in her patriarchal blessing that he would "take the Gospel to her native land."[6] Gaeth was called as the president of the Czechoslovak Mission along with five other missionaries: Alvin Carlson, Wallace Toronto, Charles Josie, Willis Hayward, and Joseph Hart.[7]

The Church obtained permission from the Czech government to allow missionaries to preach the gospel in Czechoslovakia and set out to send elders to the newly opened nation. There were only seven members in the country at the time, two of which were the Brodil sis-

---

5. Ruth McOmber Pratt and Ann South Niendorf, "Her Mission Was Czechoslovakia," *Ensign*, August 1994, 53.

6. Kahlile B. Mehr, *Mormon Missionaries Enter Eastern Europe* (Provo, UT: Brigham Young University Press, 2002), 46–47.

7. Mehr, *Mormon Missionaries Enter Eastern Europe*, 49.

First Czechoslovakian missionaries with Arthur Gaeth (left center) and Wallace Toronto (seated on far right). Courtesy of Church History Library.

ters. Only a few weeks after Wally arrived in the country, Elder John A. Widtsoe of the Quorum of the Twelve Apostles dedicated Czechoslovakia for the preaching of the gospel on July 24, 1929.[8] The site was beautiful and full of the Holy Spirit as the leaders and missionaries gathered at a magnificent castle. They found a nearby wooded knoll suited for the dedication. The morning started with rain, but by the time they got to the hill at eight o'clock in the morning, the weather had cleared for the dedicatory prayer.[9]

After the dedication, Arthur Gaeth was called as the mission president, even though he was still unmarried. In November 1929, Elder Widtsoe

8. Mehr, *Mormon Missionaries Enter Eastern Europe*, 48–49.

9. Kahlile Mehr, "Czech Saints: A Brighter Day," *Ensign*, August 1994, 48.

introduced President Gaeth to his future wife, Martha Kralickova. Two years later, Gaeth baptized and married her.[10] They purchased a villa in Prague, which became the new mission home. To get the word out about the presence of the new religion in Czechoslovakia, President Gaeth relied upon an acquaintance that had contacts that worked with Prague Radio. Two broadcasts aired, on August 3 and August 7, 1929, informing the small nation that "the Mormons had opened a mission in Czechoslovakia."[11]

In addition to the broadcasts, Gaeth had scheduled a lecture to be given at a German adult-education institution and written an article for a German-language newspaper about the Church's arrival in Czechoslovakia.[12] Wally came to recognize that the newly appointed president had quite a journalistic disposition and a booming voice.[13] Indeed, seventy-two articles appeared in newspapers about the Mormons within the first six months that they were there. Many of the articles were favorable. However, once they sent missionaries into Mladá Boleslav a couple of years later, "Catholic priests . . . filed police complaints . . . accus[ing] the missionaries of being 'immoral and undesirable' aliens and charged that 'Mormons are a sect forbidden in every state outside of Utah because of polygamy.'"[14]

President Gaeth sued the priest for libel. Luckily, the mission president had friends within the office of Tomáš Masaryk, the president of Czechoslovakia, and they were able to settle for a retraction in the paper. A year later in 1935, the Prague Catholic newspaper "claimed that the missionaries were German espionage agents." The statement could have generated dreadful and jeopardizing consequences. Once again, President Gaeth sued the paper and won. The paper then not only had to publish a retraction but also had to pay for court costs and

10. Mehr, "Czech Saints: A Brighter Day," 48.

11. Mehr, *Mormon Missionaries Enter Eastern Europe*, 47.

12. Mehr, *Mormon Missionaries Enter Eastern Europe*, 47.

13. Mehr, "Czech Saints: A Brighter Day," 48.

14. Kahlile B. Mehr, "Enduring Believers," *Journal of Mormon History* 18, no. 2 (Fall 1992): 127.

give money to charity.[15] By 1931, a total of 250 articles, mostly written by missionaries, had appeared in the newspapers and journals.[16]

Wally found that the people of Czechoslovakia were different than those he had known in Germany. In his thesis, he expounded on the character of the Czech people after discussing how advantageous it was to truly "immerse himself in Bohemian life," just as he had in Germany, in order to learn about the new people and about their characteristics and attitudes toward life. "He found that they were great lovers of individual freedom, and that in this respect they emulated the great reformer, John Hus; that although there was a feeling of distrust and antagonism toward the German nation, yet there prevailed a spirit of tolerance for the German and other minorities within the country."[17]

Wally experienced a wonderful blessing during the second year of service when he had become one of the first elders to master the Czech language. But even more exciting to him was that his younger brother, Joseph, was able to join him in the Czechoslovak Mission.[18] At the time that Wally left on his mission, Joseph had been helping their father with a construction business and saving money for his own mission. The business prospered, and Joseph planned to leave the following year. Unfortunately, while Wally was abroad, the stock market crashed in September of 1929. The Great Depression years were filled with heavy financial reverses for their parents. Having two boys on missions only yielded additional difficulties for the Toronto family. When buyers could not make their payments to Albert, he could not pay for materials. People were declaring bankruptcy left and right. Albert could have done the same, but he would not. He paced back and forth in his room, asking himself, "How do I get out from under this?"[19]

The family chose to put their faith and trust in the Lord and knew he would provide for their needs in one way or another. The Depression

15. Mehr, "Enduring Believers," 127.

16. Mehr, "Czech Saints: A Brighter Day," 48.

17. Toronto, "Some Socio-psychological Aspects," 7.

18. Toronto, *Forever and Ever*, 60.

19. Albert Toronto Family Organization, *Story of Albert and Etta Toronto*, 45.

often pushed people to desperation and pitted family members against each other. At one point, "the boys' bonds and insurance policies were cashed in to pay off a loan from a demanding relative."[20] But despite the challenges at home, the elders managed to remain on their missions. The boys "wanted to be there, to be in the mission field during the depths of the Depression. And how they ever managed to keep them there, was a real miracle."[21] Albert eventually went to President Grant, hoping for a loan to fend off the collectors he owed. To his great joy, the prophet graciously helped him.[22]

During the crisis, Etta continued to sustain her husband faithfully. She reassured him, "Albert, we can do it. . . . Hang in there." Because of her support, he often told Wally and Joe, "I haven't been very smart in this life, but boys, the smartest thing I ever did was to marry your mother."[23] Managing their finances, nevertheless, remained incredibly difficult for the Torontos while the boys were in Czechoslovakia. However, they felt that their ability to make ends meet was a direct result of the blessing that Grandfather Giuseppe received at the hands of Brigham Young.[24]

Joseph finally arrived in Eastern Europe near the end of 1930. He was called on a mission to Germany and arrived in Dresden on November 30. A week and a half later, on December 10, President Gaeth sent a letter to Joseph asking him to join the mission force in Czechoslovakia. Joseph had previously mentioned in a letter to Wally that he would love to serve with him, but Wally did not think it was possible. As he traveled to Prague to meet Joseph at the station, Wally was thrilled to see his brother again. They had not seen each other in over a year.[25] What a joy it was for the two brothers to serve together in the same mission!

---

20. Albert Toronto Family Organization, *Story of Albert and Etta Toronto*, 16.
21. Carma Toronto, interview, February 26, 2004, 2.
22. Albert Toronto Family Organization, *Story of Albert and Etta Toronto*, 45.
23. Albert Toronto Family Organization, *Story of Albert and Etta Toronto*, 45.
24. Carma Toronto interview, February 26, 2004, 2.
25. Toronto, *Forever and Ever*, 47, 60.

The two brothers attended a joint Mutual Improvement Association meeting the evening Joseph arrived. Everyone present joined in singing "The Holy City." Joseph bore his testimony in German because he did not know Czech. When he returned to his apartment, he and Wally caught up on how the family was doing and, of course, discussed the girl Wally left back home. Wally told Joe that Dolores had written and told him that "she never thought it would be possible for her to care for someone as she [did] for him, but a new feeling [had] entered her life." The "new feeling's" name was Tony Middleton. "Things will turn out all right," Wally assured mostly himself, but his worry about Dolores's "new feeling" did not go away.[26]

Joseph described in his personal history the experiences he had tracting with his brother. He recorded, "The only way I could manage that first morning was to, with one hand, give the pamphlet to a lady and hold the typewritten-card in the other. How I murdered the language that morning! A few were patient enough to hear me. One young woman said, 'Perhaps you speak better German than Czech.' Speaking in German, I told her we were missionaries from America. She then said in perfect English: 'Well then, let's speak English.' Czech, German, and English at the same door! And what a thrill it is to go tracting with my own brother!" But typical of many siblings, Wally took advantage of having his younger brother as a companion and constantly teased him during their meetings. One time he jaunted, "Here am I walking the road of salvation, and there is my brother struggling in the pitfalls of sin. What can I do to help him?" Wally pointed at Joe and enjoyed the expected laughter of his audience. Then he asked his little brother to prepare a lesson for the next meeting the following Tuesday on "The Injurious Effects of Sin," encouraging him to speak from experience. Joe later wrote, "What would you do with such a brother?"[27]

Wally worked hard throughout his mission, constantly growing in the love he had for the people he served. He was called to leadership

26. Toronto, *Forever and Ever*, 72.

27. Toronto, *Forever and Ever*, 65–66.

positions and fulfilled other important responsibilities as they were given to him. On September 1, 1929, Wally recorded, "I was appointed as secretary of our new mission. Not so much to do now, but we have faith in the future." A couple weeks later, he wrote, "Memories come again. It's a wonderful life with all of its diversities. A man can't read his future one day ahead. Made a list of important city officials and other prominent men and mailed them all an invitation to attend our English lectures."[28]

By October, the mission had obtained permission from the police to distribute two Czech-language tracts presenting the Church's doctrine, even though most of the missionaries could not yet speak the language. The tracts were the first two of twenty-five published during the first three years of the mission's existence. They consisted mostly of translations from works authored by Elder Widtsoe.[29] Later, Wally also wrote some of the content himself. Joseph once memorized a tracting speech that Wally had written for him. By the end of 1929, Wally could already see the progress of the newly formed mission. He wrote, "The Lord certainly is good to us. There are only six of us here, but how many friends we seem to have. We have been invited out almost every night. Yes, we are beginning to get into the homes, and our friends are asking about our message."[30]

Wally was positive, confident, and full of energy. Yet he was humble and recognized the Lord's hand in the work. He recorded in his journal, "My heart rejoices in the work of the Lord. How diligent and how humble we should be, and yet how weak we really are!"[31] Two weeks later, he wrote, "Speaking of weather, . . . it could not be more ideal for this time of the year. Sunshine, clear sky, birds, and golly, Spring is in the air. The Lord certainly has been good to us, for we have met with great success. The Czech language is difficult, but despite it,

28. Toronto, journal, September 16, 1929, 268.

29. Mehr, *Mormon Missionaries Enter Eastern Europe*, 50.

30. Toronto, journal, December 27, 1929, 370.

31. Toronto, journal, February 7, 1930, 46.

I have felt the Spirit of God in my work as never before. The mission will succeed, for God leads it on."[32]

Wally could not help but observe the tense political situation of the country. He noted multiple times the conditions and problems that he thought might arise if difficulties continued. "Again the people congregated and broke store windows in which were German signs. They cannot look far enough ahead to see the ultimate results—such as war and strife. It looks serious. Those papers which urged the people on are now begging them to stop."[33] Five months later, he recorded, "Went to Brodils in evening with brethren and had Sister Jane assist me with talk. Communist's Day. Streets are thronged with people and lined with soldiers and policemen. But no unrest is evident."[34]

Later, in his master's thesis, Wally discussed how the character of the Czech people translated to politics: "He noted in them strong traits of obedience to leadership, and sometimes almost blind devotion to a cause. For the most part they were seemingly non-militaristic, but greatly enjoyed talking about the efficiency and precision of the former army. Many of them were disturbed and dissatisfied about conditions and hoped for leadership which might again weld them into solidarity. Some saw the salvation of the country in the National Socialist Party, which was constantly gaining power. Others wondered about it. A few had grave doubts."[35]

After three and a half years, it was time for Wally to return home. President Gaeth wept as Wally gave his farewell address to the Saints in Czechoslovakia in sacrament meeting the Sunday before he left. The mission president and both Toronto boys helped Wally pack his trunk at three o'clock in the morning. They then traveled to the train station and said their goodbyes, and Wally went home.[36] Little did he suspect that in three short years he would return.

32. Toronto, journal, February 29, 1930, 68.

33. Toronto, journal, September 26, 1930, 278.

34. Toronto, journal, February 25, 1931, 64.

35. Toronto, "Some Socio-psychological Aspects," 6–7.

36. Toronto, *Forever and Ever*, 72.

4 "THE MISSION PRINCESS"

Wally brought a precious commodity back from Europe: a diamond for Dolores.[1] He had every intention of marrying her, but things did not go as planned. He never even had the chance to present her with the ring because the two ended their relationship soon after he returned. Since his intentions were thwarted, he decided to continue his education back at the University of Utah instead. In addition to his schooling, he obtained a job as a bookkeeper and office manager at the LDS Hospital.[2] Around that time, another young woman would enter his life: Martha Sharp.

Unlike her future husband, Martha Sharp grew up in a highly privileged situation. Because of her circumstances, in comparison to Wally's, she seemed like somebody from another world, even another planet. As she grew up, she became the stable one in her family

1. Carma Toronto, interview, February 26, 2004, 10.
2. Martha Toronto Anderson, *A Cherry Tree behind the Iron Curtain: The Autobiography of Martha Toronto Anderson* (Salt Lake City: Martha Toronto Anderson, 1977), 12.

as far as the gospel was concerned. Her brothers and sisters were not very solid. According to Carma, Wally's sister-in-law, nothing but a testimony of the gospel would find a girl like her ending up with a guy like Wally.[3]

Martha was born in Salt Lake City on February 27, 1912, to John and Sally Luella Ferrin Sharp.[4] She was named after her grandmother, Martha Bronson Ferrin, and would someday endure the same experience that her grandmother had once endured: bearing the difficulties of supporting her husband, Josiah, when he was called to serve a mission.[5] Like some of the experiences that her future granddaughter would have, Martha Ferrin's experiences were "hair-raising and showed how the Lord took care of her and the family during those years."[6]

Grandmother Ferrin would often "give all the food in her house to Indians, both hostile and friendly." She learned their language and could talk to them as they made demands. "They always came when she was at home alone with the little ones. These were often terrifying experiences for her, but she was always kind and generous to the Indians. She was courageous, and very spiritual as well, in bringing up her family of eleven children."[7] Martha Sharp would also someday experience the Lord taking care of her and her family while her husband served a mission. Martha's mother, Luella Ferrin, was youngest of those eleven children in the Ferrin family. Little is recorded about her except that she was extremely talented, especially in singing.

Martha's father, John Sharp, grew up in Salt Lake City. As a young man in his twenties, he went to New York City to study medicine at New York University. While there, he studied voice with Madam Von Klenner. He had a beautiful baritone voice and sang in groups and quartets as "an outlet from the rigors of his medical studies." By

---

3. Carma Toronto, interview, February 26, 2004, 7.
4. Anderson, *Cherry Tree*, 1.
5. Anderson, *Cherry Tree*, 1, 4.
6. Anderson, *Cherry Tree*, 1.
7. Anderson, *Cherry Tree*, 1.

no coincidence, Luella also took lessons from Madam Von Klenner. Through this association John and Luella met, "fell in love, and after a brief courtship . . . were married in the Salt Lake Temple on September 18, 1903." The couple first lived in New York City, where John obtained his MD. They then returned to Salt Lake City, where he practiced medicine.[8]

Martha was the second of John and Luella's five children. During her childhood, her father "worked out of [their] home in caring for the sick and delivering babies." Her father also served in the Army Corps during World War I, eventually going overseas and taking care of wounded troops in France from 1917 to 1919. After the armistice, Martha remembered her father being a little more stern but still loving. After World War I, he frequently took her on hunting and camping trips, and he established offices in the Deseret Bank Building. "He was very busy." In fact, "he was known as the best surgeon in the west."[9]

While her husband practiced medicine, Martha's mother continued to pursue her musical career as much as possible while raising her children. She performed in leading roles as a member of the Salt Lake Opera Company. She was also a soloist for several years in the Mormon Tabernacle Choir. She directed and produced operas, a hobby that would have a great bearing on Martha's future interests, as Luella encouraged her children to develop their talents.[10]

Martha went to grade school at Columbus and junior high school at Irving. In high school she "loved being in the operas and plays, dance reviews and pageants at the school." And, like her future husband, she particularly enjoyed being on the swim team. She later attended LDS High School, where she graduated in 1930. Once graduated, she enrolled at the University of Utah, where she mainly studied French and German for a degree in modern languages. Martha also took up private lessons on the harp and became a gifted harpist. She danced in church-sponsored shows and operas and was asked to do

8. Anderson, *Cherry Tree*, 1, 3.

9. Anderson, *Cherry Tree*, 4–6.

10. Anderson, *Cherry Tree*, 7.

choreography for several productions. She also joined the Lambda Phi Lambda sorority and had an active social life. The Sharp home on Ashton Avenue in Salt Lake City became a wonderful place for the university to have parties and formal dances because the home had four rooms that opened up into a beautiful ballroom.[11]

In the summer of 1932, Martha took a vacation with her sister, Marion, and some other friends to a resort in Emigration Canyon, called Pinecrest. They had a wonderful time hiking, playing tennis, throwing horseshoes, and singing around the campfire at night. It was there that Martha met a certain young man who directed the activities at night and worked in the office during the day. His name was Wallace Felt Toronto. As the two became acquainted, she learned that her oldest brother, Harlow, who likewise had attended LDS High School, knew Wally when he was the student body president and the captain of the swim team. Harlow had been a favorite speed swimmer as well. When Martha met Wally, Martha was still studying the German language at the university, and Harlow was on a mission in Germany, where Wally had originally served. The couple had much in common and had no problem finding things to talk about. "[Wally] was funny and we joked a lot, and he even broke the blisters on my fingers that I had from plucking the strings of my harp. He was interested in my playing, and we talked about it quite a bit as he was dressing my fingers."[12]

About the first week of September, after Martha returned home from Pinecrest, she got a phone call from Wally. He had finished his season at Pinecrest and had helped the owners, Mr. and Mrs. Chapman, close up the resort before returning home to register for the fall semester at the University of Utah. Martha was delighted to talk with him again. She grew especially excited when he invited her to go to the Peach Days celebration in Brigham City. She had never been on a date that lasted all day long before, but after talking about it with her parents, they thought it would be okay.[13]

---

11. Anderson, *Cherry Tree*, 9.

12. Anderson, *Cherry Tree*, 11.

13. Anderson, *Cherry Tree*, 11.

Wally picked Martha up early on the morning of their first date. She remembered as the day progressed that she had "never been treated so nicely by a young man before." Peach Days with its carnival atmosphere thrilled her. The festivities ended with a big dance that night. But it was what happened after the dance that Martha tells us was the most memorable:

> Driving home late, after midnight, we rounded a curve on the highway and witnessed an accident that was quite a shock to us both. The car had rolled over several times and some of the young people had been killed. We pulled over to help, and as other cars came along we were able to get injured and dying young people wrapped in blankets and into cars and ambulances. I held up fine while we were working there, but after we started home I began to shake. Naturally we drove home slowly because it was such a shock to us both.[14]

Experiencing such trauma together brought the young couple closer to one another. From that first date on, they dated only each other, eliminating former boyfriends and girlfriends from their dating schedules. Martha took Wally to sorority parties, and he took her to missionary frat parties. On September 15, 1933, a year after they first met, Wallace Felt Toronto married Martha Sharp in the Salt Lake City Temple with David O. McKay, a member of the Quorum of the Twelve Apostles, officiating. After the wedding, Martha dropped out of college in her junior year, but Wally continued studying at the university and working as a bookkeeper and office manager at the LDS hospital. Together they managed the apartment house they rented that was owned by the Chapmans, who had been Wally's employers at Pinecrest.[15]

Their first child, Marion, was born on November 5, 1934. When she was barely a year old, Wally and Martha were called into the First Presidency's office for an interview with President David O. McKay, then of the First Presidency. Neither of them had any idea why a member of the First Presidency would want to see them, and both were in

14. Anderson, *Cherry Tree*, 12.

15. Anderson, *Cherry Tree*, 12.

<< Marion, Martha, and Wallace Toronto passport photo, 1936. Courtesy of Church History Library.

shock when President McKay asked if they would preside over the Czechoslovak Mission. At only twenty-four years old, Martha remembered feeling that "it was a distinct honor to be included in this calling, because [she] would, as a mission president's wife, have a great responsibility—not only as a leader in the auxiliary organizations, but as a mother to many missionaries. It was a sobering thought."[16]

After much preparation, many goodbyes, and a missionary farewell, President and Sister Toronto left Salt Lake City in May, traveling by way of Nauvoo and other LDS historical places. They also spent a couple of days at Niagara Falls before they boarded the SS *American New York*. Martha had never traveled before, and even though she was pregnant and had a small child in tow, she grew to love traveling because she was with Wally. They landed in Amsterdam and then stopped in Paris and later Berlin, where they visited with other mission presidents on their way to Prague.[17] They arrived in Czechoslovakia on June 1, 1936.

The first experience Martha had with using her French and German skills outside of the classroom differed from her expectations. "I'll admit I was thoroughly confused, but the languages did look and sound familiar, at least, which is more than I can say about the Czech language, which I had to learn from scratch. That language was something I can't quite describe." Wally tried to teach her a few phrases, but it still sounded very strange to her. She enrolled in a language class at the Berlitz School. As she studied, worked, and prayed, she surprised herself when she found that she learned the language quite well.[18]

Wally felt that her Czech was improving daily.[19] She had a talent for language. After all, she had learned French and German at the

16. Anderson, *Cherry Tree*, 13.
17. Anderson, *Cherry Tree*, 13.
18. Anderson, *Cherry Tree*, 14.
19. Toronto, journal, August 15–21, 1937, 138.

University of Utah.[20] He was especially proud of her when she bore her testimony well without using any notes.[21] Not only did she need to learn a new language, but she also had to learn a lot about the Church from an organizational standpoint. Before this calling, she had just been a bystander; now she was part of a leadership team. Early on, she admitted to Wally that because of the experience she was facing, she had really begun to recognize for the first time in her life the meaning and depth of the gospel of Jesus Christ. She realized how much there was for her to learn.[22]

The sense of humor that Wally developed growing up did not change with his calling to be a mission president. While Martha was more refined, he still nurtured his funny bone. She often felt his humor was inappropriate for his station. For instance, one night in a particularly tender moment during an opera, he began whistling. Marion, their daughter, later described similar experiences that her mother endured on more than one occasion. Even though her father seemed to appreciate the arts,

> His devotion to opera was suspect, even though he went with us. He wasn't especially interested in the lyric quality of the singers or the tonality of the orchestra. He seemed to enjoy the performances, but his greatest pleasure was in watching my poor mother's ecstatic sufferings as she watched. She responded to every strain of pathos with tears of sympathy and understanding. Father would always lean over and pat her knee at a crucial moment and say, "Now, Mamma, it isn't real." And she would glare at him through tear-filled eyes and wish he hadn't come.[23]

Wally's bird imitations also irritated Martha. He often practiced them at the most inopportune times. One time was during a perfor-

20. Bob and David Toronto, interview by Mary Jane Woodger, August 20, 2013, Sandy, UT, transcription in author's possession, 8; and Anderson, *Cherry Tree*, 14.
21. Toronto, journal, April 4–10, 1937, 94.
22. Toronto, journal, November 1–7, 1936, 51.
23. Marion Toronto Miller, "My Story: The Dream (The Early Years)" (presentation, December 1998), printed copy, 12–13.

mance of the opera *Madame Butterfly*. The death scene commenced, with its sadness and grief, when all of a sudden, everyone could hear the twitter of birds above the orchestra. Everyone in the house started looking around, except for Martha, who was both fuming and weeping. Wally had decided to add a little "special interest into the orchestration." Martha did not speak to him for some time after the performance.[24]

While Wally refused to act more mature and dignified, Martha struggled to appear older than her years. At the age of twenty-four, she was younger than most of the missionaries she was supposed to mother, and she had grown up in provincial Utah. Suddenly she was thrust into an unfamiliar world, new and frightening in its challenges. She squared her shoulders and met the task before her with a dignified grace that Wally found remarkable. The missionaries started calling Martha the "mission princess." The typical title of "mission mother" did not seem to fit since she was younger than most of them. She was an attractive woman and so very young for such a position of responsibility, and both the members and missionaries alike came to revere her.[25]

When September of 1936 arrived, the Torontos celebrated their third wedding anniversary and recorded, "So many blessings have come our way. We have a delightful child, and expect another one in a short time; we are in Czechoslovakia, enjoying the greatest call that can come to a person, officiating in missionary work; somehow or other our bills seem to be paid up. We rather married on a 'shoe string'. And most delightful of all, we seem to become happier as the days, weeks, months, and years go by." Wally then described what a wonderful companion Martha had been. "No finer companion could one find in the world. She has been willing to cooperate, to sacrifice, to work, to study diligently—and all in the spirit of love and devotion. My greatest blessing is my darling sweetheart. How can I help but love and cherish her. May we have many more wedding anniversaries together."[26]

24. Miller, "My Story: The Dream," 13.

25. Bob and David Toronto, interview, August 20, 2013, 25.

26. Toronto, journal, September 13–19, 1936, 38.

Wallace, Marion, Robert, and Martha Toronto, Prague, 1940. Courtesy of Church History Library.

Martha's main Church responsibility was with the Relief Society. Each of the large branches had a Relief Society, and she was the one who assigned local sisters to leadership positions, who in turn did very well. Martha decided that when they had literary lessons about American authors, they would instead substitute Czech authors and writers. Such lessons had to be very clear; many concepts could be lost in literal translation. Martha transplanted some fun ideas from the activities that her Relief Society implemented in Utah, one of which was having bazaars. At one bazaar hosted under her direction, more than 150 attended, and every bit of food and handiwork was sold. The bazaar also included an outstanding program of music. Under Martha's direction, they were able to bring in over 1,100 crowns to fund future Relief Society events.[27]

27. Toronto, journal, December 5–11, 1937, 168.

One of the problems that Martha faced in the Czech Relief Societies was gossip. Wally called it a "great evil from within" among the sisters.[28] At one point, when the Boleslav Relief Society president and a few other sisters had generated some problems, he told them that he was going to "close the branch and send the missionaries into more fruitful fields" if they did not stop gossiping. "There were tears shed, and statements made that it was the 'other fellow' who was to blame." Speaking right to the point, Wally reminded them that the Church had a bad reputation because of the gossip in Boleslav, which started in the Relief Society.[29] He told them that he would come after the New Year, hold a special meeting, and give them a definite decision; if things did not change, the branch would be closed.[30] The gossiping ceased after that.

There was one other constant worry for both Martha and Wally: their finances. Quarterly mission allowance from the Church was about $180, but the bills continually stacked up. They would have to do some "tall stretching" to make the budget work. Although the allowance had been set at $180 per month ($20 less than President Gaeth and his wife had received), they had been told they would receive $200. Wally always wondered why their budget had been reduced. The most probable reason was the Great Depression back in the states. The Torontos consequently had "to ask the First Presidency to take care of Martha's confinement" as she prepared for their next baby.[31]

Both of the Torontos were happy about the prospects of a new baby, and Baby Marion, whom they called "Knoflíček" (Buttons), was growing up quickly. She was even beginning to speak a few Czech words. The change of climate and country had not bothered her in the least.[32] However, Martha did struggle with some difficulties being pregnant in a strange land. At one point, she suffered a terrible sore throat and called on a throat specialist for help. She then developed a bad case of sinus

28. Toronto, journal, July 26–August 1, 1936, 21.

29. Toronto, journal, January 10–23, 1937, 67.

30. Toronto, journal, December 20–26, 1936, 61.

31. Toronto, journal, June 28–July 4, 1936, 11.

32. Toronto, journal, July 26–August 1, 1936, 21.

trouble, possibly because a doctor in Prague punctured her sinus bones.[33] She was miserable, and within a week she had two more operations on her nose.[34] Her troubles with the doctors yielded a yearning for home. To her great sorrow, her mother also passed away while Martha was still across the ocean, which made her only more homesick and "blue."[35]

On November 28, 1936, while the Torontos were at a member's home for dinner, Martha fainted at the dinner table and moaned about some pain in her side. Thinking it might be appendicitis, she went to the doctor, who put her to bed and said that the new arrival would come that evening. He gave her a few pills to stimulate labor pains, but nothing happened. Then they gave her an injection to induce labor. Because of her limited Czech language, an interpreter had to assist with the childbirth.[36] By 8:30 in the evening, she was in full labor, and at 9:30 "a fine healthy seven pound son was born." The baby's "cries could be heard all over the hospital. And Marty took it all like a 'brick'—as brave and as fine as anyone could have done."[37] They decided to name their new son Robert Sharp Toronto.[38]

Although Wally and Martha were serving a mission, they did not neglect to enjoy many things that, as a young family, they would not want to miss. Like any ordinary Christian family, they decorated a big pine tree for Christmas. They filled stockings and put the gifts beneath the lowest branches of the beautifully decorated tree, and they played Santa Claus.[39] Little Marion woke up at the crack of dawn and, in ecstasy, played with her new dolly. The Torontos' Christmas was completely normal, except for the myriad of missionaries that accompanied them in all their festivities.[40] It was a great ending to a wonderful year.

33. Toronto, journal, February 14–20, 1937, 80.
34. Toronto, journal, February 21–27, 1937, 81.
35. Toronto, journal, March 14–20, 1937, 89.
36. Mehr, *Mormon Missionaries Enter Eastern Europe*, 67.
37. Toronto, journal, November 21–28, 1936, 56.
38. Toronto, journal, December 15–19, 1936, 60.
39. Toronto, journal, December 19–25, 1937, 176.
40. Toronto, journal, December 25–31, 1938, 307.

5

"HOW CAN OUR BRETHREN BECOME MORE ZEALOUS?"

When Wally first presided over the mission, he had grave misgivings about being able to carry on the successful work of mission president Arthur Gaeth. Wally called Gaeth "a man of great ability, foresight and humility." On arriving, Wally voiced his fears and apprehensions to the newly released mission president. President Gaeth's reply to Wally's concerns "sunk deep into [his] heart." He told Wally, "Just remember, Wally, that one and the Lord are always a majority."[1]

Wally was less flamboyant than Gaeth and decided to continue only a portion of Gaeth's public activities, which included serving as secretary for the English Club Union and lecturing frequently. "Overall, [Wally] spent less time in social activities and more time nurturing a growing membership."[2] As he energetically visited

1. Wallace F. Toronto, "Lord's Help Indispensable," *Hvězdička* [*The Star*, Czechoslovakian Mission newsletter], July 1938, found in Jiří Šnederfler papers, Europe Church History Center, Bad Homburg, Germany, transcription in author's possession.
2. Mehr, *Mormon Missionaries Enter Eastern Europe*, 67.

each branch every month, he found turmoil in the Mladá Boleslav Branch but was encouraged with the stability of the branches in both Brno and Prague. These visits resulted in a revamping of the missionary effort. Consequently, the Mnichovo Hradiště and Kolín Branches were opened in 1936. "Furthermore, he removed missionaries from cities where meetings were poorly attended or where lack of baptisms prohibited the organization of a branch. The revamping closed Pardubice in 1936 and Mladá Boleslav in 1937, and the missionaries [who had served previously in those branches] were reassigned elsewhere."[3]

Wally studied the Czech people. He found them to be a thriving, happy, progressive people who leaned heavily towards becoming a great world democracy. "He found them sincere and loyal, but always suspicious of new influences from the outside [world]." He was very conscious of the difference of behaviors between the Czechs and Germans. He kept a careful record of the attitudes that were reflected in his daily contracts with the people.[4] At times, Wally was a bit distraught with the Czechs because, as he saw it, they had "no organizing ability" and often made arrangements without enough consideration. Wally found that the Czechs simply said, "'Yes, we will have it this way or that way,' and then the affair usually [flopped] because they [did] little or nothing about the details."[5]

The work in Czechoslovakia changed under Wally's direction. Missionary Edward B. Morrell said that they did not have street meetings. Instead, under President Toronto, they had very large public meetings, often with 100 to 370 people present. However, on other occasions they could only get 10 to attend. The elders, particularly in Prague, worked out a strategy for attracting people. After meetings on Sunday, they wrote down the names of the visitors and went to their homes. That way, they were able to hold meetings in the investigators' homes.[6]

3. Czechoslovak Mission Manuscript History, June 20, 1936, December 20, 1936, and September 20, 1937.

4. Toronto, "Some Socio-psychological Aspects," 7–8.

5. Toronto, journal, December 6–12, 1936, 59.

6. Ed and Norma Morrell, interview, May 8, 2013, 10.

Wally had some concerns about how to preach the gospel in Czechoslovakia. One was that there were only two large cities. The majority of the fourteen million Czechoslovakians lived in small, scattered villages. Wally wondered how he could have elders learn Czech sufficiently enough to be able to travel from village to village preaching to "the honest in heart."[7] To answer the quandary, the missionaries went tracting. Wally sensed that they did make some progress that way. The Czech missionaries had about seven tracts written in Czech. Those assigned to smaller villages went to every house; sometimes they visited the same home two or three times.[8] One lady wrote to Wally to tell him that she could hardly wait for the young man (a missionary who had come to her door during one of their tracts) to return with more.[9]

Even when missionaries were not assigned to a certain area, the meetings were still important, and the Czech Saints continued holding them even without missionary influence. In October 1938, the Saints in Tabor held a meeting at a sister's home. Wally intended to go to that meeting, but he was unable to find the house until about nine o'clock that evening. Everyone was still there—three members and two friends that had not given up hope that he would come. They had a song and prayer and then discussed their Sunday School lesson while they waited. When he got there, Wally blessed the sacrament. They stayed until almost midnight talking about recent events in light of the gospel. Regarding the late night meeting, Wally recorded, "It is glorious to feel the spirit of these splendid 'lone' members, who, although without missionaries, meet together each week and conduct meetings of their own." Wally became convinced that "people can do the work if we only give them the necessary suggestions and place our trust and confidence in them."[10]

While tracting was successful, the most important part of Wally's "modus operandi" was not tracting; rather, it was holding these

7. Toronto, journal, August 15–21, 1937, 137.

8. Ed and Norma Morrell, interview, May 8, 2013, 9.

9. Toronto, journal, August 23–29, 1936, 32.

10. Toronto, journal, October 23–29, 1938, 285–86.

Wallace Toronto (right) with Czechoslovakian missionaries, 1937. Courtesy of Church History Library.

public meetings. Wally did all he could to get as many investigators to meetings as possible. On one occasion, he personally distributed three thousand handbills. However, only thirty people showed up to the meeting. Wally titled his talk "Is Death the End of All?" There were some new faces there, and Wally felt that some good had been accomplished even with such a low turnout. At the meeting, Wally had given the first part of his speech without paper and knew he was blessed by the Lord to be able to speak without notes. "The people were interested and seemed eager to know the truth," Wally wrote. "I am convinced more and more that the only way we will make headway here is to preach the Gospel as straightforward as we know how. We are not here to please the people, but are here to give the message."[11]

Holding meetings was rarely easy. Wally was frequently required to petition the local government or police for permission to hold meetings in certain

11. Toronto, journal, October 25–31, 1936, 48.

locations. For instance, in Plzeň, when the police had denied to see him, he succeeded in getting to see the chief commissioner. He told Wally that the missionaries had been denied the privilege once before because there had been a Mr. Craig—who was not a Mormon—who had applied to give lectures under the title of "Mormon." When the police commissioner learned that Craig was not LDS, he "changed his demeanor" and asked for the names of all the missionaries in the area "as well as a letter of appeal from their former decision."[12] In one particular location, Wally was told he could not receive permission to hold meetings because only Czech citizens had that right. When he told the police officer that they held English lessons after the meetings, the officer changed his mind. Permission was granted, and the officer even attended one himself.[13]

President Toronto's practices did begin to bear fruit. The number of baptisms increased the first year that Wally served, reaching a high of thirty in 1936. But then, as political conflict developed, they declined to seventeen in 1937 and to just six in both 1938 and 1939.[14] The baptisms were held in various places: in the dead of the night in a river with ice cut away, in a swimming pool in Prague, in a bathhouse, and on the Beroun River.[15] Wally attended each and every one.[16] Nevertheless, he began to become very concerned that those being baptized were not truly converted. He was worried that some missionaries were baptizing people without making any effort to prepare the converts for living the gospel. He recorded, "Many of them have no conception of the real meaning of their baptism. They probably consented in a moment of spiritual up-lift or to please some missionary. And when a crisis came, they had no solid foundation upon which to stand." Sub-

12. Toronto, journal, October 17–23, 1937, 157–58.

13. Toronto, journal, December 26–31, 1937, 179.

14. Mehr, *Mormon Missionaries Enter Eastern Europe*, 69.

15. Marion Toronto Miller and Judith Toronto Richards, interview by Mary Jane Woodger, May 3, 2013, Salt Lake City, 16, 20, in author's possession; Toronto, journal, July 12–18, 1936, 13; and Toronto, journal, October 9–15, 1938, 280.

16. Gad Vojkůvka, "Memories of President Wallace Felt Toronto," email to Mary Jane Woodger, November 9, 2013, transcription in author's possession.

sequently, he encouraged missionaries to be sure that the converts' testimonies were strong.[17] He developed instructions for missionaries to use in deciding when it was time to baptize a convert. He requested that missionaries follow an outline of eight important steps in teaching and guiding people to the gospel and then to baptism.[18] One could possibly look at these eight steps as a pre–*Preach My Gospel* handbook for missionaries of that day and age.

One of Wally's biggest struggles was opposition from the Catholic Church. Priests constantly caused trouble for him and the missionaries by fostering anti-Mormon feelings. In Kolín, there was a Catholic priest who worked very hard against allowing Wally and the Church to hold meetings. Wally traced all the problems in the location to that particular priest, who had given a lengthy lecture about Mormons. Wally informed Mr. Potter, the American Consulate, of the problem. Potter became very upset about the treatment that Wally and the missionaries, as Americans, were receiving.[19] The situation in Kolín was finally escalated to a judiciary hearing.

At the hearing, the police commissioner testified that the missionaries had been denied permission to hold meetings on the grounds that they were foreigners. His conclusion was based on an 1867 law that forbade foreigners to meet. Ironically, the same law had given the missionaries permission to remain in the first place. After examination, the commissioner finally admitted that the problem was not the 1869 statute, but rather Catholic intolerance. A denial had been registered against the Mormons. It was decided that they would have to put in an appeal to the Land Office in Prague. Wally wrote an appeal that afternoon to Prague.[20] He then found out that part of the problem was that he was not forming his application correctly. He had been asking for permission to hold a series of lectures, but the law required him to ask for one meeting or lecture at a time. Wally was very surprised that

17. Toronto, journal, December 12–18, 1937, 174.

18. Toronto, journal, February 20–26, 1938, 200.

19. Toronto, journal, September 6–12, 1936, 36.

20. Toronto, journal, January 1–8, 1938, 181.

the local police officers had not informed him of that requirement.[21] He decided to lie low for a month and then make a new application. In the meantime, the missionaries worked quietly among their friends.[22] Wally later prepared individual applications for each separate meeting and handed them to the police officers. Permission was finally granted.[23]

Getting permission was also a problem in Benešov, stemming again from Catholic party objectors who accused the missionaries of being a threat to the public peace of the city. Wally thought, "This is just like in the dark ages!" He visited an official of the country office who had previously denied them permission to hold meetings there because of a deliberate uprising from the Catholic party to get rid of them. He had a long gospel talk with the country official and pointed out the virtues of the gospel. The official happened to be a Catholic and said he could never conform to Mormon views. But when Wally explained that the teachings of the Church "were those of Christ and of his early church, and that the present day religious organizations had changed and despoiled much of the former truth, he became very interested." They talked for about an hour. When Wally left, the official told him that if he wanted to go to Benešov again, he should visit the official, who would do all he could to grant them permission. Wally truly knew that the Lord had blessed him and that he had made a fine cause to have the official understand the nature of the work.[24]

When Wally spoke, he often found big crowds gathered to hear him. In Benešov, he had a packed hall of 180 people. Part of the crowd was probably there because of the "advertising" that the Catholic priest had given against it "from his pulpit the Sunday before." Some of the missionaries had gone to that meeting. They heard the priest "denounce the new Christian sects which had arisen as a result of an apostasy from the Mother church and 'especially the newest of them,

21. Toronto, journal, January 16–22, 1938, 186.

22. Toronto, journal, February 6–19, 1938, 197.

23. Toronto, journal, February 27–26, 1938, 200.

24. Toronto, journal, August 7–13, 1938, 253.

the Mormons.'" Many people who attended simply out of curiosity were impressed by Wally's lecture on the life of Christ.[25]

However, at other places, attendance was sparse. In Olomouc, Wally gave a lecture to just twenty-three people. Following the lecture, he held a short meeting with the missionaries and insisted that they find a new hall near the heart of town. He had a feeling that the problem was that the location of their hall was unfavorable. "Time will tell the Gospel story of Olomouc too—the seat of the Archbishopric of the Catholic Church." Wally felt like they were "blasting boulders to get those people interested in religious matters."[26] He found it strange that some places were inclined toward hearing the word of God and that others totally rejected it.

A priest in Hradiště had forbidden his congregation from attending an upcoming LDS meeting and had spoken against the missionaries. But at the meeting, Wally was delighted when they counted eighty people in the hall. Some even had to stand. Wally talked about why he had come to Czechoslovakia. One of the missionaries also gave a talk on the important principles of Mormonism. The crowd seemed pleased with the meeting. Wally observed, "I am afraid that the priest actually helped out our attendance by railing against us. At any rate the Lord blessed us in our undertaking."[27]

Catholic interference became a constant problem for Wally. Priests caused havoc wherever and whenever they could. After one member's funeral, a police officer stopped Wally and asked him if he had conducted a service at the cemetery. When he affirmed that he had been in charge, the police officer asked him if he had received permission to do so. Wally was astonished. He had never needed written permission before to conduct a funeral. He later learned that someone had seen them at the cemetery and had run to the police to tell them about it, hoping to get them in trouble; permission to hold public meetings was then denied temporarily. "The Catholics do seem to rise up against us

25. Toronto, journal, December 19–25, 1937, 176.

26. Toronto, journal, February 2–March 5, 1938, 202.

27. Toronto, journal, September 6–12, 1936, 35.

Torontos with Czechoslovakian missionaries, 1938–39. Courtesy of Church History Library.

in that town. I offered to go to the police station with the officer. On the way we met the Chief Inspector, who told him to merely take my name and address, and to have the Bensov missionaries come in the following morning, and fix the matter up. He indicated that there would be no difficulty about it."[28]

Catholic opposition even began to appear in some newspaper articles, containing what Wally called "a rather unfriendly smack." However, in the long run he did not think it did the Church much damage.[29] He was sure that the Catholic or clerical party was trying to eliminate Mormons in Czechoslovakia. But he was intent not to let it happen. "They will not do these things without a fight on their hands. Encouraged, possibly, by the Benešov

28. Toronto, journal, January 23–29, 1938, 188.

29. Toronto, journal, March 28–April 3, 1937, 93.

incident, they seem inclined to carry it farther."[30] Wally decided one time to join them instead of fight them. On an Easter Sunday, he and Martha went inside St. Vitus Cathedral to attend Easter Mass. They wormed through the throngs of people and "went to the great cold edifice, where [they] saw the archbishop and all his bishops" proceeding through what Wally called "pompous and monotonous ceremonies." He and Martha "didn't have the patience to sit through it all, and so [they] wended [their] way home, thankful that [they had] no convictions which [led them] to that kind of pitiful worship—nothing but show, pomp, ceremony and pageantry—perhaps soothing and edifying if one likes it."[31]

When political unrest developed, Wally often had to inform the missionaries that some activities in Czechoslovakia could be dangerous. In June 1938, he warned the elders, "It is our great desire to have nothing come up which will endanger the good name of the Church and our mission. We as a mission want to 'come through clean,' and particularly in connection with the Czech people and government." He reminded his missionaries, "These folks are going through trying times and must seek every avenue of precaution against outside interference. Let us be aware of the fact that we are foreigners among them—thus subject to suspicion, and let us remember that the unwise use of a camera increases this suspicion a hundredfold." He then told the elders to never take photos without first securing permission from a police officer.[32]

Despite Wally's warnings on that front, his missionaries got into trouble on multiple occasions for taking pictures, and he was constantly exerting effort and time getting them out of it. Two elders who had ignored Wally's rules had taken unauthorized photos and immediately received notice to leave the country. They were given fifteen days to make an appeal. Wally formulated a letter for the missionaries stating the reasons why they were in Czechoslovakia and what their

30. Toronto, journal, April 3–9, 1938, 213.

31. Toronto, journal, April 10–16, 1938, 216.

32. Toronto, "Restricted Use of Cameras," *Hvězdička*, June 1938.

official connection was to the mission office. He sent the letter to the judge. With such goings on, it seemed to Wally "like the devil himself is busying himself in our work. But we must fight him as best we can—and above all avoid issues which cast suspicion on us. It may be that I shall have to forbid the use of cameras."[33] He warned, "If you do not follow this out, we shall have to call all cameras into the mission office and keep them for you until you are released—and thus forbid their use entirely. We must take every precaution."[34]

The next morning, Wally went to the district court with the three missionaries in question, along with C. D. Wallenfels from the American Consulate in Prague. The judge said he had received Wally's letter concerning the situation. Each elder was then called in and questioned as to what he was doing there, why he had taken the trip to the Sázava in the Benešov district, why he had taken pictures, what he had taken pictures of, and so on. The whole proceeding lasted about forty minutes. The missionaries were then required to sign a written statement that ultimately ended the hearing.[35]

However, just a few days later, one of the elders sent an express letter to Wally that startled him profusely. The elder had received an order from the police to leave the country at once. Wally turned the letter over to a lawyer, who informed him that the orders were given because the missionaries were under suspicion of being spies. Wally called the judge who had handled the previous case. After discussing the matter, the case was dropped.[36]

Then the problem with taking illegal photos surfaced again in February 1937 when another elder was ordered to leave the country. Wally called Mr. Chapman of the American Embassy, who had been in touch with the Ministry of Interior. The Ministry of Interior was actually surprised that the case had not been concluded. Mr. Chapman, however, was optimistic and promised that he would see that the Prague police

33. Toronto, journal, September 6–12, 1936, 37.

34. Toronto, "Restricted Use of Cameras," *Hvězdička*, June 1938.

35. Toronto, journal, September 13–19, 1936, 39.

36. Toronto, journal, September 20–26, 1936, 41–42.

did not interfere with Wally's mission work again.[37] Sure enough, the elder received a notice the next Saturday to report to the police station, and he found that all charges of espionage had been dropped. Wally was relieved by the news. A considerable number of comments had been in the newspapers about internal spies and how the death penalty was inflicted on citizens who betrayed the country's secrets. He knew of one officer who was condemned to die that very week. The laws were tightening up to thwart espionage. Wally again reiterated to his missionaries, "We cannot afford to be tangled up with any charges even when such charges are groundless." He warned and forewarned the missionaries that they had to be very careful about their actions.[38]

Unfortunately, that was not the last time that missionaries got into trouble with the Czech government for breaking various rules. On January 5, 1937, two elders made their appearance in Prague because the county police refused to register them. They ordered the missionaries out because of a new military law regarding border zones in Třebová, where the missionaries were working. Wally secured copies of the laws of the counties and attempted to discover which bordering counties the elders could not go in without the consent of military authorities. On behalf of the American Consulate, Mr. Potter offered to attempt to find out what the missionaries' rights were. He certainly helped to clarify the situation. Wally was constantly on alert. "One mis-step and all twenty of our brethren could be ordered out of the country. We must be so very careful."[39]

It was one worry after another for Wally; however, he had decided that this was why he was there—to handle the problems. Everything the missionaries did required that they receive permission. Even when Wally ordered some radio tunes from home, he discovered that he had to get permission from the Ministry of War because they were the ones in control of everything that had to do with communication.[40]

---

37. Toronto, journal, February 21–27, 1937, 82.
38. Toronto, journal, February 21–27, 1937, 82.
39. Toronto, journal, January 1–9, 1937, 66.
40. Toronto, journal, February 14–20, 1937, 80.

Again, one elder wrote Wally to tell him he had been called into the police station and questioned about his permission to stay in the country. Previously, in February of 1936, the elder had received a note from the police that he had neglected to read. At the police station, he found out that he had been in the country without permission since the time the note was issued. It was then September of 1937. "Another head-ache," recorded Wally. "But I think that we will be able to pull the right strings and fix it up. I advised him immediately that we would get to work on it, and I called Mr. Chapin of the American legation concerning the matter."[41]

Another missionary neglected to read the orders issued to him and was only permitted to stay in Czechoslovakia until September 1, 1937, because of the technicality. Wally remarked that the incident would surely add another gray hair to his head. "Great guns, if I can only get the brethren to look out for themselves and take a little responsibility in this matter." He "wrote a long letter of explanation and excuse to the Zemský Úřad in Brno." The matter was cleared up without difficulty.[42]

Although he was frustrated at times, Wally's sense of humor was part of his missionary leadership. He once dressed up in one of Martha's dresses, put on makeup, and went to a masquerade ball that was hosted in the Prague Branch hall by the Mutual Improvement Association. A total of 150 people attended. Among the group was a host of new faces who laughed at Wally's antics. The program that followed was excellent. He recognized it as "one of the finest evenings" that had ever been held "since the mission was organized."[43] An event called an anniversary social was held at Prague Hall with more than 130 people present. It was full of entertainment. The "Melody Boys" (a quartet that Wally put together) performed at the social and sang humorous Czech melodies that brought down the house. During the intermission, the kitchen sold sandwiches, cakes, and drinks.[44]

41. Toronto, journal, August 29–September 4, 1937, 140.

42. Toronto, journal, October 3–9, 1937, 152.

43. Toronto, journal, February 19–25, 1939, 335.

44. Toronto, journal, July 16–22, 1939, 386.

And, despite all the difficulty with the Czechoslovakian government and the Catholic party, Wally and his missionaries continued to find ways to spread the gospel. One way was through music—hence, the "Melody Boys." In Brno, he discussed the plan of having a musical quartet made up of missionaries. He suggested, "We need some kind of a plan to draw the people to us during these times of stress and tension. We need to get also within the reach of the better-to-do classes and acquaint them with the message as well. A musical quartet, if good enough, might be able to find openings on the radio, receive press comments and be invited to perform for all kinds of clubs and organizations—but only along with a talk on Mormonism."[45] However, his plan was not so easy to carry out. He found that he did not have the essential talent in his elders for the quartet, so he wrote to the First Presidency and asked for missionaries to be sent to Czechoslovakia with the necessary skill set. President McKay replied that he would try to send some new missionaries before May 1, including both a pianist and a first tenor. In addition, President McKay impressed upon Wally the "necessity of carrying on the mission work, even though conditions [were becoming] unfavorable."[46]

When the quartet was finally formed, they made great strides, just as Wally had envisioned. In his journal dated February 1939, he recorded that they had been practicing quite regularly and that at a Mutual Improvement Association meeting in Prague, they were called back by applause several times. He also saw the possibility of the elders singing over the radio in Brno and performing at the Brno and Prague English Clubs. He hoped "to be able to establish a reputation and do some good for the work [there] through the medium of music."[47] Wally had become a regular at the English clubs, an interesting practice that he used in his missionary work. In particular, the English Club Union, which he attended frequently, began to be a great blessing in the work of the mission. He often gave talks at the Private

45. Toronto, journal, August 14–20, 1938, 255.

46. Toronto, journal, March 5–11, 1939, 339.

47. Toronto, journal, February 26–March 4, 1939, 337.

Members in Prague Mutual Improvement Association meeting hall, 1949. Courtesy of Church History Library.

English Circle of Prague. On one occasion, he gave a talk to about forty people and spoke about "A Crisis with the U.S. Constitution" and about President Roosevelt's plan to reconfigure the Supreme Court. Usually he felt like his talks were well received.[48]

Wally was invited to attend various other clubs as well. One member arranged for Wally to give a "Utah" lecture at the Pansky Club, one of the most exclusive men's organizations in Brno. There, Wally became acquainted with several influential men, including Dr. Jar Lorek (reputed to be a millionaire) and Dr. Nedela (a famous builder), with whom he had a fine gospel talk. He was glad that he had the chance to meet the "monied men" and that they had an opportunity to hear something about Mormonism. He distributed a number of booklets at the clubs. Wally used his club meetings to make headway.

48. Toronto, journal, April 4–10, 1937, 95.

However, when there was a little progress, there was also backlash. He noted, "Wherever we work the devil is on his toes." The same evening that he gave his lecture at the Pansky Club, "several people [had] stood outside . . . and passed out anti-Mormon literature to all who had been in attendance." In typical optimistic fashion, he said, "It may do us more good than harm. I never fear such things."[49]

Though both the quartet and Wally's work in the clubs received some favorable attention, Wally met with several elders back at the mission home to discuss why missionary work was not progressing faster in other areas. It seemed to Wally that they were continually "undertaking a process of gleaning" and that few were accepting the message. He asked the elders, "What can we do to improve our methods and our efficiency?" Wally admitted that the question burned in his heart "most of the time. How can our brethren become more zealous in the work?"[50] He spent much of his time over the three years that followed working on that question.

49. Toronto, journal, December 5–11, 1937, 172; and Toronto, journal, July 11–17, 1937, 125.

50. Toronto, journal, October 24–30, 1937, 158.

6 MAKING THE CZECH PEOPLE "MORMON CONSCIOUS"

Wally's efforts to refocus missionary work and open new areas were boosted by a visit from the prophet, President Heber J. Grant, and President J. Reuben Clark Jr. in July 1937.[1] Throughout that summer, Wally spent a great deal of time preparing for their visit by distributing news articles among a number of newspaper editors. During their stay there, forty articles appeared about them and their visit in various publications. Wally also wrote articles for the *Deseret News*, such as one he titled "Czechoslovakia Welcomes the President," and sent them home with a number of photos of President Grant.[2] And Wally was sure that the visit of these great leaders would never be forgotten by the missionaries who clustered about them and received their inspiration and blessings.

When the prophet arrived, everyone was impressed with his appealing and fascinating manner and keen intellect. He and his associates in turn voiced their

---

1. Mehr, "Czech Saints: A Brighter Day," 48.
2. Toronto, journal, July 4–10, 1937, 121; and Toronto, journal, July 25–31, 1937, 131.

President Heber J. Grant's visit to Czechoslovakia in July 1937. Marion Toronto, with President Grant, Elder Richard R. Lyman, and Wallace Toronto (centered). Courtesy of Church History Library.

appreciation of the work of the Latter-day Saints in Czechoslovakia and of the quality of the missionaries. As they traveled from village to village, President Grant enjoyed the journey greatly. He sang, as was his custom, a number of hymns along the way, including "A Poor Wayfaring Man of Grief" and "O My Father." In recent years, some thought that President Grant was tone deaf, but he delighted in singing and often referred to being able to sing as his single greatest accomplishment. Wally made mention that never in the mission had they had the opportunity to meet and listen to so many General Authorities at one time. He thought, "This visit will go down in our history as one of the fine events which helped renew our courage and faith, and which assisted in making Czechoslovakia 'Mormon conscious.'"[3]

3. Toronto, journal, July 4–10, 1937, 122.

President Grant told the elders of his own mission to Japan and of the discouragement he had felt when they only baptized three people, all of whom were later excommunicated. On the other hand, he also referred to the marvelous work still to be done in the world and to the successes he had experienced in Great Britain, parts of Europe, and the Hawaiian Islands. President Grant was emphatic that the Lord's work cannot be stayed. He "stressed the fact that missionary training is better than a college education. . . . [He also] repeated his favorite saying that that which we persist in doing becomes easy to do—not that the nature of the thing changes, but that our power to overcome it increases." Wally felt it was a great and glorious opportunity to come "to know President Grant intimately to feel his warmth, his spirit, his kindness and his love."[4]

Wally was equally excited to become acquainted with President Clark. Describing him in his journal, Wally wrote: "What a keen mind; what a level head; what a vast variety of experiences. The government officials almost bowed and scraped to him. And yet how humble and delightful he was all of the time. The more I see of the Church leaders and the more intimately I can observe them, the more humble I feel in their presence. I know that they are men chosen of God, for they stand far in the lead of ordinary men. They radiate humility and inspiration and their testimonies of this great work are unshaken." Wally felt "blessed beyond measure" to have had the privilege of meeting with the General Authorities of the Church and humbly wondered if he was worthy of those blessings.[5]

While accompanying the prophet, President Clark was interviewed by a number of journalists for several papers. A long article that included his picture appeared in the *A-Zet*, as well as in other papers. His arrival in Czechoslovakia was announced over the radio because, apart from being a member of the First Presidency of the LDS Church, he was also a former undersecretary of state. He, along with the group, also visited the American Consulate. They met with

4. Toronto, journal, July 11–17, 1937, 123, 127.
5. Toronto, journal, August 8–14, 1937, 136.

a Mr. Jan Broz, who was a former member of the Foreign Ministry of Czechoslovakia and a Czech official in Mexico. It became an unexpected reunion when he saw President and Mrs. Clark, for he knew them when they served in Mexico in government service.[6]

Wally was amazed by the stamina of the eighty-one-year-old prophet.[7] Wally recorded his feelings about the events that had occurred. "We have been unusually blessed by the presence of the President of the Church and his party in Czechoslovakia." He knew that no one would ever fail to remember "the memorable missionary meetings in which we had the marvelous opportunity" to listen to so many General Authorities of the Church. "It was an occasion which comes usually but once in a life time." Wally believed that the visit of President Grant and his party's visit to Czechoslovakia had "done more than any other single thing to make the Czech people 'Mormon conscious.'"[8]

Right after President Grant's visit, a satirical article appeared about Mormons, specifically about Brigham Young, accompanied by ugly caricatures, in a Czech magazine named *Světozor*. Wally visited the editor, Dr. Altscule, and expressed his dislike of the article and his disappointment that Mormons were made the focus of such satire and irony. The editor apologized and agreed to print an article, with pictures, to compensate for any damage done. Wally gave him an article on polygamy and the Mormons with some photographs. He noted, "If he doesn't print [then] we have recourse to the courts and the press law, which demands the printing of a counter article when requested by the offended party."[9]

When negative articles such as the one in *Světozor* were written, Wally often reminded the editors of the 27,000 crowns that the Mormons had given them to help the "starving German children in Czechoslovakia." One such editor was chastised through the Foreign

6. Toronto, journal, August 8–14, 1937, 135–36.
7. Mehr, "Czech Saints: A Brighter Day," 48–49.
8. Toronto, "Mission President's Message," *Hvězdička*, August 1937.
9. Toronto, journal, August 15–21, 1937, 138.

Office Bureau for a story that was without foundation. Wally told him that he would be "glad to have them print an article about us [the Latter-day Saints], of our own writing, and call the matter settled."[10] Indeed, Wally made great strides with the Czechoslovakian press.

Under Wally's direction, the mission formed a tradition celebrating Pioneer Day, which was also the day when the Czech mission was formed in 1929. Since then, an ever-increasing group gathered at Karlstejn, the dedication site, every year on its anniversary to express gratitude to God for the blessed privilege of being able to hear and accept the gospel in the Czech language. They commemorated the young, courageous men, including Wally, who had made that day and their progress possible. And, of course, they also remembered the faith and courage of the Mormon pioneers.[11]

Wally established another tradition: publishing a monthly mission newsletter. In many of these newsletters, he often reminded the missionaries of the importance and value of fasting. In August 1937, he wrote, "No brother should deprive himself of the spirituality which comes from an occasional day of fasting and prayer, and of the added blessing which follows the payment of a fast donation. This kind of thing will help to put you in spiritual tune for the work you are attempting to do."[12] Wally frequently asked both missionaries and members to pray and fast. He once fasted for two days straight. He believed that it would "humble [him] a little more to carry the responsibility of leading the mission" during distressing times. He received "considerable spiritual strength" from his fast.[13] He asked the brethren of different branches to fast specifically in behalf of his missionaries and the troubles they faced. Some of those troubles, at times, were physical, not spiritual. For instance, one missionary struggled with a bad back. Wally urged the Prague brethren to fast and pray in his behalf. The very next day, the elder was able to sleep for ten hours undisturbed,

10. Toronto, journal, November 21–27, 1937, 166.

11. Toronto, "Our Ninth Anniversary," *Hvězdička*, July 1938.

12. Toronto, "Mission President's Message," *Hvězdička*, August 1937.

13. Toronto, journal, April 16–22, 1939, 353.

which was unusual for him. Wally thought, "If there is any place in the world where faith and administrations ought to be effective it seems to me it ought to be in the mission field, where we are working closely to the Lord."[14]

One of the most important teachings Wally shared in the newsletters was of the truthfulness of the Book of Mormon. The reprinting of the Book of Mormon in the Czech language helped the Church to grow in that nation. The original translation, published in 1932, had been done by a translator who was not a member. The Czech Saints kept copies of the new translation all throughout the German period.[15] Wally frequently wrote in his journal about his study of the Book of Mormon. In one entry, he recorded, "I utilized the rest of the day in study—particularly of the Book of Mormon. Although I have read it, I find so much that is new and inspiring every time I pick it up. I cannot see how anyone with a sincere heart could read it and then deny its divinity. Martha is also reading it. Then too, we are attempting to read each day from it in Czech."[16]

Wally wrote about a lot of different things he did and related the events back to teaching about or reading from the Book of Mormon. He wrote about the meetings that they held where people were really interested in hearing its message. He wrote about an event where everyone participated in "community singing, devoured two dishes of delicious soup, read from the Book of Mormon, and then played games."[17] He talked about a time when he "sent off a leather-bound Czech Book of Mormon to Dr. Alice Masaryk, together with other material, to be placed in her father's library at Lany."[18] When meeting with officials, he would give them leather-bound copies of the Book of Mormon that President Grant had signed upon Wally's request.[19] At one point, Wally

14. Toronto, journal, June 13–19, 1937, 115.

15. Ed and Norma Morrell, interview, May 8, 2013, 18.

16. Toronto, journal, August 2–8, 1936, 22.

17. Toronto, journal, March 28–April 3, 1937, 93–94.

18. Toronto, journal, March 27–April 2, 1938, 211.

19. Toronto, journal, July 11–17, 1937, 124.

had more than 2,000 copies in his garage and was anxious to sell them to investigators.[20]

Although the Book of Mormon was extremely important to the Czech Mission, another volume also found prominence: *Articles of Faith*, by James E. Talmage. Early on, Wally wished to develop a two-year study course for his missionaries based on Talmage's *Articles of Faith* that involved some memory work, chiefly of passages of scripture but also of all the Czech pamphlets. He felt incapable of undertaking such a work; thus, he wrote to President Richard R. Lyman of the Quorum of the Twelve Apostles and asked him to have some of the best heads of the Church work up a study course on *Articles of Faith* for all the missions of the Church. He asked if it could possibly include examinations and assigned papers that students at Brigham Young University could correct. He "even suggested that college credit be given for such a course, if properly worked out and approved. Maybe it is a 'pipe dream,' but I believe it could be made a vital part of our work."[21]

Even though Wally felt incapable of writing such a course, he at least wanted to make sure that *Articles of Faith* was translated into Czech, and by February of 1939, the translation was completed.[22] When he first saw two bound copies of the Czech *Articles of Faith*, he noted what "a beautiful book" it was and had over a thousand copies printed for distribution.[23] Wally sent 140 books to various public libraries in Bohemia, Moravia, and Slovakia. Some were returned, but scores of libraries sent letters of thanks and appreciation for the gift. He was pleased that 130 books were in the libraries of Czechoslovakia and its neighboring nations to spread the message of the gospel to those who would be led to seek it out.[24] He desired to have the Pearl of Great Price and a new Relief Society handbook published and translated into Czech as well. He hoped that the Relief Society handbook in

20. Toronto, journal, January 9–15, 1938, 183.

21. Toronto, journal, July 24–30, 1938, 249.

22. Toronto, journal, January 1–7, 1939, 321.

23. Toronto, journal, February 5–11, 1939, 329.

24. Toronto, journal, June 18–24, 1939, 376.

particular "would stimulate the work of the fine women and give them a more definite idea as to the organization and program of the Relief Society."[25]

In visiting the wards and branches over which he presided, Wally found that marriage was frequently a topic that came up in his conversations with the singles. Many young Czech converts wondered if they would ever be married in a temple. It truly broke his heart. He, too, wondered if it would ever happen. One particular sister asked him if "not being married in the temple would hold her [back] from the blessings of celestial glory." Wally replied, "This is a great question among the members here, who have no opportunity to marry in the temple, and oftimes [have] no opportunity to marry at all." He made the sister a special promise. "A just God would take all of these things into consideration. . . . In the millennium such adjustments would be made."[26]

A young LDS couple went to the mission office one day to talk about some of the problems with their marriage. He "warned them of some of the pit-falls, and urged them to live the marriage bond as though it had been performed for eternity, telling them that some day they would be eternally joined by temple ceremony."[27] However, when two sisters got engaged to Church members on another occasion, he remarked that the "Brodil girls are going to enjoy all of the blessings of the Church, including marriage in the temple—a thing I have secretly prayed for during many months. They are wonderful girls."[28]

Wally found that weddings were quite different in Czechoslovakia compared to what he was used to in Utah. In January 1939, Wally attended the wedding of two members. He watched as six couples got married at once in an unimpressive ceremony performed by the state. Afterwards, he became even more thankful for his temple marriage. In his journal, he recorded:

25. Toronto, journal, February 5–11, 1939, 329–400.

26. Toronto, journal, July 31–August 6, 1938, 250.

27. Toronto, journal, January 22–28, 1938, 325.

28. Toronto, journal, January 1–9, 1937, 65.

My heart went out to our young members here, who do not have such an opportunity. However, I am sure they shall have it someday. We wished them well on their journey of matrimony, and of course they beamed all over, but were so wrapped up in one another that they didn't know what it was all about anyway. They are our first Mormon couple to marry in the Czechoslovak Mission field and we are proud of them. There are other prospects now though, for Brother Dlouhy and Sister Baštova are thinking seriously of it, providing finances work out and in event that her mother doesn't oppose it too vigorously, which she has done up till now. Marriage is a real problem among young people here.[29]

Wally often visited with members and tried to stay in touch with "lone" Latter-day Saints scattered throughout Czechoslovakia. His ministry understandably involved giving blessings: baby blessings, blessings of healing, and blessings of comfort. He was frequently required to "pour oil [of counsel] on the troubled waters" during those blessings. Counseling members often, he helped straighten out their quarrels. At the same time, he took to finding amusement with the members, whether it was playing volleyball with them or playing with the members' children. He thought, "We won our way a little closer into their hearts by playing with them. They saw that we were one with them, and sensing this poured out their hospitality to us."[30]

Wally was also determined that his missionaries would have "more spirituality than any other age of missionaries has ever possessed." To meet the challenge, he felt that the missionaries needed to sharpen their tools, be guided by the promptings of the Spirit, and be stimulated by a genuine love and affection for those among whom they labored. He was determined that missionary life should be based on deep, sincere spirituality and heartfelt love. If the missionaries could cultivate those two things, Wally believed they would find themselves

29. Toronto, journal, January 15–21, 1939, 324.

30. Toronto, journal, August 7–13, 1938, 252; February 12–18, 1939, 331–32; May 28–June 3, 1939, 364; February 26–March 4, 1939, 336; July 23–29, 1939, 390; July 16–22, 1939, 386; June 21–27, 1936, 9.

unknowingly polishing up tools for spreading the gospel.[31] He outlined his teachings in one of the mission newsletters:

> First, a knowledge of the Gospel is of utmost importance. Under the proper stimulus, you will thrill with each page of it. You will desire to know it so thoroughly that you can make it perfectly clear to any thinking and willing mind.
>
> Secondly, is a knowledge of the language of those among whom you labor. The Gospel message is of little use to you as a missionary, unless you can express it in plain, forceful language which all can understand. With spirituality as a guide and love as a stimulus, nothing will be able to prevent you from learning the language.
>
> Next, perhaps, is a knowledge of the people among whom you labor. You will seek to learn of them through the experiences of others as found in books of custom, tradition and history. But better still you will have the urge to learn of them first-handed, to mingle with them, study them and their habits, and appraise their accomplishments.[32]

Wally also believed that tracts, articles, and booklets would help elders if they got them into the hands of their investigators. He became aware of a new media that the missionaries could use: lantern slide machines, and he wanted them used at least once a week. Apart from the slides, he also utilized what he called "all . . . means of propaganda," including bills, posters, newspapers, and the radio. In short, he asked his missionaries, "Are you using all such to the best of your ability and to [the] best advantage?"[33]

He then told the missionaries that teaching by example was not enough. They needed to make sure that they were in the homes of friends—members and nonmembers alike. Then hopefully, those nonmembers would want to inquire about the plan of life.[34] Preaching at its best lacks the warmth of personal contact, he said, and is always one-sided. "Preaching, with rare exceptions, is never so effective in warming the heart, inducing the mind and strengthening the soul, as is

---

31. Toronto, "Lord's Help Indispensable," *Hvězdička*, July 1938.

32. Toronto, "The Missionary Tools," *Hvězdička*, July 1938.

33. Toronto, "Other Implements Furnished You," *Hvězdička*, July 1938.

34. Toronto, "Converting Friends to the Gospel," *Hvězdička*, March 1938.

personal contact."[35] His message was always that faith was a principle of progression and power.[36]

Wally was well ahead of his time in putting genealogy research immediately into the hands of investigators. Two of his missionaries once spent two hours talking about the mechanics of genealogy work. Wally's goal was "to have every member of the mission secure his genealogical information for at least three generations back."[37] He was determined that the whole Czech Mission be devoted to the stimulation of genealogical work among the Church members. Wally knew it would do immeasurable good among them.[38] He organized genealogical classes and spoke on the gathering of records by the government in Germany and of photo work that was going on the record near the border. "It does seem as though the 'spirit of Elijah' is certainly working among the people," Wally observed. He noted the prophetic words of one brother who said, "'The Lord is far ahead of us. He has many missionaries and servants in the work—although many of them do not realize it.' It is a revelation to see all of these wonderful developments, which some day will be used to complete our temple work."[39]

Czech convert Gad Vojkůvka remembered Wally's "love of people. Strong faith, knowledge of the doctrine, scriptures and acceptance of inspiration, joyfulness, kindness and empathy for all." Wally had "intelligence, courage and incredible optimism with a constant smile. He was not weary of any work or labor. He was respectful to people—regardless of their position in life."[40] Wally's sister, Norma Morrell, said that "he was optimistic and had a wonderful sense of humor, and

35. Toronto, "Preaching and Teaching," *Hvězdička*, March 1938.

36. Toronto, journal, January 1–9, 1937, 65.

37. Toronto, journal, July 3–9, 1938, 241.

38. Toronto, journal, July 24–30, 1938, 250.

39. Toronto, journal, January 16–22, 1938, 185.

40. Vojkůvka, "Memories of President Wallace Felt Toronto," November 9, 2013.

was always just very upbeat and positive."[41] Those qualities were a great boon for him as he served as a mission president.

Johann Wondra observed that Wally "was different from many other people from America. He had a feeling for the people there. . . . This was his personality. And it was his Christ-like love." Wondra described him as the people's friend, "and therefore, they responded. . . . [He] expected that the people act as he [wanted] them to act." Wondra explained that like Christ, Wally "went about doing good. . . . He understood that each person is different and that his approach must be different. . . . This is what his missionaries learned."[42]

Wally was brave and bold in his approach. Part of Wally's bravery existed because of his incredible ability to depend on the Lord. "He expected and got help from the Lord when he needed it."[43] During that time, "he was the . . . embodiment of the Czech mission. He knew it, he loved Czechoslovakia, he knew Prague, he knew Brno, he knew Pilsen, he knew all the little outlying areas, he knew everything about it."[44] He also knew that to preach the gospel in the conditions that existed in Europe during this time period required great faith. And Wally exhibited that faith to his missionaries.

41. Ed and Norma Morrell, interview, May 8, 2013, 12.

42. Johann Wondra, interview by Mary Jane Woodger, May 30, 2013, Vienna, Austria, transcript in author's possession, 4.

43. Mel Mabey, interview by Mary Jane Woodger, August 13, 2013, Alpine, UT, transcript in author's possession, 8.

44. Bob and David Toronto, interview, August 20, 2013, 16.

7 "WHAT A POWER WE COULD HAVE"

During the mid-1900s, missionaries spent only one week in a missionary training facility. Then they went directly into the mission field to which they had been assigned. It then became "the mission president's responsibility to train his new missionaries in the language and gospel study."[1] Wally took this responsibility seriously. He tried to assign elders to the right district, town, or city and then transfer them so they were with the correct companions. He once noted in his journal, "I plunged into the puzzle of trying to most effectively transfer our missionaries. . . . It is a problem and sometimes a headache to make the best matches between the brethren, and to find capable men to take the positions of leadership and responsibility and who know enough Czech to carry on."[2]

Toronto had been a mission president for less than a month when he became discouraged at the missionaries' level of conversion. He wondered why his mission wasn't having the kind of success of the early missionaries

1. Miller, "My Story: The Dream," 5.
2. Toronto, journal, March 27–April 2, 1938, 211.

of the Church did, like Wilford Woodruff. The missionaries often reported to Wally that their lack of success was accredited to the people because they were "Godless, irreligious and indifferent." Wally admitted that the attitude of the people was part of the problem; however, he believed that the main problem, instead, was that his missionaries were less spiritual than those early missionaries of the Church. "Some of these boys are so young. Some need such a conversion! I have come to the conclusion that my hardest job is to convert the missionaries and make them feel their responsibilities. And I sometimes wonder if such a thing is possible."[3]

He decided the missionaries' biggest disadvantage was that they were "life-timers" instead of converts to the gospel. He informed his missionaries, "We have been born into the church—which we cannot help. We have never had the stimulation at home, perhaps to study out the Gospel and thus gain a burning testimony of its divinity. This may not be our fault. We have been brought up to take things for granted." He then offered them some encouragement. "It is not too late. It is a sorrowful thing that some missionaries leave the field after two or three years with their spirituality little improved. It is only because they never strove to attain it. And it is the all-important thing in successful missionary work."[4]

Wally lamented in his journal about his desire to motivate the elders in his care: "If our young men—more of them—were only leaders, who could make opportunities, when they do not seem to exist, or who could push the work with the pace and the enthusiasm which is required! Had we such men the work might grow and take on larger proportions. The greatest problem seems to be with the missionary himself—to help him convert himself to the Gospel, and make that conversion so successful and so complete that he feels his obligation to use every minute in worth-while endeavor."[5]

---

3. Toronto, journal, July 26–August 1, 1936, 20.
4. Wallace F. Toronto, "Our Own Progress Depends on Spirituality and Humility," *Hvězdička*, February 1938.
5. Toronto, journal, August 2–8, 1936, 23.

Wally's schedule constantly included time set aside for dealing with the problems of missionaries. Whenever new elders got to Czechoslovakia, he could quickly identify what each missionary's problems were. In one journal entry, he observed that one missionary was a bookworm and continued to study, never joining in games or entertainment. Another lacked the qualities of leadership. Another typical problem was that the Czech missionaries "had formed a 'Dear John' club that grew as time went on," and it took a toll on the morale of the mission.[6] After dealing with that same issue with so many missionaries, he stated, "This discouragement among missionaries is one of the worst problems I have to deal with."[7]

One missionary seemed to be "somewhat soured on the work" and felt he had "done little or no good" because he had not converted anybody. He went to the mission president and suggested that he be sent "home because of some throat trouble," but Wally knew that it was just an excuse. He observed that the missionary was not happy in the field and that he had a difficult time getting along with his companion. He was not what Wally called a "pusher" and did not "know the art of getting along with people." Wally threw up his arms in defeat. "I hardly know what to do with him to help him change his attitude."[8] Similarly, another companionship was not getting along either. They got into arguments and exchanged some very unkind remarks toward one another. In frustration, Wally recorded in his journal, "If we as missionaries can't demonstrate the Christian spirit among ourselves, how can we expect anything of the members."[9]

One missionary was becoming very discouraged over the language and went to Wally and explained his concern that he didn't know how to speak Czech very well. The inactivity in the Žižkov Branch, where he was working, was very high, and the elder feared that his lack of ability to speak the language would not help matters in the branch.

6. Miller, "My Story: The Dream," 12.

7. Toronto, journal, February 7–13, 1937, 79.

8. Toronto, journal, July 26–August 1, 1936, 20.

9. Toronto, journal, February 7–13, 1937, 79.

After Wally talked with him for a long time about the problems, he felt he had been able to encourage him to succeed. They prayed together about the matter. At the end of the interview, Wally felt that the young man was a fine boy with a very willing heart.[10] Toronto also wrote in his journal about yet another such elder. "I had an opportunity to talk to Brother Ward about his work here. He would like to leave for home when two and a half years are up. He is somewhat discouraged with our results, as are many of the brethren, and in view of our results is unable to see the deeper value of missionary activity. However, he said he would leave the decision in my hands and carry on as best he could. This work is difficult and tries the faith of these fine young elders. There is no doubt of that."[11]

Wally was sometimes less successful than he hoped to be with a few of the young elders. In particular, he felt that one missionary who desired to go home was a "damper" on the work. He was only doing "enough to survive" until he was released. Wally tried a number of ways to inspire the young man, but it was useless. He eventually came to the conclusion that he would have to let the missionary go for the sake of the other missionaries because his bad influence was dampening the strength of the whole mission. Whenever Wally had to send missionaries home, it always broke his heart. However, Wally never gave up on his missionaries. Even after they returned home, Wally stayed in contact with them and would try to straighten them out if they had strayed from the Church.[12]

One very different problem also plagued several missionaries. Wally recorded one instance in his journal:

> I happened to see Brother Williams and Brother Merrell with a very attractive young lady. I went over to them, and when they saw me coming they turned color a bit. However they introduced me, and then she told me that they were taking her to a show. The brethren knew they were in a pinch. I told them in English that I would expect a complete explanation in the morning, and left them two very surprised young

10. Toronto, journal, January 10–23, 1937, 71.
11. Toronto, journal, July 17–23, 1938, 247.
12. Ed and Norma Morrell, interview, May 8, 2013, 27–28.

> men. The following morning they came out to the office and I bore down upon them and suggested that such a thing could result in a dishonorable release. They felt pretty uncomfortable about the whole thing. Brother Williams said that he just felt like "busting loose" and that he didn't know why he had done it, in the face of our strict mission rules about associating with girls. However, the brethren swore that it was the first time it had happened and that it would be the last. And I am sure that it will be. If there were ever two contrite brethren, it was them. Oh, the life of a mission president! One problem piles upon another.[13]

Likewise, when other reports reached him of missionaries seeing girls, he called the elders into the office and told them that if they continued to meet with young women, "it would mean a release from the mission."[14] One missionary became suspicious when his companion kept going out alone, and he reported it to Wally. When Wally confronted the elder, he defended his activities by saying that a young lady was making advances. Wally informed him that he would have to "overcome 'her advances,'" and if he did not, Wally would have to "do something drastic."[15]

Problems involving girls with the missionaries posed a constant frustration. In his journal, Wally recorded incidents concerning his missionaries falling in love and making promises to take Czech girls home but then failing to keep their word. As a result, Wally often had to handle the heartbroken women who were left behind.[16] For instance, when a certain elder neared his release date, he talked to Wally about his feelings toward one of the women of the branch. He informed Wally that he would undoubtedly write her an offer of marriage once he got home. Wally told him to get his feet on the ground once he returned to the states, associate with other girls, and then write to the sister in the branch after six months if he still felt the same about her.[17] Such

13. Toronto, journal, July 25–31, 1937, 131–32.
14. Toronto, journal, August 16–22, 1936, 27.
15. Toronto, journal, August 9–15, 1936, 24.
16. Toronto, journal, July 10–16, 1938, 244.
17. Toronto, journal, February 28–March 6, 1937, 83.

situations seemed to occur over and over again. Wally convinced another elder who wanted to take a Czechoslovakian sister to America not to have her go.[18] The elder had told the sister before he left Czechoslovakia that he was in love with her and would send for her soon. When six months passed, and the girl heard nothing from the returned missionary, she was heartbroken. Wally had told the elder to be careful, for she "ha[d] a bad case on him." Wally grieved, "This girl problem is difficult at times."[19]

In another instance, another elder had become involved with a young Czech woman while on his mission. He promised to send for her, but he never did. Instead, when he returned home he married someone else, but for two years the Czech girl received no letters from him telling her of his marriage. When the returned missionary finally wrote her, he told her "that he was still in love with her and always would be." Wally wrote, "The whole letter seemed empty and queer—as though he were trying to cover up his shame for not writing her earlier about his marrying another girl, when he had promised to send for her. I advised her to write and tell him that everything was over, as far as she was concerned, and that she did not care to hear from him again."[20]

When another missionary promised to send for a sister in one of the Czech wards, Wally wrote, "She expected that he would, and has been keenly disappointed. But I told her of his utter undependability, and indicated that he had had other experiences with other girls while on his mission—and that of all our missionaries he was one of our least useful. This is a hard thing to say about a brother, but it is true. He caused many a head-ache."[21]

Another challenge tested Wally's unique ability to handle difficult situations. Elder Mel Mabey described an experience he had with one of his companions who struggled with homosexual temptations. The

18. Toronto, journal, August 1–7, 1937, 133.

19. Toronto, journal, January 1–8, 1938, 182.

20. Toronto, journal, August 6–12, 1939, 394.

21. Toronto, journal, August 7–13, 1938, 254.

companion never approached Elder Mabey, even though they slept in a double bed. When Mabey discovered that his companion was struggling with same-sex attraction, he went to his mission president. He was distraught, and he sobbed as he talked to Wally. He wondered how he could best handle his companion's situation. Wally told Elder Mabey to confront his companion and tell him that he knew he was homosexual. At the time, Mabey thought that was the "weirdest advice [Wally] could give him." He was surprised that Wally did not send his companion out of the country. But Wally understood that this elder only experienced the temptation and that he had not acted on his desires. Wally knew there was no reason to send him home. Elder Mabey took his mission president's advice and talked with his companion. Mabey respected Wally's advice. He likewise appreciated the fact that he had decided not to send his companion home because his companion was, indeed, a very good missionary.[22]

In the face of such problems, Wally balanced discipline and encouragement. He believed that every missionary was worthy of whatever help he could give.[23] He tried to get the missionaries to see their possibilities. "What a power we could have in this mission if every brother were qualified to teach and preach the Gospel and had the enthusiasm and the energy, which such a calling demands! If such were the case, our work, I truly believe, would grow leaps and bounds. I am convinced that the type of young missionaries the Church sends out is largely responsible for the few converts we gain for the cause."[24]

Wally successfully encouraged many missionaries and built them up through his writings in *The Star: The Czechoslovakian Mission Newsletter*. He spent a considerable amount of time writing the monthly messages and "attempted to put into the article some thoughts which might inspire the young missionary."[25] At one time, he wrote:

22. Mel Mabey, interview, August 13, 2013, 9–10.

23. Toronto, journal, May 2–8, 1937, 102.

24. Toronto, journal, July 26–August 1, 1936, 20.

25. Toronto, journal, August 2–8, 1936, 22.

During the year many of you have become effective in the use of the Czech language. Your general tone of cooperation and your enthusiasm has been especially invigorating. You have had many difficulties to overcome, and on the whole, have been very successful in grappling with your problems. You have also been receptive to suggestion from the mission office. You have carried out, with few exceptions, the regulations necessary to missionary work. You have been successful in planning and adapting yourselves to a daily program of activities, the splendid results of which are to be readily seen in your increased knowledge of the Gospel, in your extended powers of perception and in your preparedness and ability to bring honest souls to a knowledge of the Gospel. Yes, Brethren, it is a joy and a privilege to preside over a group of fine, strong, persevering and faithful personalities such as you are. This is the richest experience of my life. You have made it so.[26]

In another newsletter, Wally wrote to his missionaries about being clean:

To come through clean, [a missionary] must not only keep himself morally upright, but that he observes every regulation and code of conduct which the great missionary fraternity, numbering hundreds of young men throughout the world, demand of him, that he deal honestly from great undertakings down to the smallest item scratched on his daily report; that he devote every minute of his time while in the mission field to hard, conscientious, diligent work; that he never lets an opportunity go by to preach and teach this gospel; that every thought for self be sublimated in the glorious light of service to others. This—yes, all this, is "coming through clean."[27]

Wally told the missionaries that the greatest desire not only of their parents or of their mission president "or even of your church itself—but of the Lord . . . is that each and every one of you can, at the conclusion of your missions, say, 'Lord, I am grateful for this opportunity. I have done my best. I have come through clean!'"[28]

Wally admonished his missionaries to pray nightly that the hearts of those they had contacted would be touched by the Spirit. He also had them pray for success with their companions and suggested that

26. Toronto, "Mission President's Message," *Hvězdička*, January 1938.

27. Toronto, "Come Through Clean," *Hvězdička*, June 1938.

28. Toronto, "Come Through Clean," *Hvězdička*, June 1938.

they go with their companions to a secluded spot and talk to God when in need of help. He advised them to fast and pay fast offerings as well. He told them that such behaviors would demonstrate to Father in Heaven that they were serious, that they were putting "service before self." He counseled them to be more sober in their work, and then they would be led with the Spirit. He encouraged the missionaries to be out of their apartments by 9:30 in the morning, eager to serve and to touch someone's heart with their message.[29] Elder Mabey explained that Wally "knew how to relate to missionaries, to get everything out of them," and he certainly upheld some high expectations of them.[30] Because President Toronto loved the missionaries so much, they returned the sentiment.[31]

Wally was still in his late twenties, barely older than his missionaries. Even with such a small difference in age, he had the ability to consider the missionaries' youth and not take incidental things too seriously. Missionary Dale Tingey recounted how he had planned to see the Nuremberg trials with some other missionaries.[32] He had wanted to stay in Switzerland for a while longer to ski. As the senior companion, he should have been a better example. Wally called him and asked where the other missionaries were. Tingey informed him that he had sent them ahead, so he did not know where they were. Wally scolded him a bit. When they met at the train station, he asked Elder Tingey again where the other elders were, to which Tingey replied that he had already told him before that he sent them on ahead. Wally was quite upset with the elder. "He said, 'Now Tingey, I have half a notion to put you on the night plane and send you home.' So I said to him, 'If you feel good about that, I would feel good about it because I really didn't

29. Toronto, "Some Ways of Gaining Spirituality," *Hvězdička*, February 1938.

30. Mel Mabey, interview, August 13, 2013, 10.

31. Bob and David Toronto, interview, August 20, 2013, 24.

32. The Nuremberg Trials were held after World War II in Nuremberg, Germany to prosecute political, military, and other leaders of the Axis forces (including Germany, Italy, and Japan).

want to come in the first place.' . . . He just says, 'I'll tell you one thing, Tingey. You're not going home.'"[33]

The missionaries had great respect and love for Wally because he was so much like them. One day, an extremely agitated Elder Abbot stormed into Wally's office waving a paper and yelled, "Look what these sons of b****** have done to me!" Abbot threw the paper across the desk and informed Wally that they were throwing him out of the country and not renewing his visa. Wally calmly looked at the elder and responded, "Brother Abbot, don't refer to my brethren as sons of b******. Refer to them as the BBBs." Abbot questioned, "The BBBs?" Wally answered facetiously, "The black belly bastards."[34] He clearly knew when to be serious with his missionaries and when to use humor. At a conference in Prague, he told the elders to bring swimming trunks. When they found themselves on the Modow River, Wally joked, "Brethren, we're all going down seeing a little more of each other in the Modow."[35]

Wally also encouraged his missionaries not to use notes when giving their talks. In a mission president's message, he said:

> I believe that the effectiveness of delivering a well prepared lecture or speech without a paper, was brought forcibly to our attention in Mnichovo Hradiště. Two of the brethren spoke without a paper . . . and held their audience spellbound. To do this with Czech requires that the talk be carefully prepared and written, and then either memorized or placed sufficiently well in mind that one can deliver it without the aid of a paper. Brethren, if you will do this, you will gain that all-important link of interest between yourself and your audience, namely, that fascinating contact of eye to eye.[36]

33. Dale Tingey, interview by Kalli Searle, Provo, UT, transcription in author's possession, 1.
34. Bob and David Toronto, interview, August 20, 2013, 24.
35. Don Whipperman, interview by Mary Jane Woodger, October 9, 2013, phone conversation, transcription in author's possession, 3.
36. Toronto, "Speaking without Papers," *Hvězdička*, June 1937.

Toronto then went on to challenge the elders:

> I would like you to give at least one talk a week without reading it before an audience from your paper. Yes, put in plenty of time preparing it and writing it out, but put in that much more time learning it. True, this is the harder way. But it is the more effective way and will pay you big dividends in the long run. If you will earnestly attempt to do this over a period of a few months, I promise you that your Czech will vastly improve and that the attendance at your meetings will greatly increase. Begin this week to do it.[37]

Wally cared a great deal about his missionaries and their success. Likewise, he felt the same way about the Czech members. He visited them in their homes and "built strong friendships."[38] He planned weeks of spiritual rejuvenation for members, and specifically for the youth. He also promoted "Hike Your Neighborhood" day, during which religious discussions ensued about doctrine or scriptures. These activities strengthened the members' friendships and assisted in forming a large Church family of brothers and sisters.

Historian Kahlile B. Mehr shared the following results of Wally's mission: "For two decades, the Czechoslovak Mission was a lone salient of the Church in Slavic Europe, which besides Czechoslovakia included Poland, Bulgaria, and states of the Soviet Union and Yugoslavia. Missionaries served in Czechoslovakia for fourteen years, from 1929 to 1939 and 1946 to 1950. A total of 286 people were baptized (137 before, 10 during, and 139 after World War II)."[39]

37. Toronto, "Mission President's Message," *Hvězdička*, June 1937.

38. Vojkůvka, "Memories of President Wallace Felt Toronto," November 9, 2013, 6.

39. Mehr, *Mormon Missionaries Enter Eastern Europe*, 43.

8 "HOW LONG CAN PEACE LAST?"

Omens of war had reared their heads for years in Czechoslovakia. As early as January 30, 1933, when Hitler was pronounced chancellor of Germany, missionary Spencer Taggart reported that "no one cared to listen" to his gospel message. Instead, everyone wanted to talk about Hitler, and everyone seemed to be "extremely apprehensive of how this [might] affect Czechoslovakia."[1] In June 1936, right after Wally once again stepped on Czechoslovakian soil, he witnessed a precursor to war himself when he visited the Aerial Exposition of the Republic held in the Stromovka. There he "saw scores of planes and war machines, and the development of all kinds of aerial defense technique." He watched people test their parachutes. There were huge searchlights and antiaircraft guns. Wally considered that Hitler must have "thousands upon thousands" of such armaments, as might Mussolini.[2] Russia was also building its air preparations. In July 1936, Wally

1. Spencer Taggart, "Becoming a Missionary, 1931–1934," typescript, 1989, 31.
2. Toronto, journal, June 13–19, 1937, 115–16.

recorded, "Oh, the fools that men are! How many other secret preparations are going on, quietly and unnoticed? The man in the ranks will never know. Such an experience makes one believe that a conflict is inevitable. When it will come one cannot know, but each nation is secretly preparing to plunge itself—the flower of its young manhood—into war and bloodshed. To ride through miles of country plunged into darkness and to hear the planes roaring overhead, chilled our blood when we reflected on its meaning."[3]

In fact, according to Wally, all of Europe was "[shuddering] to think of the havoc of the next cataclysm."[4] Wally wondered, "How long can peace last, with all of this material manufactured for no good purpose? If all the money and investments in such war machines could only be put into public education, medical research, social programs for assisting the unemployed—oh what a world we would live in. But the Devil can't seem to see it that way."[5] By November of 1937, he noticed that the tension in Europe seemed "to sway from week to week." He noted that Hermann Goering "announced that Germany [could] no longer honor the terms of the Versailles Treaty. This . . . caused much uneasy comment."[6]

Wally knew that changes were on their way to Czechoslovakia, and such knowledge only increased his missionary efforts. However, the impending war and the climate of conflict did adversely affect him and his missionaries in countless ways. When he and his missionaries were denied three times in four months the right to hold meetings, he realized that restrictions were tightening up. "This can be readily understood when one considers the strained relationship of the Czechs with the German minority here, and the recent unpleasant experiences with spies and foreigners, principally Germans. Thus I believe that

3. Toronto, journal, July 5–11, 1936, 14.
4. Toronto, journal, June 13–19, 1937, 116.
5. Toronto, journal, June 13–19, 1937, 115–16.
6. Toronto, journal, November 7–13, 1937, 161; Hermann Goering was a powerful military figure during Adolf Hitler's rise to power in Germany leading up to and during World War II.

we have been denied, not maliciously, but generally with all others. Therefore we must secure a decision in our favor through the necessary government offices."[7]

Along with everyone else in Czechoslovakia, Wally watched as Hitler reached out to various countries. In his journal, he noted the event when Mr. Schuschnigg of Austria[8] met with Hitler and had "an official meeting to bring Austria into closer contact with Germany."[9] Even an alliance with a remote country like Austria caused considerable concern in Czechoslovakia. Wally reflected on the worsening state of Europe. "Any concessions granted mean a strengthening of the Berlin-Rome axis, which democratic and free countries are wont to accept or permit. It also seems that England is having some difficulty with her cabinet and that a new foreign minister may be named in place of Eden.[10] One cannot keep pace with the changes."[11]

On the last day of 1937, Wally wrote of his devotion despite the increasing tension: "Although war and trouble seem to threaten Europe, yet our confidence is such that we and our members shall be blessed in the carrying out of our responsibilities, come what may. We have only one objective for the coming year, and that is to preach and teach the Master's Gospel of love and peace, as never before. And it is so needed in the world today. May the Lord bless us to accomplish that aim during the coming year."[12] At the same time, Wally was well aware that things were not going to get better. In February he

7. Toronto, journal, December 12–18, 1937, 175.
8. Kurt von Schuschnigg was the chancellor of Austria and did not want Hitler to take control of Austria.
9. Toronto, journal, December 12–18, 1937, 198.
10. Sir Robert Anthony Eden served as Britain's secretary of state for foreign affairs from 1935 to 1955 intermittently (due to war and health) until he succeeded Winston Churchill as prime minister (1955). Sir Eden replaced Sir Samuel Hoare as foreign secretary in 1935 and was replaced by Edward Frederick Lindley Wood (Lord Halifax) in 1938 and by Harold Macmillan in 1955.
11. Toronto, journal, February 6–19, 1938, 198.
12. Toronto, journal, December 26–31, 1937, 180.

admitted, "It seems according to prophecy, that we cannot look forward to good times in the immediate future. The earth is virtually in tumult now." The newspapers became "alive with comments" about Austria's breakdown and loss of independence "brought about by a long chain of events . . . culminating in the conference of Schuschnigg of Austria and Hitler of Germany, in which the latter succeeded in binding Austria more firmly to the Nazi program."[13]

Following the *Anschluss*, or union, of Nazi Germany and Austria in March 1938, it seemed clear to Wally—and everyone else—that the conquest of Czechoslovakia was Hitler's next ambition. The incorporation of the Sudetenland (the borderland areas around Czechoslovakia) into Nazi Germany would leave the rest of the Czech nation weak and powerless to resist subsequent Nazi occupation. Czechoslovakia would surely be the next objective of the Nazi regime because of its four million German minority. Wally recorded, "Hitler has declared and is using every means to bring his dream true, that all German peoples shall be united under his leadership. But this nation of Czechoslovakia stands invincible, cultivating closer relationships with Great Britain and France."[14] On March 16, 1939, the German Wehrmacht did move into the remainder of Czechoslovakia, at the Prague Castle, and Hitler proclaimed occupation.

With the union of Austria and Germany, tension in Prague began to surface. Wally could almost "feel it among the people." The Czech cabinet was called together and remained in session all night, "considering the events as they transpired in Vienna. And events moved fast." When Kurt von Schuschnigg, chancellor of the First Austrian Republic, was forced to turn the government over to Nazi leaders, "Austrian flags were torn down, the German Svastika was displayed, and the Austrian Legions made up of exiled Austrian Nazis who had found temporary shelter in Germany, began to march on Austria. . . . Several of the former cabinet members . . . fled to . . . Czechoslovakia." Wally observed, "It looks as though Austria has definitely become a perma-

13. Toronto, journal, February 27–March 5, 1938, 202–3.

14. Toronto, journal, February 27–March 5, 1938, 203.

nent part of Germany. The newly formed government has requested the German government to send in soldiers to quell any revolutionary movements or uprisings." Then Wally predicted, "The next few days may tell a story of blood-shed and murder. At least they will be days of high tension for Czechoslovakia."[15]

Soon after the birth of another Toronto child, Carol, things began to escalate very quickly. On May 21, Wally learned that two Germans who had attempted to cross the Czech frontier near Eger were "shot down by the border police, when they refused to stop upon command." When German troops moved toward the border, it seemed to Wally that "Hitler would seize the country. But the Czechs moved to the border as well, with a well-trained army prepared to fight to a finish." While war began raging in Czechoslovakia, British ministers deliberated restlessly through the night. They finally concluded that "they would follow France into any European struggle." France was bound by a treaty "to preserve the freedom and democracy of Czechoslovakia. Thus Hitler was stopped."[16]

In early May 1938, Wally went across the Czech border to the mission home in Berlin where he met with mission president Alfred C. Rees. On his journey to Bodenbach, a German municipality located near the border, Wally saw both the Czech and German flags waving side by side. At the border, he realized that things had changed dramatically as the guards made a more careful inspection than ever before.

> All cushions of the car we were in were removed and all door and window frames were tapped in an effort to detect hidden stores of German propaganda. . . . We also saw soldiers all along the railroad track and at every bridge, with their guns and bayonets ready for action if necessary. In the town great signs were on the buildings: "We will never surrender our rights," and, "We will persevere to the end!" The Czechs evidently are willing to give all they have—life if required—to protect their freedom and rights from German invasion. One cannot help but admire their fortitude and courage.[17]

15. Toronto, journal, March 6–12, 1938, 205.
16. Toronto, journal, May 15–21, 1938, 228.
17. Toronto, journal, May 22–25, 1938, 231.

In June 1938, Wally met with a group of other mission presidents to talk about the situation in central Europe and how it was affecting their various missions. In attendance were J. Reuben Clark of the First Presidency; Thomas E. McKay, president of the Swiss-Austrian Mission; Franklin J. Murdock, president of the Netherlands Mission; Alfred C. Rees, president of the East German Mission; and M. Douglas Wood, president of the West German Mission. President Clark felt significantly concerned about the work in Germany and wondered how long the missionaries could hold out under the stifling methods being used by the government. He was very "pessimistic about it, after talking about the religious situation in Germany with some of the officials who quite openly declared that they had little use for religious activity." He also felt that Czechoslovakia was in great danger; he suggested that Wally "take every precaution and without upsetting [his] missionaries plan routes of escape."[18] President Clark suggested to the mission presidents that they "come together about once every two months to size up the situation politically as it relates to our missionary work, and to encourage one another. It was tentatively decided that [they] should meet in Basel sometime in August, since Berlin or Prague were unsafe for the discussion of such matters." When the mission presidents said goodbye to President Clark, they felt that their "gathering had been most profitable, although none too encouraging for the future of [their] work in Central Europe."[19] Wally wrote in his journal, "'To what good purpose can it all come?' It is for defense of course. But it means that the dread of war hangs over the central European countries, and it means more than that—it means that war is sure to come, sooner or later. Oh how the people of the world need the Gospel of Jesus Christ and the peace and happiness it brings. But they seem to have no time for it. Yes, the devil is at work, and oh so subtly."[20]

---

18. Toronto, journal, June 12–18, 1938, 236.

19. Toronto, journal, June 19–25, 1938, 238.

20. Toronto, journal, July 3–9, 1938, 243.

In July 1938, Wally gathered his missionaries in Prague for a conference. Unbeknownst to them, it would be the last conference they would hold for a decade. "Between conference sessions, they attended the demonstrations of the tenth Sokol Slet, celebrating national unity and being 'one with the people.'" The Sokol Slet was an international gymnastics festival held every six years. But, as Kahlile Mehr said, "It was a unity that could not be sustained in the face of brute German force."[21]

In August, Wally went to the U.S. legation to "talk with Mr. Chapin about means of evacuating, in case of war." Although things had settled down briefly, he felt things would soon become dangerous again. The Germans were making great strides in their military preparation and holding maneuvers, which Wally thought was their attempt "to frighten Czechoslovakia into accepting the terms of the Henlein party." As Wally put it, "The problem is not one between the Czechs and the Sudete Germans but between the Czechs and Berlin, or Hitler. Thus anxiety is again in the air."[22] Chapin explained to Wally some of the issues:

> The U.S. Legation had been giving some thought to the problem of possible means of escape, but that plans made out ahead of time in such cases could not often be relied upon. He felt that the wise thing to do would be to have all of the [missionaries] in Bohemia gather at Prague, where the government might be able to arrange to remove all Americans. For the [missionaries] in Moravia [Chapin] suggested that they go east through Slovakia to Romania and then attempt to get to Switzerland from there. He felt that Hungary and Poland could be considered as potential enemies of Czechoslovakia, and that escape through those countries could not be counted on. He further stated that as soon as the Minister came from his vacation that they would consider this matter still in more detail and let [Wally] know.[23]

21. Mehr, *Mormon Missionaries Enter Eastern Europe*, 69.
22. Toronto, journal, August 7–13, 1938, 253.
23. Toronto, journal, August 7–13, 1938, 253–54.

Wally confessed, "I have no particular fears, but thought it well to have something in mind—be prepared, if such a thing be possible during international catastrophe. What I should like to do is send the brethren some instructions as to what to do in case war is declared or open hostilities arise."[24]

In September, the Czech government was forced to make a stand and "declared martial law in eleven of the border provinces in order to preserve order. Following this peace and quiet seemed to ensue."[25] Wally had a sense of how his people were coping, what they were feeling. But, sadly, he could do nothing. In September of 1938, "Hitler demanded the Sudetenland in western Czechoslovakia, where a substantial minority of Germans lived. Soon afterward, the First Presidency ordered the missionaries and the Torontos to leave immediately for Switzerland. Concurrently, the Czech government banned all public meetings. The mission temporarily ceased to function."[26]

Wally immediately sent Martha with four-year-old Marion and twenty-month-old Bob to Switzerland, where they could stay in the mission home in Basel with the McKays. Later, Wally and all the other missionaries followed. The children and Martha would "remain in Switzerland for three months." Wally then "sent the older missionaries home and the others to England to work temporarily in a mission where they could use their native tongue."[27] At the time of the evacuation, twenty-three missionaries were working in eight Czechoslovakian cities and towns. From the missionaries' standpoint, the year was successful because the membership in organized branches stood above the previous year's average, and many people had heard the gospel message.[28]

Wally wrote to the missionaries' parents to let them know about the situation. In one such letter, he wrote:

---

24. Toronto, journal, August 7–13, 1938, 253–54.

25. Toronto, journal, September 11–17, 1938, 263.

26. Mehr, *Mormon Missionaries Enter Eastern Europe*, 69; and Czechoslovak Mission Manuscript History, December 20, 1938; June 20, 1939.

27. Anderson, *Cherry Tree*, 17.

28. Toronto, journal, December 25–31, 1938, 309.

Prague, Czechoslovakia
September 19, 1938

Dear Parents:

I am happy to inform you at this time that your son, who has labored so splendidly among these people and who despite the trying political conditions in Central Europe has maintained his morale, fine spirit and enthusiasm, is now safe and sound in Basel, Switzerland.

Upon the advice of the First Presidency this move was made, since it was felt that conditions in this country were too precarious to permit further missionary work at the present time. Thus, the last group of missionaries left Prague on Saturday, September 17th. I have since been advised by President Thomas E. McKay of the Swiss-German Mission that all arrived safe and sound and are comfortably taken care of. The missionaries shall remain under his direction until I, myself, am able to join them.

I suggest that until further notice you address all mail to your son to the following address:

Swiss-German Mission
Leimenstrasse 49
Basel, Switzerland

We are very hopeful that negotiations in the near future will tend to clear up the present nervous tension in Central Europe, and that we shall all be able to return and carry on our work as formerly. However, in the meantime our group of missionaries will carry on in Switzerland, and thus continue to be a credit to you and to the Church.

You may well be proud of the conduct of your son during these trying times, for he has persevered despite many difficulties. We thank the Lord that you have been able to give us such a fine, capable representative.

May the Lord continue to bless you in your undertakings and give you the assurance that your son is safe, well and happy in his work. Praying the choicest blessings of heaven upon, I remain

Cordially your brother,
Wallace F. Toronto
Mission President[29]

When all the missionaries had been reassigned, Wally joined Martha and the children in Basel, resigned to accept the inevitable events of the future, come what may.

---

29. Toronto, journal, September 11–17, 1938, 264.

9 "BACK TO THE UNCERTAINTY OF CZECHOSLOVAKIA"

The evacuation of Wally, Martha, their children, and the missionaries in August of 1938 was called by Church personnel a fire drill. Some Church members were critical of the way the 1938 evacuation took place, calling it a "false alarm rather than a fire drill." But a year later, when Wally was required once again to evacuate, "some felt the exodus of the American elders might have failed if they had not benefited from the mistakes they made the year before."[1]

Things began to calm down later that fall. While in Switzerland, Wally called local leaders in Czechoslovakia to take care of the branches until the missionaries

1. Gilbert W. Scharffs, *Mormonism in Germany: A History of the Church of Jesus Christ of Latter-day Saints in Germany between 1840 and 1970* (Salt Lake City: Deseret Book, 1970), 92. See Alfred C. Rees, in *One Hundred Tenth Semi-Annual Conference of The Church of Jesus Christ of Latter-day Saints* (Salt Lake City: The Church of Jesus Christ of Latter-day Saints, 1939), 73, as cited in David F. Boone, "The Evacuation of the Czechoslovak and German Missions at the Outbreak of World War II," *BYU Studies* 40, no. 3 (2001): 123.

were allowed to return. Jaroslav Kotulán in Brno and Josef Roubíček in Prague took charge during Wally's absence. In September 1938, Adolf Hitler sent an ultimatum demanding that the Czech government surrender all of the Sudetenland. When the Czechs refused to comply, the Germans invaded the borderland areas anyway. Representatives of some of the soon-to-be Allied powers (France, England, and Italy) called a conference in Munich, demanding an immediate halt to Germany's expansion or else they would face the possibility of war. Hitler signed an agreement, the Munich Diktat (Munich Pact), on September 29, 1938. He promised he had gone as far as he needed to go and would invade no further. Much to everyone's surprise, Czechoslovakia believed him.

In early October, President Thomas E. McKay, who served as the supervisor over all the missions in Europe, urged Wally to send a telegram to the First Presidency suggesting that all of the former elders from Czechoslovakia be sent to England and that Martha and the kids return home. Wally complied, reluctantly writing the letter, though he still believed that he and Martha were supposed to go back to Czechoslovakia. Martha was pregnant at the time, and President McKay was very worried about her condition. He thought she would fare much better elsewhere. On the other hand, Wally felt that she would be fine giving birth again in Czechoslovakia, but he still sent the telegram to Church headquarters at the request of President McKay, who suggested that Martha either stay in Switzerland and seek medical care or go to London.[2]

Wally was right! In juxtaposition to what he said in the telegram, he would return to Czechoslovakia. After a month, many people believed that the crisis was over, and Wally's mission secretary, Asael Moulton, was sent back to Prague to make sure it was safe for their return to Czechoslovakia. Wally arrived back in the country in mid-October. He sent a long report to the First Presidency, informing them that they were back in Prague and that conditions appeared to be quieting down. He hoped that Martha, the children, and the other missionaries would be

---

2. Toronto, journal, October 2–8, 1938, 274–75.

able to return in the near future as well. He missed Martha immensely and hoped that by mid-November, she would be at his side again. He eagerly awaited her letters, devouring them once they arrived, and was very pleased when he read that all was well with her in Basel.[3]

On arriving back in Czechoslovakia, Wally checked up on the work that had gone on during his absence. He explored the possibility of holding meetings again, something that seemed to plague him regardless of the conditions of the country. He took an application to police headquarters for permission to conduct meetings for the Mutual Improvement Association and genealogical work. He visited Latter-day Saints, including Frieda Veněčková. She told him about how she had given up hope, after many vain attempts, that her atheistic husband would ever join the Church. She nevertheless kept the faith. She showed Wally the genealogical work that she had been able to do and gave him 270 crowns in tithes and fast offerings. "That is not a sign of faith wavering! Oh, if only some of our members in the branches where they have every opportunity to develop and grow in the Gospel, had but a particle of the faith of this beloved little Jewess, Frieda!"[4]

As Wally traversed around the mission, he found that the people were "depressed and shot-to-pieces mentally. They put on a bold cheerful front, but as we circulate among them, we feel and sense the depression of soul that grips all of them. Distrust, intrigue, betrayal, sold-out, are the terms running through their minds day after day. Perhaps the institution of the work camps will help stall this mania which is stirring within. At least, all is not yet well. They feel a crushing defeat at the hands of their 'friends'—England and France."[5] However, after seeing what had transpired with the Saints while he was in Switzerland, he was encouraged by what local leaders had accomplished.

During October and into November, Wally visited various branches, renewed the faith, and shared his testimony. On one trip to

3. Toronto, journal, October 16–22, 1938, 283.
4. Toronto, journal, October 16–22, 1938, 282.
5. Toronto, journal, October 16–22, 1938, 284.

Taber, Wally was pleased to see forty people at a meeting, including some new faces. On that occasion, Wally felt that the Lord had blessed them with an abundance of the Spirit. "The Czech flowed freely" as he spoke from 1 Corinthians 13 "without the aid of paper."[6] Wally instructed the people to keep reading the standard works and to live the gospel as they never had before.[7]

Wally acknowledged how much things had changed during his time away. Newspapers and radio shows were carefully censored so that "nothing must be done or said to offend Hitler and the Third Reich." In just two months absence, the Czech government had made a "complete right-about-face in politics." It was impossible and uncanny, he thought. He wrote in his journal, "A few weeks [before] it was democracy and freedom. Now it is Anti-Semeticism [Semitism], please Germany, scrape and bow to the whims of the Führer. But it has all been forced on them, subtly and cleverly, so that they do not detect the fact that they are betraying all that they formerly held sacred and just."[8]

Wally also mourned that newspapers had begun "attacking both the Jews and the Czechs in a horribly vicious manner." Czech Jews were doing anything they could to get out of the country.[9] By November, he had already received two telephone calls from Jews wishing to join the Church. Four other Jewish people had sent a letter to the Church offices in Salt Lake City, asking for an affidavit from the Church that would allow them to get to America and offer their services as doctors. In return, President Clark sent a letter to Wally and asked him to respond to their request, which he did. He "was instructed to get in touch with them and find out whether or not they were truly interested in the Gospel, as they had indicated, and to tell them that it was impossible for the church to supply such an affidavit."[10]

---

6. Toronto, journal, November 27–December 3, 1938, 300.
7. Toronto, journal, November 13–19, 1938, 295.
8. Toronto, journal, November 20–26, 1938, 299–300.
9. Toronto, journal, November 12–19, 1938, 296.
10. Toronto, journal, December 18–24, 1938, 305–7.

Wally sent these Jews some Mormon literature and found out that they had been attending meetings in Brno. He then made an appointment with them to discuss the situation. He wrote, "They seemed to be fine people—clean, straight-forward and honest. The two wives were beautiful, lovely women, one a dentist and the other a teacher of languages." Wally told them that he was not qualified to sign an affidavit but that he would try to find a friend who was both qualified and willing. He could help to that extent, but he could not promise anything. He noted, "They are apparently interested in the Gospel, but I had the feeling that it was only because they desired to secure help to America. But they are fine people and I would be delighted to find that my impression in respect to their interest in the Gospel is wrong. It may be that in such a manner the Jews will be turned to the Gospel of Christ."[11] Wally also met with another Jewish couple in Brno and shared with them "the story of the persecution of our own pioneers, and then of their final victory." He also added, "God has promised the same to the Jews when they recognize Christ as the Messiah."[12]

In late November, another young Jew by the name of Alexander Jacobs asked Wally for financial assistance to immigrate to Holland. Wally learned that Jacobs was an artist, so he proposed to give the young man a certain amount of money if he created some pictures for their Christmas newsletter. Alexander was very pleased to have the work rather than the charitable donation.[13] One of the most difficult things Wally now faced was the stream of Jews visiting his office in search of help, but he was unable to aid them in any way. As he learned of the atrocious persecutions of Jews, he felt completely helpless.[14] At times, the Jewish people were contacting the office so often that Wally could not complete his regular missionary work.[15]

11. Toronto, journal, December 18–24, 1938, 305–7.

12. Toronto, journal, April 2–8, 1939, 349.

13. Toronto, journal, November 27–December 3, 1938, 300.

14. Toronto, journal, July 4–10, 1937, 120.

15. Toronto, journal, April 16–22, 1939, 354.

Various problems began to develop on top of the issues he already faced. Several Jewish doctors went to the mission home and told Wally that they expected increased persecution in Czechoslovakia. They had already received anonymous letters warning them to stop practicing medicine and "get out of the country." The doctors wanted to take their families to America; however, they were not allowed to take any funds out of the country or to leave the country without first having all their immigration papers in order. The documents could not be secured unless one had at least $1,000 per person deposited in America. The "catch 22" situation made leaving the country nearly impossible for those who did not have the means. The doctors hoped that Wally could deposit funds in America for them. They told him that they would pay him in Czech crowns at double the regular rate of exchange. Wally told the doctors that he "would think it over, but [he] felt that [the request] involved too much of a risk." He wrote in his journal, "The poor Jews here are frantic. They are entirely surrounded by Germany, and have no place to flee. No nation on earth wants them."[16]

Wally was very aware that Church members were also suffering from what was happening with the Jewish population. When he had left, the Saints felt abandoned, deserted by the leadership. To make matters worse, he discovered news early that spring that a Church member had been baptizing a number of Jews for a certain sum of money to make a profit from their desperation. Subsequently, Wally knew the man would have to be excommunicated if the rumors were true. He hoped and prayed that they weren't.[17]

Wally had another Jewish friend, Dr. Mohl, who insisted on being baptized. But Wally did not have good feelings about it. When he visited Dr. Mohl, who claimed that he had stopped smoking, the house still reeked of tobacco. Nevertheless, Wally still thought that he should make every effort to acquaint him with the gospel message. Dr. Mohl had read the Book of Mormon and knew in his head that it was true, but Wally recognized that it had not reached his heart. He kept telling

16. Toronto, journal, November 20–26, 1938, 297.

17. Toronto, journal, March 19–25, 1939, 345.

Mohl that he needed to have "a period of probation to test his worthiness."[18] When Wally was able to help him get to Poland, he was unfortunately sent right back to Prague.

In December 1938, things had calmed down enough that Wally hoped he could bring his family and eight displaced missionaries back to Prague. Martha wrote, "Wally returned for us, and we left beautiful, calm Switzerland after a delightful stay there, to go back to the uncertainty of Czechoslovakia."[19] The missionaries slowly began trickling back as well. On December 8, 1938, six missionaries from England arrived in Prague. A wonderful reunion ensued, and Wally noted that just two months earlier they had all wondered if they would ever meet again. Two days later, he met all the missionaries in the mission home and outlined the conditions of the country and the policies to be followed as they worked in the already organized branches of Prague, Brno, and Mladá Boleslav.[20]

The brethren then held a testimony meeting in the mission home. Many reported they had experienced great "faith promoting incidents while in England," and they spoke of how much they enjoyed teaching the gospel in their own tongue. "But they also expressed their thankfulness," Wally noted, "at being able to return to Czechoslovakia and their determination to work as never before. The work in England seemed to be a good tonic for them, after the difficulties they experienced here just prior to the political crisis."[21] Even though less than half of the original force of missionaries were able to return after leaving the mission during the crisis, they were able to work and enjoy at least some success.[22] Though Wally had reported no baptisms for the year of 1938 prior to the evacuation to Switzerland, he reported

18. Toronto, journal, from February 12–18, 1939, 332.

19. Anderson, *Cherry Tree*, 17.

20. Toronto, journal, December 4–10, 1938, 303.

21. Toronto, journal, December 11–17, 1938, 304.

22. David F. Boone, "The Worldwide Evacuation of Latter-day Saint Missionaries at the Beginning of World War II" (PhD diss., Brigham Young University, 1981), 45.

six converts in his year-end report to the First Presidency. While the number was certainly lower than the seventeen from the year before, it was still six more than he had expected.[23]

In the Church, Wally picked up right where he had left off. In an effort to revive a mission tradition, "Toronto organized a basketball team and a male quartet to once again attract public attention."[24] During a Sunday School lesson on December 10 that forty-five people attended, he taught about prophecy and inspiration. "It is through the gospel that all men complied with laws which permitted them to come upon the earth," he declared.[25] Wally was also still determined to learn as much Czech as possible. One day in January of 1939, he wrote, "I delved into Czech and filled my mind with Czech phrases and gospel material, and then asked the Lord to bless me in my talk for the evening, which I was determined to give without using a paper. The Lord did bless me that evening and I felt his spirit in abundance."[26]

Once again, the issue of marriage arose almost as soon as Wally returned when he met with a local member who told him that most girls in the branch were only in the Church to try and get American missionaries for husbands.[27] In response, Wally again urged the members to live the gospel as they never had before. The members, in turn, became greatly encouraged, especially since the missionaries had returned to work among them again.[28]

That January, Wally prepared a four-page letter to all Church members regarding the covenants they had made at baptism. He made a list of ten things that were "required of them, and then made it emphatic that unless they were doing their utmost to comply with

23. Czech-Slovak Mission Manuscript History, June 21–December 20, 1939, 1, Church History Library, Salt Lake City, as cited in Boone, "The Worldwide Evacuation of Latter-day Saint Missionaries," 45.

24. Czechoslovak Mission Manuscript History, June 20, 1939.

25. Toronto, journal, December 4–10, 1938, 303.

26. Toronto, journal, January 22–28, 1939, 326.

27. Toronto, journal, December 25–31, 1938, 308.

28. Toronto, journal, January 1–7, 1939, 321.

these simple requirements," neither the mission, nor the Church, nor the Lord himself would be "pleased with them." Wally indicated that the amount of tithing and fast offerings they paid during the year was low. Their attendance at sacrament meetings and lectures during the past three months had declined. He had the branch presidents countersign letters of commitment.[29] He called it a "jerk-up" letter that he believed was necessary to boost them up again. "We have worked now with kindness and with diligence for almost three years among some of the members in order to encourage them to greater activity. I finally felt that a definite straight-forward statement of conditions was necessary. I expect some of the weaker ones to be perhaps offended, but most certainly they will not be able to say: 'I didn't know what my responsibilities were.'"[30]

Church members were not the only Czechoslovakians who got a wake-up call that spring. "Through a ploy the Nazi regime made the remaining territory of Czechoslovakia an independent state in early March 1939. By March 15, Germany had a firm control of the entire nation."[31] Contrary to their assumptions after the Munich Conference, "Czechoslovakia had lost territory to Germany, Poland and Hungary and the remaining Czech lands in Bohemia and Moravia had been seized and renamed the Protectorate" within only six months of the conference. "Czechoslovakia had ceased to exist, but without creating the peace and stability that Hitler and German diplomats had claimed would be the result."[32] Wally observed, "The 'up-set' of March 15 took the wind out of the sails of the brethren." He wrote about the effect of Nazi control on the missionaries in his journal. "Most of them lost the desire to dig in. Their study hours were not being maintained, neither on Czech nor the Gospel. They wanted to know what the future held for us, for evidently they expected that we would not remain long in the

29. Toronto, journal, February 19–25, 1939, 334.

30. Toronto, journal, February 19–25, 1939, 334.

31. Boone, "The Worldwide Evacuation of Latter-day Saint Missionaries," 45.

32. Patrick Crowhurst, *Hitler and Czechoslovakia in World War II: Domination and Retaliation* (London: I. B. Tauris, 2013), 22.

First Czech missionary basketball team, 1929. Wallace Toronto (second from left) and Arthur Gaeth (far right). Courtesy of Church History Library.

country. This idea I vigorously attacked and then informed them that we were here to stay, that we had asked for additional missionaries, and that they were to let the members know how we felt about it. This seemed to cheer them considerably, and they expressed the desire to plunge into the work again.[33]

But amidst all the turmoil, Wally experienced some positive upset of his own. On March 4, he had scheduled to speak at an evening meeting when Martha decided that "she had better go over to the doctor's that afternoon." Fortunately, it was a good thing that Wally skipped the meeting because on that night, Martha gave birth to a healthy, seven-pound baby girl they named Carol.[34] However, despite

33. Toronto, journal, April 16–29, 1939, 355–56.

34. Toronto, journal, March 5–11, 1939, 338.

Another pose of the missionary basketball team in 1929 with Wallace Toronto (far left) and Arthur Gaeth (left of center). Courtesy of Church History Library.

the joy Carol brought them, her birth coincided with fear brought by the German occupation.

As Martha lay on the hospital bed recovering from Carol's birth, "there were rumblings of every sort from vehicles large and small riding over the cobblestones, noise of people running and shouting, and even much unrest and chatter among the nurses." When Martha inquired of a nurse what caused all the commotion, the nurse answered that an unexpected invasion was in progress. Martha immediately called Wally, and he confirmed the terrible news. When he went to see her that afternoon, he assured her that everything was all right, except that the Germans now officially ruled Czechoslovakia. She remembered, "We wouldn't have to leave the country, however, because the bloodless takeover of the country went very smoothly. Hitler's thousands of troops had skillfully used this surprise tactic and were in complete control."[35] Most fortunately, both she and the baby were doing well and feeling fine in spite of the invasion. Wally and Martha then decided to call Carol their "occupation" baby.[36]

As the invasion proceeded, the mission had to immediately make adjustments to comply with the new government to avoid any problems with the Gestapo. Wally advised missionaries to stop tracting, not because it was against the law but because he deemed it wise that they not be any more visible than was necessary. He restricted the elders to teaching and contacting referrals from local church members only. The new government immediately implemented a general ruling that no public gatherings were allowed, which likely came as no surprise. Although the restriction really only lasted a few weeks, it had a long-term effect on the missionary work. Even faithful members felt the pressure of being forced into inactivity. "After this time, social meetings . . . still had to be approved by the government officials."[37]

The Nazis were always visible. Their constant presence reminded the Torontos that they lived in a war zone. One experience reinforced that reality for Martha on a particular day in the spring of 1939. A group of Nazis "in long lines and black uniforms and black boots . . . were goose-stepping" in front of the mission home in Prague. Marion, just five years old at the time, looked out the window and watched the soldiers march down the road and, at one point, even lift their rifles and shoot over the mission home. Terrified, Marion ran to her mother and "grab[bed] her around the knees, hiding [her] head in [her mother's] skirt."[38] While comforting little Marion, Martha looked out through the window's lace curtains. Much to her surprise and total alarm, she beheld her three-year-old goose-stepping along with the

35. Anderson, *Cherry Tree*, 18.

36. Toronto, journal, March 12–18, 1939, 343.

37. Czech Mission History, June 20, 1939, 3, as cited in Boone, "The Worldwide Evacuation of Latter-day Saint Missionaries," 47.

38. Miller and Richards, interview, May 3, 2013.

soldiers. She ran as fast she could to retrieve her little boy amidst the rumbling tanks. From the third floor, Bob had been observing the Germans marching by the house and decided to join them.[39]

The presence of the Nazis virtually always meant danger. And as such, everyone watched them with fear. During a Mother's Day program, all the members of the Prague branch experienced that tension. Martha described the events that transpired:

> The service was drawing to a close but still in progress when the back door of the meeting hall opened, and in stepped a tall Nazi officer. He was very handsome in his striking white naval uniform. The congregation, members and friends alike, froze in their seats. A German officer appearing as he did meant but one thing to us all—arrest and imprisonment. After hesitating a moment or two he smiled and started walking down the center aisle toward Wally, who was sitting in his customary place at the front of the hall, presiding over the meeting. Wally, being very skilled at not showing astonishment, rose and walked toward him and spoke to him in German. Happy to hear his own language, the young man shook his hand and they conversed for a moment. Unable to hear the conversation, we all sat like terrified mummies in our seats. At last, speaking now in Czech, Wally turned to us and announced that this young officer had something to say to us and would speak to us in German. Fortunately my college German was enough for me to understand. "Brothers and sisters," he began, "I am told that I may speak to you in German without having an interpreter because all of you speak, or at least understand, my language. . . . I am Brother Shrul from Kiel. . . . I am an Elder of the Church. . . . I would like to be accepted and worship with you, if you will allow me that privilege. . . ." By now all the women were in tears and the men were nodding in approval.[40]

After the young officer bore a fervent and moving testimony, he continued, "I come here not on an appointment from my government, but of my own choosing. I come here as a servant of my government. I know we have brought you considerable distress and dismay. We have caused much suffering already. Nevertheless, you and I have something in common which oversteps the boundaries of race, language,

39. Bob and David Toronto, interview, August 20, 2013, 20.

40. Anderson, *Cherry Tree*, 19–20.

European Mission presidents and wives with Elder Joseph Fielding Smith and Sister Jessie Evans Smith (center), Wallace and Martha Toronto (third row, far right). Courtesy of Church History Library.

and color. You and I have the Gospel of Jesus Christ. Despite the fact that I speak German and you, Czech, yet because of the Gospel, we speak in common terms."[41] The Nazi officer became a welcome visitor at the meetings in Prague. He "learned some Czech words and phrases that made him feel even more accept[ed by the] small group of Saints."[42]

On June 3, 1939, Wally received a letter from the First Presidency "notifying him of his honorable release" along with several instructions. "In view of the political changes, it is deemed advisable to attach the Branches of the Church in Czech-Slovak to the East-German Mission. You are therefore authorized to close the office of the Czech-Slovak

41. Wallace F. Toronto, in *Report of the 110th Annual Conference of the Church of Jesus Christ of Latter-day Saints*, April 5, 1940; Anderson, *Cherry Tree*, 19–21, as cited in Boone, "The Worldwide Evacuation of Latter-day Saint Missionaries," 48.

42. Anderson, *Cherry Tree*, 21.

Mission as of July 1, 1939."[43] As he read the letter, shock enveloped him. He wondered if the First Presidency was aware that things had stabilized since the German invasion. He decided to write a letter "containing his personal opinion . . . as to why the mission should stay open" and "planned to take it to the European Mission Presidents' Conference in Lucerne, Switzerland, on June 12."

Elder Joseph Fielding Smith of the Council of the Twelve Apostles, who was touring the missions of Europe on assignment from the First Presidency, was sent to preside over the conference. After consulting with Elder Smith, Wally "wrote a detailed report to the First Presidency outlining his views" and suggesting several reasons why "he felt it inadvisable to remove the missionaries and close the mission in Czechoslovakia." "With the increased tension between nationalities caused by the German invasion, leadership from Berlin was questionable. Since the Czechs were the largest population group affected, if proselyting was to be successful, contact had to continue in their native tongue. In addition, the preparation of mission periodicals was impossible without Czech translators and any other language would be useless." He continued, "Even though the German government dominated both Czechoslovakia and Berlin, money could not legally be passed between the two countries. Travel between the two countries was equally difficult if Church personnel were allowed to pass back and forth at all. And more than anyone else involved, the Czech members would suffer most from the change."[44]

Elder Smith agreed with all five of Wally's recommendations and sent the letter to the First Presidency with his endorsement. Before Wally left the mission presidents' conference, he had already received a cable from the First Presidency that "deferred his release while consideration was given to the greater problem of extending the

43. Czech Mission History, June 20, 1939, 13, as cited in Boone, "The Worldwide Evacuation of Latter-day Saint Missionaries," 49.

44. Czech Mission History, June 20, 1939, 13, as cited in Boone, "The Worldwide Evacuation of Latter-day Saint Missionaries," 49–50.

mission."[45] He was thrilled that the First Presidency had "reconsidered, and decided to retain the Czech mission as a separate entity." Much to his satisfaction, they had decided "not to disrupt the mission, or perhaps better said, make it a part of the East German Mission."[46] Because the wire from the First Presidency authorized him to remain until August 1, he was able to observe the tenth-anniversary celebration of the dedication of Czechoslovakia on July 24.[47]

Martha did not have the same attitude about leaving as her husband. For her, it was a hard pill to swallow that they were staying. They had received letters from family members at home telling them how excited they were that the Torontos would soon return, and Martha had longed to see them too.[48] But Wally believed the extension would allow them time to make preparations regarding the future of the mission and Church organization in Czechoslovakia.

Elder Joseph Fielding Smith and his wife, Sister Jessie Evans Smith, visited the Czech Saints that June. The Smiths "were enthusiastically accepted and drew missionaries and members alike to them."[49] During their visit, Elder Smith "stated that he expected more trouble in Europe and was of the personal opinion that the members of the Church should continue to gather to Zion to escape the oncoming disasters. They should not be prevented from going to America if they have an opportunity." Wally wrote, "He also reminded us that the Church has two great obligations, first, to leave no man without excuse, that he had not had a chance to hear the Gospel, and second, to gather in the seed of Israel." Elder Smith emphasized how important it was for the missionaries to "bear their testimonies forcefully wher-

45. Boone, "The Worldwide Evacuation of Latter-day Saint Missionaries," 49–50.

46. Toronto, journal, July 23–29, 1939, 389.

47. Toronto, journal, June 11–17, 1939, 371.

48. Toronto, journal, July 9–15, 1939, 379.

49. Anderson, *Cherry Tree*, 24.

ever they went," even if the result was a severed friendship. "This," he explained, "is our chief responsibility and calling."[50]

On July 21, 1939, the last baptisms in the country took place before World War II in Brno. Brother Dees baptized Otakar Karel Vojkůvka and his daughter, Valerie, who had just turned eight years old.[51] When Valerie decided to be baptized, she was very sick with pertussis, or whooping cough. Wally was concerned about her health and was not sure it was wise to let her be baptized. She declared that if she was not baptized on that day, she would never be baptized. He could not deny her request. As she came out of the waters of baptism, she was healed of her cough. She was somewhat correct about that particular day, that it would be her last opportunity: all the missionaries, who had the Melchizedek Priesthood and could therefore baptize, were forced to leave the country the following week. There would be no one who had the power to baptize and confirm in Czechoslovakia again until 1943.[52]

After Elder Smith confirmed Brother Vojkůvka, Wally confirmed little Valerie.[53] Three days later, sixty-eight people met on a wooded knoll at Karlstejn to celebrate the anniversary of the country's dedication for missionary work.[54] Sister Smith favored them with a song, and Elder Smith spoke. Elder Smith testified, "I want you to know that I am telling you the Truth. On the last great day we shall both stand at the Judgment Seat of God—you and I—and I shall be there to testify that I told you the Truth."[55] He then "uttered a beautiful prayer, asking the Lord to bless this people with peace . . . [and] to grant that the missionary work might be permitted to go on unhindered in

50. Toronto, journal, June 11–17, 1939, 370.
51. Toronto, journal, June 11–17, 1939, 370.
52. Vojkůvka, "Memories of President Wallace Felt Toronto," November 9, 2013.
53. Toronto, journal, June 11–17, 1939, 370.
54. Czechoslovak Mission Manuscript History, December 31, 1939. Mehr, *Mormon Missionaries Enter Eastern Europe*, 72.
55. Toronto, journal, July 23–29, 1939, 388.

[Czechoslovakia]."[56] It was a great joy for Wally to spend several days with Apostle Smith and his wife, and he felt extraordinarily blessed to know them.[57]

Regrettably, the Apostle's plea to the Father for "unhindered missionary work" was unanswered. Within a few short weeks, peace for Czechoslovakia became a luxury of the past.

---

56. Toronto, journal, July 16–22, 1939, 386.

57. Toronto, journal, July 23–29, 1939, 389.

10 "THIS BOILING CAULDRON OF POLITICAL MADNESS"

A degree of apprehension stifled the level of enthusiasm surrounding the spiritual feast accompanying the visit of an Apostle of the Lord. Just two weeks before Elder Smith's visit, something happened that tested Wally's faith and fortitude like nothing else. On July 10, 1939, two missionaries, Robert E. Lee and Rulon S. Payne, disregarded mission rules—and numerous warnings from the mission president—and made contact with a person who was willing to exchange German marks for American dollars at the black market rate (several times greater than the legal exchange rate).[1] The man was an agent for the Gestapo. Consequently, the elders were thrown in prison.

The German government had passed a law against people possessing American dollars for longer than two weeks without converting them into crowns. They also demanded that any transaction from dollars to crowns was to be done in a bank. Wally had warned the missionaries about the laws and given strict orders "not

---

1. Boone, "The Worldwide Evacuation of Latter-day Saint Missionaries," 51–52.

to exchange money with any individual, no matter how many crowns they were offered per dollar, or how much they pleaded. Dollars were in great demand, and one could sell them for five or six times what they were worth at the legal exchange rate." One of the missionaries had been approached previously by a stooge (agent) of the Gestapo to arrange the money exchange. When they arrived at the scheduled spot, the Nazi officer arrested the elder and his companion.[2] He immediately took them to Gestapo headquarters and then to prison.

Historian David Boone described the arrest of two other missionaries:

> Two other elders, Asael Moulton and Verdell R. Bishop, who had not seen these missionaries all day, went to their friends' apartment just in time to be arrested by Gestapo agents who were searching there for evidence against the offenders. They too, were incarcerated in the Pankrac Penitentiary, but unlike the first elders, they had no idea why they were arrested. The latter two may have been set free except for checks bearing their names on the person of the first two elders. Under German law it was illegal to have foreign currency in one's possession because it was worth more in Germany than the local tender, and therefore was highly prized by the government.[3]

Martha recorded the events leading up to their discovery that the four elders had been arrested. That night, she had gone to the YMCA on the trolley to attend a Mutual Improvement Association meeting, or "VOS" as it was called in Czech. To her surprise, the hall was still locked when she arrived. Previously, the four incarcerated missionaries had almost always been there early to set up chairs and prepare classrooms. She unlocked the door and went about the business of Mutual, assuming that the elders had been delayed. But the missionaries never got there. When she got home, she told Wally that they never showed up.[4]

2. Anderson, *Cherry Tree*, 22–23.
3. Boone, "The Worldwide Evacuation of Latter-day Saint Missionaries," 51–52.
4. Anderson, *Cherry Tree*, 21.

The next morning, Gestapo agents knocked on the mission home door. They entered followed by Asael Moulton, the mission secretary, who was one of the missionaries who had gone missing before the Mutual meeting.[5] The Gestapo then informed Wally of the elders' arrests. They "had found a key which Elder Moulton kept on a chain around his neck. The key opened the office cash box, which contained the mission emergency fund in English pound notes and American bills."[6] The money was reserved for missionaries in case they needed to get out of German territory quickly. When they were in Wally's office, Elder Moulton was somehow able to distract the agents long enough for Wally to take some of the cash and hide it in one of the desk drawers. However, the Gestapo agents took the rest of the money in the mission box—along with Wally's passport. They then left and took Elder Moulton back to the jail at Pankrac.[7]

Wally went to the jail to secure the missionaries' release the next day. He was told that their bail of $10,000 was nonnegotiable, but the charge against the missionaries was not disclosed. He wired the First Presidency and asked that they send the $10,000 by wire. He wanted it on hand in case there was no other way to get the missionaries out of jail. But when he tried to send money to cover the bail, they raised the price. He called Mr. Potter, the American consul, who promised to get started on the case. Wally tried to get permission to see the elders at Pankrac jail, but he was denied the visit.[8] In fact, the elders were denied all visitors. For over a month, Wally remained uninformed as to why the missionaries had been arrested. He constantly sought out the American consul to secure their release. The charges against the

5. Anderson, *Cherry Tree*, 21–22.

6. Boone, "The Worldwide Evacuation of Latter-day Saint Missionaries," 52.

7. Boone, "The Worldwide Evacuation of Latter-day Saint Missionaries," 51–52; and Toronto, journal, July 9–15, 1929, 380.

8. Toronto, journal, July 9–15, 1939, 381.

missionaries constantly changed, "ranging from political excitement and insurrection, to black market fraud."[9]

When he went to retrieve the mission's emergency money and his passport, Wally was forced to sign a statement verifying that his money was legally confiscated. Once he had his passport back, he would be able to go to Vienna the following week to meet with Elder and Sister Smith at the conference for the mission presidents. In addition, signing the statement ensured that Wally would not have to have a formal court trial for failing to exchange the American dollars and British crowns.

After a week, Wally secured 25,000 crowns, went to the Gestapo office and offered to pay the bond to release the elders. To his great disappointment, he learned that because the protectorate was not interested in the case, the elders could not be released, not even on bond, until a decision came from there. The process was becoming overwhelming. "One hardly knows what to do and how to handle such situations, especially under a new and dictatorial regime. During the whole week we have prayed mightily to the Lord for guidance and wisdom in this matter, and I believe that we shall see that events will work out for the best."[10]

The next Monday, Wally visited the Gestapo office again "only to be told that some new developments had come up which would necessitate the brethren's remaining in jail another several days." He felt powerless. "We are doing all we can—but it seems to be so little." He later learned that the Gestapo had discovered an anti-Hitler poem in one elder's possession. They also found some pro-Czech books in another elder's possession. As a result, the four missionaries' case now took on a political aspect and was transferred to the chief Gestapo headquarters.[11] Wally visited the American consulate yet again to talk with Mr. Potter, who had fortunately been admitted to see the four

9. Wallace F. Toronto to the First Presidency, September 18, 1939. Manuscript in possession of Allen Toronto, Brigham Young University, as cited in Boone, "The Worldwide Evacuation of Latter-day Saint Missionaries," 53.

10. Toronto, journal, July 9–15, 1939, 382.

11. Toronto, journal, July 16–22, 1939, 383, 385.

missionaries. Potter told him that they appeared to be all right and "as happy as they could be under the circumstances."[12]

After a week, Wally took some laundry to the prison for the elders. "However, they refused to accept it, for they said it was the wrong day for it." Czech officials at the prison told him that the missionaries were being well treated and that "he did not have to worry about them." They expressed their apology to Wally that he couldn't do anything "since they were in the German section."[13]

When Wally went to visit the office of the Gestapo chief, he found that the elders' case had not yet been transferred to them. "We seem to be so helpless in all of this. We must certainly depend upon the Lord for guidance and assistance." He ran to various offices, attempting to chase down information about the status of the case. He observed, "The secret police just [seem] to pass 'the buck', from one office to another. They are doing the same thing with Mr. Potter, [at] the American Consulate, who is working on the case for us."[14] Wally wrote letters to the parents of the four missionaries to inform them that their sons had been detained and therefore could not write. He also promised that he and the people working with him were doing everything possible for the missionaries with the hope that they would be granted an early release.[15]

The price to release the elders varied with each person Wally asked. "One agent promised their release for approximately fifteen hundred dollars, while others demanded ten thousand dollars." After the missionaries had been held for a month, he came to the startling realization that the purpose of their confinement was to squeeze out "as much money as possible from the Church." According to his report to the First Presidency, some American or English citizens living in

12. Toronto, journal, July 23–29, 1939, 389.

13. Toronto, journal, July 23–29, 1939, 390.

14. Toronto, journal, July 30–August 5, 1939, 391.

15. Toronto, journal, August 13–19, 1939, 397.

German-occupied territory had been held in lieu of as much as ten thousand dollars each.[16]

Throughout the ordeal, Wally kept his sense of humor intact. After every meeting with German officials, he bragged to Martha that the Gestapo meetings gave him an opportunity to learn new German words. During one visit with a high-ranking Gestapo official, however, his lack of German fluency put him into a state of panic. His patience spent, Wally finally got mad and began calling the official some pretty hard names, the meanings of which he was unsure. When he got home, he immediately looked the words up in a German dictionary. When he found out what he had said to the official, he exclaimed, "Oh, my!" and "immediately sat down and wrote a letter of apology" to the offended agent.[17] Fortunately for him, no harm stemmed from his loose tongue.[18]

From what his father Wally had told him, Allen remembered:

> There is no indication that the missionaries were abused, tortured, or excessively mistreated, although other political prisoners were commonly physically punished. The missionaries were separated and each was kept in an isolated cell. No talking between prisoners was allowed, even during periods when they were allowed into an exercise yard to stretch their legs. Elder Moulton later related that sometimes the missionaries were able to communicate through tapping on cell walls or winking at each other to build morale. Much of the time was passed by remembering scriptures that had been memorized, wondering why they were there, and questioning how long their incarceration would last. One elder suggested that anything helped, and remembered a time when he had used his bread as playing dice to roll on the floor.[19]

Finally, after nearly six weeks, Mr. Potter told Wally he thought that he could secure permission for Wally to see the four missionaries at the prison. Wally went to the Gestapo headquarters on Bre-

---

16. Anderson, *Cherry Tree*, 24.

17. Anderson, *Cherry Tree*, 24–25.

18. Boone, "The Worldwide Evacuation of Latter-day Saint Missionaries," 56.

19. Asael Moulton, Czech missionary, interview, by Allen Toronto, date unknown. Notes in possession of Allen Toronto, as cited in Boone, "The Worldwide Evacuation of Latter-day Saint Missionaries," 54–55.

dovska Street and met with Dr. Bäumelburg, the second in command. Bäumelburg finally revealed the charges against the missionaries. He told Wally that they were politically dangerous because of certain books and literature found in their possession but that they had been absolved of the charges. However, he said they had been involved in illegal money transactions and would have to stand a fine—one of $2,500. He ordered that a letter be written entitling Wally and the two men with the consulate to visit the elders at Pankrac under the condition that Wally only speak Czech or German. He sent a young man along with them by the name of Baum to make sure Wally said nothing subversive. Wally delighted to have roughly ten minutes with each missionary. He met "first with Brother Bishop, then with Payne and Moulton together, and then with Brother Lee. They all looked well, despite their six weeks of confinement, and had no major complaints to make. They were delighted to see me and to know that we were doing all we could for their release."[20] "An English-speaking guard was with them the whole time, so they couldn't discuss their case at all. But Wally was able to see that they were all right—dirty, but shaven and cleaned up for the visit."[21]

After going home from a visit to the prison, Wally had no idea what else he could possibly do. He woke up the next day confused by "the strange feeling that [he] should go down to the Gestapo office" that day. He told Martha about his impression, to which she replied, "Well, why don't you go?" He explained, "I'd never get in. . . . How could I ever get in without the American Consul's presence today?" He dismissed the thought at first, but it would not leave him. Finally, he gave in to the prompting. "I was greatly surprised at the rapidity with which I gained entrance and was admitted. Despite the guards, and questions of the many attendants at the Gestapo office, I found myself soon in Dr. Bäumelburg's office. I knew that the Lord was with me that morning. He accepted me very cordially."[22]

20. Toronto, journal, August 13–19, 1939, 396–97.

21. Anderson, *Cherry Tree*, 24–26.

22. Toronto, journal, August 20–26, 1939, 398.

After talking to Wally for a long time, Dr. Bäumelburg finally said, "Your church is a rich church. You could pay that ten thousand with no problem at all." Wally thought to himself, "You old rascal—if you can bluff me I can bluff you."[23] So he went out on a limb and told Bäumelburg about many "fine articles" he had written about Germany. He told him that his wish was to tell the world about the fine German people. He showed him some news articles in the *Deseret News*, which had just gone to press that morning. He then informed him about the number of missionaries in Germany who received a sum of money every month, which brought "much good" to Germany.[24]

Wally declared:

> It becomes perfectly clear that there are no serious charges against our missionaries, but that they are being held only for the purpose of exacting from our Church a great amount in American dollars, which the German government sorely needs at the present time. We are willing to pay a reasonable fine for our men breaking the currency regulations of the country, but not the great amount which you require of us. . . . If it is foreign currency you want, then let me point out that you are endangering one of your finest sources of income. Do you know that for the past few years there have been from 250 to 300 Mormon missionaries laboring in Germany to teach you people the Gospel of Jesus Christ? Do you know that each one of these [missionaries] brings into your country each month from 40 to 50 dollars? . . . Figure it out for yourself, Doctor, and you will find that it totals from approximately 10,000 to 15,000 dollars each month. Now, Doctor, unless you come to terms and deal reasonably with us, I shall request our Church to immediately withdraw every American missionary from German Reich.[25]

Wally was bluffing. There were no longer that many missionaries serving in Nazi-run territory, and he also had no authority to remove missionaries from his own mission, let alone from all of Germany. But the bluff worked. Dr. Bäumelburg "immediately took the phone, called Herr Wegner, and explained the situation to him, saying that he

---

23. Anderson, *Cherry Tree*, 24–26.

24. Toronto, journal, August 20–26, 1939, 398.

25. Czech Mission History, December 31, 1939, 9.

would be willing to pay one thousand dollars, and that in light of the things I had told him, some consideration should be given us. He then informed me that something would be done, and inferred [*sic*] that one thousand [dollars] would suffice."[26]

"Two days later, on August 23, 1939, the finance administration agreed on a fine totaling approximately $1,000. . . . Within a few hours, the four missionaries were released."[27] Nevertheless, they had been ordered to evacuate the country. The rest of the mission was already in the process of evacuating. They had to pack what few belongings they had as hastily as possible. Despite his earlier resistance to being released, Wally "had begun to evacuate the Czechoslovak mission, on the advice of the American consul, even before he received a cable from the first presidency directing him to do so."[28] Martha and the three Toronto children were supposed to be the first to leave. However, Martha insisted that she cook a big meal for the newly released prisoners. After subsisting on a diet of bread, water, and soup for forty-four days, the missionaries' stomachs could not handle the dinner that Martha had prepared, and each of them became quite ill.[29]

After the last four elders left the country, Wally pondered on the significance of their prison experience. He summarized that although it had been a great and very disagreeable worry, it had brought him into contact with official personalities whom he otherwise would never have met. Not to mention, he had been able to tell them something about the gospel of Jesus Christ. He concluded, "It is certain that blessings have flown [*sic*] from it. Such contacts may be very helpful to us in our future work and activities."[30]

Some complications, however, had arisen during the evacuation of the family and of the remaining missionaries that impeded their

26. Toronto, journal, August 20–26, 1939, 398.

27. Boone, "The Worldwide Evacuation of Latter-day Saint Missionaries," 54.

28. Boone, "The Evacuation of the Czechoslovak and German Missions," 128–31.

29. Anderson, *Cherry Tree*, 23–27.

30. Toronto, journal, August 20–26, 1939, 399.

progress. It was against the law to take U.S. dollars out of Czechoslovakia. Wally realized that they "could not enter another country as penniless refugees." He needed to figure out a solution, "a way to get the money safely over the border in spite of impossible rules." As the mission president, he "had wisely told the missionaries to save some of their American dollars and to bring them to the mission home in Prague." He promised he would find some way to get their money back to them while they were in Denmark. He made the situation a matter of fasting and prayer. And he got his answer. He "rolled more than $3,000 in paper bills into a bundle" and give it to Martha, who would carry it out of the country in the pocket of her coat. If she was caught, she would be thrown in prison.[31]

On August 24, 1939, Martha gathered her children and left first, traveling through hostile territory. Although the Gestapo agents were less likely to search her than to search a man, the possibility still existed.[32] "As the customs officers meticulously searched her luggage and purse, they did not touch the pockets of the coat she carried over her arm. They never suspected tender, young, innocent [Martha], with three tiny tots, of such larceny. And miraculously, the money was waiting for the missionaries in Denmark as planned."[33] While traveling through Berlin, "she observed the people screaming, pushing, and crowding aboard the train to ensure their own escape. Fortunately, an elder from the East German Mission helped her get seats" at the end of one of the train cars. She waited there, trusting in God "that her husband and the missionaries would also escape."[34]

On the same day, at about 6:30 in the morning, Wally received a call out of Berlin from President Thomas E. McKay. "He told [Wally] that the American Minister in Berlin was warning all Americans to

---

31. Miller, "My Story: The Dream," 3.

32. Anderson, *Cherry Tree*, 27–29; Mehr, *Mormon Missionaries Enter Eastern Europe*, 72.

33. Miller, "My Story: The Dream," 3.

34. Mehr, *Mormon Missionaries Enter Eastern Europe*, 72; Anderson, *Cherry Tree*, 27–29.

leave the country in view of the tense political situation between [Germany] and Poland. . . . He also informed [him] that he had received a wire from the First Presidency authorizing the mission presidents to act as it seemed wise under such conditions."[35] That next Sunday, Wally conducted Sunday School and asked the Latter-day Saints to remain afterward. He then "told them that it was necessary . . . to leave . . . again because of the German threat of war over . . . the Polish corridor."[36] He assured them that Martha and the children were already safe in Denmark.

Wally put the affairs of the mission in order so that he and the remaining elders could leave. On August 27, 1939, he set Rudolf Kubiska apart as acting mission president and branch president in Prague until he could return.[37] That day, Wally wrote a letter to all Church members, "announcing that we would have to leave, and encouraging them to continue on with the work and to remain faithful to the Gospel."[38] He made arrangements for the local Church leaders to take over and urged the members to continue studying *Articles of Faith*.

Wally had "intended to follow [Martha] and the children with the remainder of the missionaries within a few days but was delayed by the re-arrest of Elder Rulon S. Payne. When Elder Payne had gone to the American consul to obtain an exit permit as required by law, he was taken into custody, frisked, strip-searched, and arrested by Gestapo agents. After he sent the rest of the elders to Denmark, Wally demanded an immediate investigation. He learned that Elder Payne had been arrested "because he had the same name as a British spy the Nazis were looking for, a Mr. Payne."[39] Through the prompt

35. Toronto, journal, August 20–26, 1939, 400.
36. Toronto, journal, August 27–September 2, 1939, 401.
37. Mehr, *Mormon Missionaries Enter Eastern Europe*, 86.
38. Toronto, journal, August 27–September 2, 1939, 403.
39. Martha S. Toronto Anderson, James Moyle Oral History Program, interview by Richard O. Cowan and David F. Boone, February 1978, typescript, 1, Church History Library. See Czechoslovak Mission History, December

intercession of the American consul, "it was finally learned," Wally recorded, "that Elder Payne had been seized because of mistaken identity. Another individual of the same name was apparently being sought for espionage activities, and thus our brother was apprehended."[40] Wally and several American consul representatives verified Elder Payne's identity, after which "Elder Payne was released amid profuse apologies and immediately granted his exit visa. That night, August 31, 1939, Wally and Elder Payne left Czechoslovakia for Berlin; they arrived in Copenhagen on the evening of September 1."[41]

Wally and the missionaries were not the only ones trying to get out of Czechoslovakia. He recorded observing that many Americans and British were "headed anywhere, just to get out of Central Europe. . . . Hitler had given an ultimatum which Poland had refused to answer. England and France were frantically doing all they could to make Germany talk sense, but without success." At the time, Wally "knew little of what was going on outside of Germany for the Czech papers had to either print German propaganda or suffer the consequences." Despite it all, Wally was certain that they would return soon enough to carry on the work.[42]

Meanwhile in Copenhagen, Martha wondered what had happened to her husband. Elder Joseph Fielding Smith was in Denmark too, with the special assignment of directing the evacuation of all seven hundred young men and women.[43] As Martha went three days without any word from Wally and the other missionaries, she grew more and more anxious. "Naturally, I was very upset over the whole thing and expressed my concern and worry to President Smith. As a group of mission leaders we met often in prayer circles and discussed the

---

31, 1939, 11, as cited in Boone, "The Evacuation of the Czechoslovak and German Missions," 132.

40. Czech Mission History, December 31, 1939, 11, as cited in Boone, "The Worldwide Evacuation of Latter-day Saint Missionaries," 58.

41. Boone, "The Evacuation of the Czechoslovak and German Missions," 131–32.

42. Toronto, journal, August 27–September 2, 1939, 403.

43. Anderson, *Cherry Tree*, 30.

situation as it changed from day to day, watching the progress of the German army as it swept across Europe to the borders of Poland. . . . Seeing that I was very worried and getting more upset by the minute, President Smith came over to me, putting his protecting arm around my shoulders."[44] Sister Evelyn Wood, wife of West German Mission president M. Douglas Wood, recalled Elder Smith's special promise to Martha. "Don't worry, the war cannot start until Brother Toronto and those missionaries are out of there." Naïvely, Sister Evelyn Wood asked, "Do you mean to say they'd hold a whole war up, all of the negotiations that are being made while we get those missionaries out of there?" President Smith turned and declared, "The war will not start until those men . . . are out of the country."[45]

David Boone explained President Smith's promise in more detail. "This becomes an interesting prophecy when compared with the events as they were occurring in Europe. President Toronto and Elder Payne left Czechoslovakia at midnight of August 31. The invasion of Poland did not occur until the morning of September 1, at five o'clock A.M.[46] That they were already in Berlin can be further documented by a letter to the First Presidency from President Toronto. He relates, 'We were in Berlin the morning Germany began to bomb Polish cities, but had no trouble in reaching Copenhagen.'"[47] All the elders had left Czechoslovakia by the time the Polish offensive began. In that respect, the evacuation fulfilled Elder Smith's prediction. "If the prophecy referred to the outbreak of war between the Allied Powers and Germany, the prediction was also fulfilled."[48] President Toronto and Elder Payne

44. Martha Toronto Anderson, Czech Mission President's wife, interview, Salt Lake City, February 1978, as cited in Boone, "The Worldwide Evacuation of Latter-day Saint Missionaries," 59.

45. M. Douglas and Evelyn Wood, East German Mission president and wife, interview, Salt Lake City, February 3, 1978, as cited in Boone, "The Worldwide Evacuation of Latter-day Saint Missionaries," 59.

46. Czech Mission History, December 31, 1939, 10; *New York Times*, September 1, 1939, 1.

47. Toronto to First Presidency, September 18, 1939, 6.

48. Boone, "The Worldwide Evacuation of Latter-day Saint Missionaries," 60.

obtained passage on a special train carrying the British Legation out of Berlin. It was the last train to leave before war engulfed Europe.[49]

Wally and his missionaries safely escaped the onslaught of the Nazis in Prague, but 250 children who were assigned to leave the train station on September 1 for safety in England were not so lucky. They waited on the train in anticipation to meet what would have been their foster families.[50] Many Jews had sought Wally's aid, knowing that he had money from the Church, but he had been helpless. Not even he had known about a young London stockbroker named Nicholas Winton who had been working with the British bureaucracy for the last several months before the war to rescue hundreds of refugee Czech children, most of whom were Jews. Winton organized the escape of 669 children in total. To do so, he had to meet with over a thousand parents who were desperate to save their children from the war, convince as many families in England to take the children in, and remain undetected.

Winton's "office" for organizing the *Czech Kindertransport* was initially his hotel room at Wenceslas Square in Prague. Parents lined up to discuss with him the possibility that he could save their children.[51] His colleagues, Doreen Warriner and Trevor Chadwick, managed to ward off the Gestapo and maintain secrecy, a feat that Winton mentioned much later in his life was far more worthy of praise than anything he had done.[52] One of the main obstacles for him was the cost. Britain had agreed to take in the children as long as each child could provide a fifty-pound guarantee to the foster families. Winton sent a letter to President Franklin D. Roosevelt in hopes that America could provide him with at least some assistance. He received the reply from an official at the U.S. Embassy in London that they could spare no help. Winton

49. Anderson, *Cherry Tree*, 27–32. For information on mission evacuation in Europe see Boone, "The Evacuation of the Czechoslovak and German Missions," 123–54; Mehr, *Mormon Missionaries Enter Eastern Europe*, 72–73.

50. "Nicholas Winton," http://www.jewishvirtuallibrary.org/nicholas-winton.

51. "Nicholas Winton."

52. Stephen Moss, "'British Schindler' Nicholas Winton: I Wasn't Heroic. I Was Never in Danger," https://www.theguardian.com/world/2014/nov/09/british-schindler-nicholas-winton-interview, November 9, 2014.

did his best to raise the money for those families that were too poor to produce the funds. Even then, the British authorities were taking too long drawing up the travel documents necessary for their passage out of the country. Consequently, Winton forged the travel documents for each child. The whole process "took a bit of blackmail on [his] part. March 14, 1939, was the day that the first train car (holding twenty children) left Prague for safety. The next day was when the Germans occupied Prague and the rest of the country, followed by the persecution of and confiscation of property from the Jews that had occurred so heavily already in the Sudetenland. The Nazis, instead of terminating Winton's efforts, allowed him to continue letting the children leave since the process "[kept] with their policy to 'cleanse' Europe of the Jews."[53] They likely did not know that the children's documents were not actually valid. Another six trains left throughout the following months, but the last scheduled train never departed, and the children were never heard from again. They had presumably been moved to concentration camps. The 250 families intended to foster the children stood at Liverpool Street waiting for a train that never arrived. The level of desperation and helplessness that Winton felt spread throughout Czechoslovakia, and much of Europe, and escalated dramatically.

Wally, as well as his family and his missionaries, no doubt felt abundantly blessed to have escaped when they did. He and Elder Payne cut it close, but they were protected. They succeeded in getting a second-class compartment. At about two o'clock in the morning, they crossed the border. They then journeyed through Dresden and Berlin, where they were met by two other missionaries, Elder Klopfer and Elder Moulton. They crossed the border on the day Germany declared war. "On Friday, September 1, 1939, President Toronto and his eight missionaries arrived safely in Copenhagen. President Mark Garff of the Danish Mission recorded, 'President Toronto and his missionaries arrived safely on the last train tonight from Berlin. . . . They are tired and worn out and have had many experiences. . . . It was a real thrill to

53. CBS News, "Saving the Children," *60 Minutes*, April 27, 2014, https://www.cbsnews.com/video/saving-the-children/.

see him again united with his good wife and three small children.' The offensive that threw Europe into another conflict and the world into a second World War began the following morning when France and Great Britain declared war on Germany."[54]

When Wally arrived in Copenhagen, Elder Smith told him the disheartening news that all missionaries were to be released and that he and his family were to return home. Wally had strongly believed that he would only have to leave the Czech members for a few weeks, just as he had the previous fall. But he was ready to leave, the war had begun, and it appeared that it would not be for a short duration a second time.[55]

Several reports claimed that "Warsaw had surrendered after terrific bombing, and that Germany and Russia were ready to divide the conquered but stubborn country." Wally later found out that the reports were actually false. In reality, Warsaw "held out until the following week, and then [was] crushed by cruel aerial attacks [and] finally gave up."[56]

Some of the missionaries—Elders Lee, Moulton, and Dees—decided to remain on their missions in the states instead of in Europe. The others wanted to write to their parents and secure permission to remain on the mission. In his journal Wally wrote, "The work in the States will be especially fine and helpful to those brethren who spent forty-four days in prison at the hands of the German Gestapo." Eight missionaries left on a freighter, with a group of about sixty elders. They were all in good spirits. As Wally left, he could not help but wonder "how long it would be before missionaries would return to Czechoslovakia. I hope that the Lord will see fit to renew the work again, and give our Saints the advantage of missionary leadership."[57]

Kahlile Mehr wrote: "The achievements of ten years, 1929–39, had been minimal. Fifty-six missionaries had preached in nineteen

54. Mark B. Garff, daily record, September 1, 1939, 10, as cited in Boone, "The Worldwide Evacuation of Latter-day Saint Missionaries," 61.

55. Toronto, journal, September 3–9, 1939, 406.

56. Toronto, journal, September 17–23, 1939, 414.

57. Toronto, journal, September 10–16, 1939, 409.

cities, published 350 articles in the Czechoslovak press, and publicized the Church widely through sports, public displays, lectures, and other activities. There were 141 names on the membership record and only seventeen priesthood holders. Czechoslovakia was much better informed about the Latter-day Saints, but clearly not disposed to accept its teachings in significant numbers."[58]

Wally later said that he had gained insight into the Nazi methods of control and domination. "The German attitude, that it is *the* superior nation, renders an unhindered approach to this device, . . . an indication of the submissiveness of the German population to authority and of their blind obedience in time of crisis, as well as of their desire to enter the World War."[59]

All missionaries in Europe were to leave the country. When the First Presidency said that all seven hundred missionaries were to leave Europe, Wally felt that the First Presidency must have felt that "a great catastrophe [was] impending." All he could do was pray for them. "May God bless the Saints and the good souls whom we have left in this boiling cauldron of political madness."[60]

58. Mehr, *Mormon Missionaries Enter Eastern Europe*, 73.
59. Toronto, "Some Socio-psychological Aspects," 105.
60. Toronto, journal, September 24–30, 1939, 414.

11 "PUT THE PIECES BACK TOGETHER"

The Torontos had mixed feelings when they left their mission in September 1939. Wally wrote in his journal, "It seems that we have merely kept it going during these perilous times, and that little progress has been made. Going home! A queer feeling comes over one, when the reality of it strikes—partial sadness and partial joy. Sadness because we must leave this glorious work and these fine wonderful people who have meant so much to us in our experiences of the past three years, and joy in anticipation of seeing our loved ones again."[1]

The Torontos crossed the Atlantic by ship, landing in New York City, where they stayed at a hotel. As if the experiences of the past several months had not been enough, hair-raising incidents never seemed to cease. In New York one night, Marion and Bobby snuck out of the hotel room and managed to walk "down onto Broadway with its roaring traffic." Martha frantically searched "high and low" for them before finally running downstairs, finding them "in the care of some strange

1. Toronto, journal, May 28–June 3, 1939, 366.

lady, who had pulled them off the street from in front of an on-rushing truck." The woman who had found them said she could not understand the children when she asked them where they lived or who they were. After all, Marion and Bob still knew only how to speak Czech.[2]

The Torontos arrived in Salt Lake City soon thereafter. Now that they were home, Wally and Martha had to figure out how to move forward. Early in his mission presidency, Wally had already started to consider his future and what he would do when he returned home after his release. In 1937, he had had a conversation with Elder Richard R. Lyman of the Quorum of the Twelve. During their lengthy discussion, Elder Lyman "urged [Wally] to go on in the seminary work." At the prospect, Wally wrote, "I told him of the uncertainty I felt in such work because of the frequent changes in administration and how a number of well-qualified men had been dropped like 'hot potatoes' because [they] had had college training in theology at the Eastern colleges. He seemed to feel that the seminary work was founded however on a solid basis of scholarship, and would become even more so in the future. I learned much wisdom and many things from [Elder Lyman] that evening."[3] After his talk with Elder Lyman, Wally began thinking of teaching as a postmission career.

In June 1939, when going home seemed inevitable, Wally had anticipated that the Church board of education would be sending contracts to him, offering him a part-time teaching position in Salt Lake, allowing him time to secure a degree as well; however, none had arrived before they left Europe.[4] Regarding the transition from Czechoslovakia to home, Martha wrote, "The adjustment of being home after a mission is a difficult one, and we had to go through this period along with all the other mission presidents and missionaries."[5] The family returned in a very poor financial condition. To improve their situation, they decided that Wally should go back to school and work on obtaining his master's degree. It was then that he decided to use his mission experiences as

2. Toronto, journal, October 8–14, 1939, 422.

3. Toronto, journal, January 24–February 6, 1937, 74.

4. Toronto, journal, May 28–June 3, 1939, 366.

5. Anderson, *Cherry Tree*, 35.

the basis for his master's thesis: "Some Socio-psychological Aspects of the Czecho-Slovakian Crisis of 1938–39."[6] They borrowed money so that he could get a job with the state's welfare department while they waited for a contract to teach. Finally, one came through authorizing him to teach early-morning seminary at South High School.

Students who entered Wally's class keenly felt his influence as a seminary teacher. He had "a great love, wherever he taught or whatever he did," and the students had a lot of respect and love for him in return.[7] One of Wally's students was young Henry B. Eyring—later to become First Counselor in the First Presidency. He remembered that Wally had "brought something intangible to [his] teachings." Though he had not fully appreciated it at the time, he realized that Wally had "reached him in ways that went beyond curriculum, teaching style, or even personal testimony."[8] Elder Eyring remembered a story that Wally once mentioned in class about a spiritual experience he had enjoyed as a missionary. While tracting with his companion, they knocked on a certain woman's door. Wally introduced himself and told her that they wanted to tell her about the Church, to which the woman replied, "No, I don't want to hear about it. I'm very sad right now because I've lost a child." At that moment, it occurred to Wally to teach her about the Atonement and the subsequent blessings of eternal life. He promised her that she would see her child again. As he testified, he spoke in the Czech language perfectly, the language he did not actually know yet. The woman felt the Spirit and ended up going to church.[9] That story and other remarkable lessons left a lasting impact on Wally's students.

In July of 1939, Wally received a letter from a Dr. Beeley of the University of Utah, informing him of a fellowship that would greatly enable him to finish his schoolwork.[10] In June the following year, the university bestowed upon Wallace F. Toronto a master's degree of

6. Toronto, "Some Socio-psychological Aspects," 6–7.
7. Ed and Norma, interview, May 8, 2013, 25.
8. Robert I. Eaton and Henry J. Eyring, *I Will Lead You Along: The Life of Henry B. Eyring* (Salt Lake City: Deseret Book, 2013), 122.
9. Ed and Norma, interview, May 8, 2013, 30.
10. Toronto, journal, June 25–July 1, 1939, 377.

science. Two years later in 1942, he became the director of the Red Cross for Utah.[11] Along with his new position, he became a member of the Salt Lake Kiwanis Club. Wally grew extremely busy during the war years in a variety of endeavors.[12] Nevertheless, the Czech people were undoubtedly never far from his mind.

In Church service, Wally became a member of the Mutual Improvement Association General Board and traveled a great deal and even spoke as an emissary of the board. His sister-in-law, Carma, recalled how straightforward he was in that position and how he affected the people around him. She particularly remembered one stake conference at which he was the visiting authority. Local leaders were talking about a certain boy who was traveling in a wayward direction. A moderator panel, which included the bishop, the young men's president, and the elders quorum president, gathered to discuss the problem. They wondered how they could help the young man. He had stopped going to church. Each of them mentioned what they were going to do. Finally, right in the middle of the meeting, Wally raised his hand and inquired, "Do you mean all you people are going to jump on this one kid and scare the hell out of him?" Not surprisingly, all ears were on him. "He said, 'We're shooting buckshot when we should be shooting with a rifle here. One person, one on one. Build a relationship with the kid first. Don't everybody pile on him.'"[13] As was typical, his forthright manner caught the attention of all the rest, and his words influenced them for the better.

While Wally remained busy teaching, Martha attended to their ever-growing family. Their son, Allen, was born on June 2, 1945, the day after Judy's fourth birthday.[14] Martha had settled back into life in Utah. She was seen as a "sophisticated lady with her harp," and her harp meant a great deal to her, as did many other things. She once again enjoyed wearing fine clothes and going to the beauty parlor

11. "W. F. Toronto Dies in S.L.," *Deseret News*, January 10, 1968.

12. "W. F. Toronto Dies In S.L."

13. Carma Toronto, interview, February 26, 2004, 5–6.

14. Anderson, *Cherry Tree*, 37.

every week to have her hair done. Carma remembered that Martha was always dressed perfectly when she went to church. She had her hat, gloves, purse, and coat—the entire ensemble that matched from an exclusive store in Salt Lake City: Maycotts.[15]

A few months after the armistice was signed on August 14, 1945, something completely unexpected transpired. Wally and Martha were called into the office of the First Presidency, where President David O. McKay asked how they would feel about going back to reopen the Czechoslovak Mission and "to put the pieces back together for preaching the gospel again in that land." Wally had never actually been released anyway. He had retained the title of mission president throughout World War II, "keeping in touch as much as possible with the [Czech] Saints." Neither he nor Martha had any "doubt in [their] minds about accepting [the] call from the Lord."[16] So Wally gave up his three jobs to accept an overwhelming responsibility of restoring the mission to a nation he loved deeply.

His second stretch as mission president did not start out under the most ideal circumstances, for he had to go alone. He first had to find a house to live in. "It would be impossible to take a family of five children over into a European country that had been so recently ravaged by war, with no place to stay and no plans for a mission home." Martha readied her husband for his departure and bade him farewell at the train station along with two young elders, Victor Bell and Heber Jacobs, who would accompany Wally to Europe and assist him in fulfilling his many responsibilities.[17]

Wally traveled for quite a while before arriving in Czechoslovakia. He and his elders traveled by ship to Europe and spent several weeks on the ocean. They decided to spend their time doing what they would do if they were already in their areas. On their very first day, they and the presidents and missionaries of other European missions organized a gospel class that would take place from ten to eleven o'clock each

15. Carma Toronto, interview, February 26, 2004, 12.

16. Anderson, *Cherry Tree*, 37–38.

17. Anderson, *Cherry Tree*, 38.

Victor Bell, Wallace Toronto, and Heber Jacobs in Prague, 1945. >>
Courtesy of Church History Library.

morning. They prepared and taught the lessons assigned to them. The mission presidents held classes for their missionaries to learn their separate languages. "Brother Weber takes the four new missionaries going to Switzerland and teaches them German, I have a Czech class for our two brethren, and the Hollanders get into a huddle on Dutch." They often became acquainted with the passengers on board and engaged in gospel conversations with whoever was willing, keeping themselves quite busy.[18]

The leaders encouraged their young elders to attend the services and meetings held by the other denominations, including the Catholic and Protestant churches. They felt that "they might gain some insight into the viewpoints of members of other faiths, and thus be better prepared to introduce them to the Gospel." They knew that their elders could benefit greatly by having a foundation of knowledge about other faiths. "These denominations know the truth in part only, and very often they misinterpret what they do know. They lack the depth and the vision, the stimulation and the inspiration of the restored Gospel. I came away from these meetings, fine as they were, realizing the more how blessed I was to be permitted membership in the Church of Jesus Christ."[19]

When they reached the harbor in Le Havre, the ship's captain announced that "[they] would remain outside the port all night since there were no facilities for unloading and checking until Monday morning." The engines were turned off, and the boat stopped moving as everyone settled into bed. Wally did not fully understand what the captain meant until the following morning. The passengers were up early to prepare their luggage and rush to see Le Havre, which appeared rather beautiful in the night, the distant lights twinkling afar off. They were taken by surprise at what they saw instead. "The sight

18. Wallace F. Toronto to Martha Toronto, June 15, 1946, Church History Library, MS 16693, Salt Lake City.

19. Wallace F. Toronto to Martha Toronto, June 26, 1946, Church History Library.

was sickening. This sparkling gem of the night before, now flooded with the light of the morning sun, lay there a mass of rubble. . . . The wanton destruction of war lay on every side. The huge bombed and burned-out carcasses of proud ships, half submerged in the harbor, bore evidence of frightful days. The docks and warehouses were heaps of debris and stone, now partially cleaned up. Most buildings in the immediate background of the harbor itself stood half demolished, their remaining glassless windows staring over this once proud harbor in death-like silence."[20]

They traveled through France and Switzerland by train. As they passed through France, they noticed that Paris was one of the few large cities nearly untouched by the war.[21] They arrived in Switzerland and proceeded to secure train tickets to Prague, but the next available train would not depart until the following Wednesday. However, Wally and the elders were not completely unhappy by setback, "for to remain in Switzerland, is like a sojourn in paradise." In a letter to Martha, Wally wrote, "Switzerland profited by the war—and more particularly by staying out of the war. It truly blossoms with the fruits of peaceful living. Everyone seems to be well off. The store windows are full of everything that most countries lack—even our own. . . . Remember the delicious Swiss chocolate and sweet cakes? The shops are full of it."[22]

They passed through the Austrian Alps on their way to Prague. They tried hard to study Czech on the train, "but the scenery was too fascinating. Hour after hour [they] stood at [their] compartment window marveling at the rugged peaks, oft times at the snow-capped mountains in the distance, the high string-like waterfalls dangling as it were from the top of sheer cliffs, and at the surging mountain streams below us." The beautiful "glories of Nature" were marred only by "the destruction wrought by man." Many "bridges had been blown up." Temporary ones had been built in place of them. "Railroad yards were full of turned and twisted equipment. Parts of fine stations were in

20. Wallace F. Toronto to Martha Toronto, June 26, 1946.

21. Wallace F. Toronto to Martha Toronto, June 26, 1946.

22. Wallace F. Toronto to Martha Toronto, June 26, 1946.

ruins. A number of factories in these beautiful valleys along the way had been gutted by bombs and shells." Wally thought, "Yes, here is the destructive, ugly side of man's make-up against a background of God's perfect creations; and man's evil designs are so futile and so puny in comparison to the good things of life. How can man, or the devil himself, ever hope to win out against such odds!"[23]

After reaching Salzburg, they headed onward expecting little sleep as they had to pass through several zones early in the morning and eventually the Czech border. A group of U.S. soldiers went around to check everyone's passes. They honored the French military passes that Wally and the elders had, but they warned them that there was a possibility that the Russians would throw them off the train because they did not accept anything that was not written in Russian. The soldiers suggested that, if they were "bounced," the missionaries carry their bags across the bridge to the American border station. Presumably, the officers there would put them up for the night. Wally found the news discomforting since he had been assured by those in Paris that it would not be a problem. "The man in my sleeper—a Czech—hid all of his money, his wristwatch, and other effects, and suggested that I do the same, for, as he said, these Russian soldiers take anything they have a liking for, no matter who the victim is. This, too, was a pleasant thought to add to our apprehension. We must have waited upon this border for almost two hours—all of us lying in bed wondering about the situation."[24]

He recounted to Martha what happened:

> Finally footsteps. The door opened and there appeared a young Russian soldier, bulky in his heavy uniform, but pleasant appearing. I handed him my French Military Pass. He looked it over carefully—upside down, first, and then with my help, right side up. He could find no Russian words and seemed a bit dismayed. However, had he found some, I think he could not have read them. Finally, I took my Passport and helped him compare my name there with my name on the military pass. That seemed to satisfy him, so he smiled, grunted something

23. Wallace F. Toronto to Martha Toronto, June 26, 1946.

24. Wallace F. Toronto to Martha Toronto, June 26, 1946.

> and went on to the next compartment. I heaved a sigh of relief. Later I crept out of bed and two compartments down checked on Brothers Bell and Jacobs. The Russian boy had apparently noted that their arrangement was the same as mine—although they said he checked their permits upside down—and caused them no trouble. And so we thanked the Lord silently that we had encountered no difficulties in entering Russian territory.[25]

All throughout the journey, Wally seemed to enjoy the company with which he found himself on the train. Many of them were Czechs. He talked with them about the war and about the conditions of the country. They seemed friendly enough. "The only disquieting tone at all, was that some of the Czechs on the train were not sure just how the new Communist government, and the new Communist Prime Minister were going to work out. . . . The sentiment seemed to be, 'We are lovers of freedom and the democratic form of life, but we must work with Russia and cater to her, for we have no other alternative. We cannot be sure how our experiment of walking the fence between the ideologies of the East and the West will work out.'"[26]

The three Latter-day Saints reentered Czechoslovakia on June 28, 1946. "The membership had waited seven long years for this reunion."[27] Wally was happy to find that the city, like Paris, had escaped much of the damage that most of Europe had endured. "We walked to the [Prague] Hotel, our first home, just around the corner from the Powder Tower (Prašná Brana). Outside of being a little dirty in some corners and a bit run-down because of lack of materials, Golden Prague still glittered." President Ezra Taft Benson visited the sparkling capital of Czechoslovakia soon after Wally arrived, and Wally noted: "It is thrilling, indeed, how these members welcome the missionaries, and especially an apostle of the Church. It makes me feel that at home we don't appreciate these leaders nearly enough. To have the guidance and association of such a man was a rare privilege. Here was a man, young in years, but rich in wisdom, directing the Lord's work in

25. Wallace F. Toronto to Martha Toronto, June 26, 1946.

26. Wallace F. Toronto to Martha Toronto, July 2, 1946.

27. Mehr, "Czech Saints: A Brighter Day," 50.

Karlstejn monument, dedicated July 29, 1944, commemorates the opening of Czechoslovakia for preaching the gospel. Courtesy of Church History Library.

Europe during its most distressing period. . . . His presence in Europe has been a blessing far beyond earthly value."[28]

While the prophet was there, Wally took him to the dedication site at the ancient fortress at Karlstejn. "There was the monument—erected when everyone thought it would be impossible. . . . The

28. Wallace F. Toronto to Martha Toronto, July 7, 1946.

Church members at the Karlstejn monument on July 29, 1946, commemorate the opening of missionary work in Czechoslovakia. Courtesy of Church History Library.

chiseled stone plate reads something like this: On this spot the Czech Mission of the Church of Jesus Christ was organized July 24, 1929." The place meant so much to him, as he was one of the missionaries present during the dedication seventeen years earlier when he was a young missionary.[29] He had always maintained the tradition of visiting the site on its anniversary every year. He, and likely everyone present, felt the sacredness of the spot, still standing even amidst the terrible tragedy of war.

After they left the dedication site, they visited Brno, which presented a stark difference to Prague. The once beautiful city had been bombed heavily in many areas. The home of the Vojkůvka family was destroyed. "It is miraculous how they escaped alive." Wally and the others went up the hill toward the infamous Spielberg Nazi concentration camp. They

29. Wallace F. Toronto to Martha Toronto, July 7, 1946.

looked over the valley of Brno. It still seemed the same, apart from the war damage, "all of it the work of American fliers."[30]

Despite the damage caused by the American army, the people of Czechoslovakia recognized that the Americans had saved their lives. "They loved Americans. Every person had a story to tell about Americans, how nice they were when the soldiers came."[31] While Wally was at the embassy, "a Czech military and civilian convoy brought the fragments of an American B-29 and some article of clothing from a dead American flier, shot down somewhere over Czechoslovakia, and presented them to [representatives of] the American Army." Several speeches were given after flower girls lined up as the Czech band played. "The Czech representative, a soldier, said that this was symbolic of Czechoslovakia's great regard for America, and that the Czechs had given . . . some three hundred fallen fliers decent burials throughout the land."[32] About a week later, Lieutenant Alden Anderson—a new friend of Wally's—made sleeping arrangements for two hundred men of the Graves Registration Division of the army who would "begin the task of locating and disinterring the bodies" of the three hundred or so American fliers who had "lost their lives over Czechoslovakia soil."[33]

Wally set out to finding a house as soon as he could, but he had no idea that it would take so long to find a mission home. So many other responsibilities required his attention on top of house hunting. He was endlessly busy. In the end, it took an entire year to find an adequate villa before he was successful and could reunite with his wife and children. The year that he spent in Prague without his family was "one of extreme hard work, both physically and mentally." "He spent many hours trying to find . . . Church members, some of whom had become lost or moved to other countries, or had been imprisoned for one reason or another."[34] In fact, members of German ancestry had either been

30. Wallace F. Toronto to Martha Toronto, July 7, 1946.

31. Dale Tingey, interview, 3.

32. Wallace F. Toronto to Martha Toronto, July 14, 1946.

33. Wallace F. Toronto to Martha Toronto, July 19, 1946.

34. Anderson, *Cherry Tree*, 38.

deported or imprisoned by the Czechs.[35] Wally wrote Martha, "The Czech government had followed the policy of sending all Germans, who did not prove themselves worthy of Czech citizenship during the war years, back to Germany. This is done on the principle that they are as guilty as the Germans in the Reich, and that the Germans in Czechoslovakia therefore should not escape the punishment which is being suffered by the German nation." And that punishment was to be stripped of everything and forced to build up an economy of their own and "pay reparations for war damage to the Allies and former occupied countries."[36]

Consequently, almost two million people were forced to leave within the year. The population of the country then decreased by millions. Wally found that the Czechs at least offered what he called "a most magnanimous gesture." To those who could prove that they had taken no part in Nazi citizenship, the government "offered citizenship and the right to retain their land and property." All others were allowed to take only what belongings they could carry, except for their jewelry, which would be confiscated. They were given a supply of food to last them three weeks. Wally noted, "Families were kept together wherever possible, and fair treatment is being accorded them."[37]

With the help of the two missionaries, Wally distributed a train carload of welfare supplies, which Church headquarters had sent from Salt Lake City, to the Saints in the mission, as well as to any others who were suffering from afterwar effects. He was able to provide clothing and various kinds of food. Later, several people said that he had practically saved their lives.[38] Near the end of July, the boxes that had been lost during the long journey finally arrived. Some were regular boxes of food for distribution, but they had also put large portions of food in their own pieces of luggage. "Brother Bell brought four gallons of honey. Every one of his four cans sprung its lid, and his trunk was

35. Anderson, *Cherry Tree*, 39.

36. Wallace F. Toronto to Martha Toronto, July 19, 1946.

37. Wallace F. Toronto to Martha Toronto, July 19, 1946.

38. Anderson, *Cherry Tree*, 39.

nothing but honey from top to bottom." The honey had seeped through all his extra clothes and shoes. "In short, it looked as though bees had been there for years. We cleaned it up and were able to salvage three of the four gallons." Wally considered it "the sweetest day" of the elder's young life.[39]

Czech Church members had survived every hardship imaginable. Elfrieda (Frieda) Glasnerová Veněčková, a Jewish convert who was baptized in 1932, spent two years with her husband and two sons in a concentration camp. "Eleven members of her extended family had perished at Auschwitz."[40] When they finally released her, her feet were so frozen that she could not walk, and she had to be sent to a hospital.[41] Near the end of July 1946, Wally visited her in the hospital. She cried when she saw him and thought she was "looking at a vision."[42] She told him the story she lived during the war. "Two thirds of the nine million Jews of Europe were annihilated—her own sisters perished in the gas chambers in Poland—and the other third were tortured and plagued behind barbed-wire." Frieda felt blessed that she only spent "a relatively short time in a slave labor camp, totaling six months. Her husband was confined and forced to hard manual labor for three months longer, and in another camp, for no other reason than that he had married a Jewess and would not give her nor their little family up."[43]

Despite months of hunger and intense suffering, Frieda's face was "radiant and bright" as she talked with her beloved mission president. Wally continued listening intently as she relayed the account. "The Nazis, now knowing that they could not win the war, had ordered all the Jews in the Terezín concentration camp to be shot on the morning of May 5th. Frieda was in Terezín. She prepared with the rest of her dissolute countrymen to lose her life before a Nazi firing squad—but somehow felt that it would not be so. In the early morning of that very

39. Wallace F. Toronto to Martha Toronto, July 27, 1946.

40. Mehr, "Czech Saints: A Brighter Day," 50.

41. Miller and Richards, interview, May 3, 2013.

42. Miller and Richards, interview, May 3, 2013.

43. Wallace F. Toronto to Martha Toronto, July 19, 1946.

same day the Allies liberated the camp, and her life was spared." When she found herself in need of an operation, the doctors knew it was pointless. She was far too weak to survive it. "But she seemed to feel that the Lord had work for her to do." Following the operation, the doctors called her the "miracle" because she had survived against the odds. "With the help of the Lord, she cheated the Nazis out of another Jewish death."[44]

Wally knew that he had "been in the presence of true greatness" after his visit with Frieda. He was impressed by her goodness and her conviction and love for the Lord. She recognized all the blessings that he had bestowed upon her and her family. When he was ready to leave, she called over to him and said, "When I am better, please come and visit me in my home. I have been saving up my tithing and would like to give it you."[45]

Before he rejoined the Czech Saints, Wally had learned about the demise of a small Czech village that had fallen victim to Hitler's indignation. Lidice was nestled a short distance northwest of Prague near Kladno, a small mining town. Close to midnight on June 9, 1942, Nazi officers stormed the small cottage homes and ordered the inhabitants out on the street with all their valuables. The men, including any boy over the age of fifteen, were separated from their families and placed in a cellar for the remainder of the night; the women and children slept in a school. The following day, just outside Horák's farm, the men were lined up a few at a time next to a wall and shot.[46]

Before the executions began that morning, the Nazis transferred the women and children to Kladno, where they then separated mothers from their children. All girls fifteen and older were sent with the women to concentration camps. The officers picked out nine of the children to be adopted into German families. The rest of the children were to receive "special treatment" in the gas chambers. Based on certain defined criteria, 89 of the 105 children were killed after they

44. Wallace F. Toronto to Martha Toronto, July 19, 1946.

45. Wallace F. Toronto to Martha Toronto, July 19, 1946.

46. Eleanor Wheeler, *Lidice* (Prague: Orbis, 1957), 10.

failed the tests. The mothers "did not learn the truth about the fate of their husbands and children until they were crossing the border into Czechoslovakia, after the liberation in 1945" three years later.[47]

Some of the men in Lidice had been working a night shift at the mines. When they returned home, the Nazis transferred them to Prague, where they too were shot and killed. By noon on June 10, "not a single male inhabitant of Lidice remained alive." Nazi officials thrust the corpses into a common grave and proceeded to demolish the town primarily by blowing up and burning the houses and buildings. They documented their work during the course of their destruction. "Motion picture film and still camera shots were found in Nazi files under the heading 'Instructional and Cultural Films.' . . . Nazi soldiers are pictured as they desecrated the graveyard in their search for the gold teeth of the dead" and threw what they found into a basket. The purpose of the film was not only used to show their leaders that they had successfully carried out their duties, but it was also used as "an indoctrination film to instruct the Nazi youth in the methods of razing villages."[48]

The revulsion of the events was only augmented by the official Nazi declaration drafted to justify their horrific actions:

> In the course of the search for the murderers of SS-Obergruppenführer Heydrich, incontestable proof was found that the population of Lidice near Kladno had given support and assistance to the perpetrators of the crime. The relevant evidence was, in spite of interrogations, collected without the co-operation of the inhabitants. The attitude toward the crime revealed hereby is still further emphasized by other activities hostile to the Reich, by stores of seditious matter, dumps of weapons and munitions, an illegal radio transmitter, and also rationed goods in great quantity, and by the fact that inhabitants of the village were actively serving the enemy abroad. Since the inhabitants of this village have in the most uncompromising manner opposed the published laws through their activity, and have given support to the murderers of SS-Obergruppenführer Heydrich, the male adults have been shot, the women sent to a concentration camp and the children

47. Wheeler, *Lidice*, 10.
48. Wheeler, *Lidice*, 10–12.

placed in suitable educational institutions. The buildings have been razed to the ground and the name of the place has been erased from the records.[49]

Of course, none of it was true. "They [had] searched the town inside and out and found nothing."[50] The small town of Lidice, along with the smaller town of Ležáky two weeks later, suffered the undeserved consequences ordered by an angered Hitler against the actions of two Czech paratroopers, Jan Kubis and Josef Gabcik, who had just killed his right-hand man, Reinhard Heydrich. Heydrich was the SS-Obergruppenführer, one of the highest-ranking officers in Hitler's army. He had been sent to Czechoslovakia in 1941. His reign of terror commenced as soon as he entered the capital. "Immediately after his arrival in Prague, he had two hundred Czechs shot and several thousand imprisoned. Before his violent death, Heydrich was scarcely known outside of Germany, yet he was the architect of the death camps that annihilated six million human lives." Within two months of his arrival, he and the Gestapo agents "delivered four hundred death sentences followed by immediate execution. Four thousand patriots and intellectuals were put into prisons and concentration camps. The Czechs had to be shown by forceful means that any resistance, however slight, would have disastrous consequences for them."[51]

The two Czech patriots were hired to kill the despised Heydrich by the exiled Czech government, headed by former Czech president Eduard Beneš, seeking refuge in London. "The operation was organized by Frantisek Moravek, chief of the Czech secret service, who had fled to London, taking several boxes of secret documents with him, before the Germans arrived in Prague." Moravek relayed all the details of the mission "of killing the cruelest enemy of their people" to Kubis and Gabcik, who were then given "special training in England.

49. Wheeler, *Lidice*, 12–13.

50. Wheeler, *Lidice*, 2.

51. Edouard Calic, *Reinhard Heydrich: The Chilling Story of the Man Who Masterminded the Nazi Death Camps*, trans. Lowell Bair (New York City: William Morrow and Company, 1985), 13, 249.

On the night of December 28, 1941, they parachuted into the protectorate with two other groups from a British Halifax bomber. Until May 27, 1942, they lived in hiding, making preparations to insure the success of their mission."[52]

For five months, they lay in wait. "On the morning of May 27, when Gabcik stepped in front of Heydrich's car and tried to shoot him, his . . . gun failed to fire. But then Kubis threw [a] bomb. It exploded under the right rear wheel of the Mercedes, wounding Heydrich. Klein, the chauffeur, ran after Kubis in vain. The two Czechs escaped."[53]

While the explosion failed to kill Heydrich, his wounds proved fatal. He was rushed to a hospital nearby in Bulovka. Hitler sent doctors from Berlin to Prague. They tried to save Heydrich's life while over 60,000 policemen searched for the assassins. "On June 4, 1942, the Prague radio station announced that Heydrich had died of his wounds. Hitler ordered that the body be brought to the Reich Chancellery in Berlin. . . . The leaders of the Nazi party mourned their 'irreplaceable' policeman, the man who . . . in 1936 had become the dreaded chief of the Security Police."[54]

Only two weeks later, "a traitor named Karel Curda told the Gestapo what he knew about the agents who had come from England. . . . Kubis and Gabcik took refuge in the Karel Boromaeus Greek Orthodox Church" in a crypt underground. At least 750 SS officers surrounded the church on June 18. "When Kubis and Gabcik refused to surrender, they were killed. All the priests involved in hiding them were sentenced to death and executed."[55] However, killing Heydrich's assassins was not enough. Hitler chose Lidice and Ležáky as the unfortunate recipients of his revenge because the villages were wrongfully alleged to have aided Kubis and Gabcik. Hitler needed to remind Czechoslovakia that they were not to defy his rule. Two years after the villages

52. Calic, *Reinhard Heydrich*, 253–54.

53. Calic, *Reinhard Heydrich*, 254.

54. Calic, *Reinhard Heydrich*, 9.

55. Calic, *Reinhard Heydrich*, 254.

were razed to the ground, the land was surrounded by a barbed wire fence to warn the Czechs against rebellion.[56]

Hitler's plan backfired. Nations around the world felt sorrow for the people of Lidice. While Hitler intended for the name to be erased from the world, the world chose instead to react differently. As a sign of respect, several countries chose to change the names of cities, streets, and town squares to Lidice so that its name would never be forgotten. Ordinary people from dozens of countries raised funds to send to Czechoslovakia to rebuild the city after the war ended. When work began on rebuilding the village, young people from all over the world—India, France, America, the Soviet Union, Vietnam, Canada, China, and many others—went to Czechoslovakia to help "lay the foundations for the road leading to Lidice."[57]

The tragedy that befell an unsuspecting, peaceful town generated the deepest sorrow among the people of Czechoslovakia. The events were horrific and appalling. Wally visited the site to see for himself the ruins of a once beautiful and thriving town. In a letter to Martha, he described the experience with respect and awe. "From the brow of this low hill we looked down on what was once Lidice—now nothing, absolutely nothing, except a barren, rolling country-side, marked only by the stark remains of a few white foundations, leveled to the ground, of former happy homes, where contented, loving families once lived; by the outline of a simple country schoolhouse, where formerly children learned, laughed and played; by a level rectangular area where stood a village church, where once were uttered humble prayers and supplications; by a few remaining shade trees and a quiet brook, which the former inhabitants of Lidice loved and enjoyed." But behind it all stood a "simple wooden cross watching over the common grave" of all the men who had been martyred in cold blood.[58]

Wally, touched by the reverence surrounding the little valley, walked over to the wooden cross and the common grave of the Lidice

56. Wheeler, *Lidice*, 11.

57. Wheeler, *Lidice*, 17–20.

58. Wallace F. Toronto to Martha Toronto, August 12, 1946.

martyrs. Beside him "stood weeping a lean brown weather-beaten old woman with a peasant shawl drawn around her sad wrinkled face." She told Wally that her son and her brother lie in the spot. The woman had traveled from a neighboring village to "place an offering of flowers upon their resting place." Wally spoke to her with love and sympathy. "Her tear-stained face [brightened] somewhat when I told her that these loved ones, although robbed of life in the flesh, were yet living in the not-too-far-distant spirit world, and that she would see and embrace them again." This experience alone "was worth the trip to Lidice, if for nothing else, to see [a] new hope kindled in the soul of this care-laden woman."[59]

Later, Wally gave a talk titled "Truth Must Prevail" that focused on the solemn fate of the Lidice people. Echoing his words that he wrote to his wife, he described the site of desolation and expressed his feelings as he bowed his head "in reverent silence as the evening shadows deepened over the valley." He expressed how the people of Lidice were symbolic of the suffering and heartache of the entire Czech nation. They had been "stripped of every earthly possession" and their lives had been stolen from them "by an overwhelming power of evil, simply because they dared to believe in their hearts and in their actions that 'Truth Must Prevail.'"[60]

While Wally was experiencing such remarkable spirituality in Czechoslovakia, Martha was attending the farewell addresses of missionaries who would soon be joining Wally (and eventually she would too) in Czechoslovakia. She often wrote to Wally about the future missionaries. On one occasion, she went to the farewell of a missionary in the Yale Ward in Salt Lake City and wrote to Wally about the young man's previous experiences, "He's a fine fellow, and has quite a story to tell. . . . During the war he was shot down. . . . The Czech people hid him from the Germans who came looking for him. They cared for him and were finally able to get him out of the country through the underground. . . . Some of the people lost their lives because they

59. Wallace F. Toronto to Martha Toronto, August 12, 1946.

60. Wallace F. Toronto, "Truth Must Prevail," 1946–47, Church History Library, MS 17103.

aided him. His greatest desire ever since has been to go back to that country and bring the Gospel to the Czech people."[61] She also attended the farewell address of Donald Whipperman where former missionary Ed Lyon spoke, painting a "gloomy picture of [the] mission." Lyon told the people, "It [was] the most difficult mission in the Church" because, among other things, it had the hardest language.[62]

During the long year apart, Martha wrote to Wally of her longing for him and the troubles she encountered while he was away. In November 1946, she wrote of severe winter conditions and expressed that she was glad that the children were not with him in Czechoslovakia. She wrote, "I'm even worried about coming over at all unless conditions improve for the next winter. It would be very hard for them, and me too for that matter, to live in a cold house when we're used to such a nice warm one. Golly, hon, I must be a sissy but I remember how cold it used to be even when we were there before and I get weak knees thinking about it."[63]

Wally replied with a thorough description of the conditions in Czechoslovakia. Martha shuddered at the things he was experiencing and began to have cold feet about joining him at all. "Darling, I just couldn't bring these children over there to be cold all the time and be sick all winter. It worries me to think of it. Honey, *be sure* of the situation before sending for us. If only I could come alone, I know I could stand it if I didn't have to see the kids suffer. If they didn't *need* a father so very badly it might be best to go on like we are now. I'm sure we could live through the separation even as hard as it is. I'm just all mixed up about it. I know the Lord will see it through for the best so I shouldn't worry about it."[64]

61. Martha Toronto to Wallace F. Toronto, March 23, 1947, as found in Anderson, Martha Sharp, Letters to Wallace F. Toronto, 1946–47, 1956–1958, 1961, Church History Library, MS 17103.

62. Martha Toronto to Wallace F. Toronto, April 14, 1947.

63. Martha Toronto to Wallace F. Toronto, November 10, 1946.

64. Martha Toronto to Wallace F. Toronto, December 1, 1946.

Czechoslovak mission home, ca. 1947–50. Courtesy of Church History Library.

Wally and Martha remained apart during Christmas of 1946. Martha watched as their little "Gus" embraced a family friend. She knew the "poor little guy [wanted] and [needed] a Daddy."[65] This realization disturbed her, and she started to cry. However, Wally sent a telegram later that day, a tender mercy that cheered her up and helped her make it through the day. By the end of December, Martha was praying constantly with the children that Wally would find a house. In one letter, Martha wrote, "It will be a glorious day when you send word that you've found

65. Martha Toronto to Wallace F. Toronto, December 29, 1946.

one. If you only could find one *now*, then I'd go ahead on getting passports, visas and what not. You know, dear, it's only four months until school is out. . . . At least the longest part of this year is over and I'm sure these next four months will go by quickly."[66]

During 1946, Wally missed out on some very important milestones in his family, such as Marion's first date and Carol's baptism.[67] But as time went on, he was finally able to find a mission home, a three-story villa in Prague that had all of Martha's requirements: a washing machine, an electric iron, a refrigerator, a stove, a sewing machine, and some toilet paper. In an effort not to leave anything out, she wrote him again to ask if she should take bedding, towels, dishtowels, soap, toothpaste, pans, kitchen utensils, pie plates, and cake tins.[68]

In the spring of 1947, with the villa rented to serve as the mission home and as their residence, Wally was ready to have his family join him. Martha applied for visas in New York City at the same time that four new missionaries sent in applications to the Czech consulate in New York City. All of them received their visas at the same time, boarded the ship, and sailed across the Atlantic. In June 1947, at Le Havre, France, Wally met all of them on the docks, ready to serve in Czechoslovakia with his eternal companion once again.

---

66. Martha Toronto to Wallace F. Toronto, January 26, 1947.
67. Martha Toronto to Wallace F. Toronto, February 16, 1947.
68. Martha Toronto to Wallace F. Toronto, March 27, 1947.

12 "THE LITTLE SPY"

Martha and the children traveled by ship to Europe. They were finally reunited with Wally in June of 1947 at the port in Le Havre. They brought with them a brand-new 1947 Ford. They might have expected a typical harbor, but instead they were greeted by an artificial one made of floating docks. The original dock had been decimated by the war, as Wally had described in his letter the year before. Martha and the children watched people from the ship throw cigarettes down to those gathered below on the docks. Wally told Martha that he too had cigarettes on hand. He explained, "I took cigarettes and soap with me because you could buy anything with cigarettes and soap." From the docks, the Torontos went to the Le Havre mission home, where they were delighted to eat french fried potatoes, "nice little chunks of potatoes french fried." After the meal, they proceeded to drive across Germany in the new Ford. Bob remembered stopping in one of the main cities in Germany and seeing a statue, "riddled with bullet holes," in the middle of the square. Because of World War II, "there was nothing as far as the eye could see except for destroyed buildings—[in] every direction."[1]

Martha was obviously a little older the second time in Czechoslovakia. The missionaries wanted to give her a nickname as they had in the past. She was still an attractive woman and not very old compared to the wives of other mission presidents. However, "Princess" no longer seemed very fitting. Instead, they began to call her "Dynamite" because of a lovely dress that she had with little rectangular patterns that looked like sticks of dynamite. They later shortened the nickname and simply called her Sister T.[2]

The work of the Church quickly began to take semblance in the Czech Mission once again. Missionaries arrived at various intervals: four with Martha in June and then six in August. They began to build a workforce that could learn the language and proselyte effectively. As the missionaries gained more experience and confidence, they were sent to other parts of the mission, taking younger companions with them. Soon, they had branches set up in small towns and regular meetings were being held in the cities. Church membership began to grow. Auxiliary meetings were held in the mission home as well since its rooms were big enough to accommodate crowds of twenty to fifty. Eventually, people from all over the city started attending the meetings, and "they enjoyed them very much."[3] And two young women entered the country as the first sister missionaries there. They had to stay in the mission home with the Torontos. Wally gratefully watched as they became quite effective.[4]

The missionaries followed a particular process in their work. After opening a city for teaching, they rented a hall. Then they went from door to door teaching people and trying to encourage them to go to the meetings in the hall. They put up flyers that encouraged people

1. Mehr, *Mormon Missionaries Enter Eastern Europe*, 83; Bob and David Toronto, interview, August 20, 2013, 19–20.

2. Bob and David, Toronto interview, August 20, 2013, 25.

3. Anderson, *Cherry Tree*, 47–48.

4. Anderson, *Cherry Tree*, 47.

Czechoslovak mission home as it appears today. Courtesy of Church History Library.

to "come and see [a] film about the Mormons and Joseph Smith." As was usual for nearly all missionaries, they also tracted. They left the tracts, which were translated into Czech, with people everywhere they went. After the missionaries finished their preparations, Wally went to that town and shared a film and a presentation, which he had previously prepared about the Church. The missionaries followed the same process in virtually every town of Czechoslovakia.[5] And even though his growing family required considerable attention, he "energetically visited every branch each month."[6] Because he and Martha were so busy with mission affairs,

5. Miller and Richards, interview, May 3, 2013.
6. Czechoslovak Mission Manuscript History, June 20, December 20, 1936; September 20, 1937.

they hired a very "motherly nursemaid" named Marenka to care for Carol and Bobby.[7]

The three-story villa in Prague that they used as a mission home from 1947 to 1950 served as Wally's office and as the residence for his family of five children, ages two to thirteen. It had a huge yard of orchards and trees as well as a pool with little frogs in the water.[8] A total of twenty-seven rooms surrounded a two-story foyer with a beautiful balcony. Sometimes when Wally was gone, Martha helped her children take the cushions off the couch and lay them out all over the floor below the balcony. They then ran upstairs and jumped over the balcony onto the pillows. The mansion had a large staircase that ascended up three floors and down into the dark basement below. Concrete lions protected the front doors of the large, pink brick structure. A gargoyle spouting water from its mouth stood at the pond in the garden, and an ornate wrought iron gate surrounded large, beautiful lawns and gardens. A lovely cherry tree stood outside the window of the kitchen.[9]

There was also a large sunroom with a "whole wall of glassed windows" and a ping-pong table next to the office. In Wally's office there was a copy machine—or as the children called it, the "ditto" machine—at the back of the room. They regularly played with it to make copies, turning the handle, cranking out each sheet, and getting ink all over their hands.[10] On the main floor, Wally's office was off to one side while the dining room and kitchen were on the other.[11] A piano room adjoined the dining area. Marion often played the piano to soothe herself whenever she was distressed or unhappy. The kitchen had stairs leading up to a missionary dormitory with four or five beds for the young men, and one room reserved for the sisters.[12]

---

7. Miller, "My Story: The Dream," 1.
8. Anderson, *Cherry Tree*, 71–72.
9. Miller, "My Story: The Dream," 3–6.
10. Miller, "My Story: The Dream," 6.
11. Bob and David Toronto, interview, August 20, 2013, 22.
12. Bob and David Toronto, interview, August 20, 2013, 22.

Their second mission was a little different for Wally and Martha because they now had six children who needed to attend school. Wally was determined that his children be immersed in the language and culture. People respected him for that, and his family became a good example to the missionaries and others.[13] The Torontos decided not to send their children to a private school. Instead, they sent them to the Czech public schools. For the children, public school was often challenging.[14]

Carol and Judy became close buddies during those years. They regularly did things together that made them and their older brother, Bob, late for school, the consequence of which was standing in the corner with a dunce cap on.[15] Judy remembered one particular day when Bob ran about two miles to get to school on time. Carol and Judy, with no desire to run, said, "We just can't make it." They decided to stop at a sugar beet field, where they sat and filled their stomachs with sugar beets instead of getting to school late. About the time that they believed school was out, they went home. Carol wrote a note pretending she was her mother and explained to her teacher why she had missed school that day. She also typed up a note for Judy to take to her teacher. When she gave the note to her teacher the next day, he asked her, "Who wrote this note?" She replied, "My sister did," for she could not lie. Both of them got in trouble, and the school called Wally and Martha to inform them about what had happened.[16]

Tardiness, however, was not the worst of their problems. The Toronto kids were constantly bullied. Their classmates would write things on their backpacks to tease them. They would also tell them to say certain things in Czech that were out of order or inappropriate, knowing that the Torontos did not know what the words meant, and laugh hysterically when Bob or Carol repeated the words. One day on the way home, about twelve kids chased the Torontos, who tried

13. Dale Tingey, interview, 3.

14. David Toronto, interview by Daniel Toronto, 2010, 4.

15. Judy Richards, interview, 3–4.

16. Judy Richards, interview, 3–4.

to hide in a doorway of some apartments to get away from them. The schoolmates lined up and would not let them out of the doorway for a long time.[17]

The children did learn enough Czech words to get along with their friends, but not enough to understand schoolwork. Bob found himself sitting in a Czech classroom, "not knowing what was going on" for the three years he attended.[18] He remembered when "the pictures of Masaryk and Beneš, democratic presidents, came down; Stalin and Lenin went up." The requirements also changed. Instead of learning just Czech, they had to learn Russian.[19] In class, Bob was to learn Russian in Czech but he still did not know Czech well enough to figure out what the Russian was about.

At one point, Wally tried helping Bob with his schoolwork in his office. They were supposed to copy notes into a blue book, but Bob struggled because penmanship had to be "virtually perfect" by the second grade. He just could not do it in the foreign language. Wally tried to help him for a while. But after some time, Bob didn't remember his father being in his life too much. He was just too busy. Wally had "fifty missionaries spread out all over the country doing things." And as things worsened politically, Bob remembered losing his dad altogether.[20] It was just a downside of having a mission president as a father. Wally sometimes became rather distant. He treated his children without a great deal of warmth. Wally's being gone a great deal of the time was especially hard on Bob because Wally was "never around for the family. He was off doing mission stuff all the time." Bob felt his absence "very keenly," and it affected his life later.[21]

On the other hand, David, the youngest, remembered his dad being very fun to be with. David was born in Czechoslovakia in July 1947. After he was born, Wally called his kids "Czech, double Czech, triple

---

17. Judy Richards, interview, 3–4.

18. Bob and David Toronto, interview, August 20, 2013, 4.

19. Bob and David Toronto, interview, August 20, 2013, 4.

20. Bob and David Toronto, interview, August 20, 2013, 6.

21. Miller and Richards, interview, May 3, 2013, 19.

Czech."[22] When they left the house, He called them the "cancelled Czechs."[23] Being the youngest, David realized that Wally probably paid more attention to him than to his other children. When Wally was in Czechoslovakia, the family "probably got pushed back a little bit because there was so much else going on." When he was finally in a position where he could be with his family, they were able to develop a personal relationship with their father.[24]

"I think the relationship between me, and Al, and Dad is probably a lot different than it is with the older kids," David observed.[25] When David was born, Wally would "take [him] around to the branches and . . . introduce [his baby] as his little spy" because he was born in 1949, the year after the Church was branded as a spy organization. "So [he] was the little spy." When David returned to the Czech Republic as an adult in 2007, he visited Plzeň. While there, he saw Sister Marková, who had been Wally's secretary and translator in her early twenties at the time. When she saw David, she looked at him and said, "You must be my little spy."[26] The experience brought him deep emotions.

Along with feeling somewhat lonely in Wally's absence, Bob also remembers being hungry almost all of the time he was in Czechoslovakia. He remembered having snack time every day at school. The children would arrive at 8 o'clock in the morning. Snack time was at 10 o'clock. They could bring their ration stamps to school and exchange them for things such as a liter of milk. After World War II, the country used ration stamps to control how much food people could buy. For some reason that Bob cannot remember, everyone would have milk and braided bread except for him most of the time. When he did get to have some, it was "the most delicious thing [he] could ever remember in [his] life." He recalled, "I don't know why I didn't [get the snack]. . . .

22. Bob and David Toronto, interview, August 20, 2013, 3.

23. Bob and David Toronto, interview, August 20, 2013, 3.

24. David Toronto, interview by Daniel Toronto, 2010, 6–7.

25. David Toronto, interview by Daniel Toronto, 2010, 6–7.

26. Bob and David Toronto, interview, August 20, 2013, 23.

I just never asked my Mom and Dad or anything like that, so I'd just go around and bum what I could off the other kids."[27]

School would go from eight o'clock to noon and then from two to six o'clock. During the two hours off, Bob would go to the mission home and eat whatever he could find. The Torontos were given enough ration stamps to get milk and butter for their six children, but nobody else could get any because they lacked stamps. Instead of butter, they would spread goose grease on their bread. They would "cook a goose, let the grease solidify, put a little salt on it, put it on the bread, [and] eat it." Having at least half a dozen missionaries constantly staying at the mission home at any one time cut down on how many rations were available. Luckily, they had a cook for the mission home as well as an older woman who would help out around the house, but the children still had to wash most of the dishes.[28]

Bob would "climb right out the window of the kitchen" onto the branches of the cherry tree and "torment the elders." One day the missionaries decided that they had had enough of Bob's pranks. They took him upstairs onto the balcony and hogtied him with his hands behind his back and his feet up. "I thought this was no big deal," he recalled. "I . . . snuck the pocketknife out of my pocket [and] was going to . . . free myself. But they came and took my pocketknife." He was stuck until Marion went over to them and gave them "the devil." Then they released him.[29]

For Bob, being tied up was nothing compared to the scary experiences of his Czech classroom. One particularly frightening experience occurred in a class on Czech literature. There were four rows of desks, and Bob was in the fourth row at the back. The students started reciting a poem row by row, but he did not know it. By the time it got to him, he had heard the first stanza enough times to memorize it and recite

27. Bob and David Toronto, interview, August 20, 2013, 12–13.

28. Bob and David Toronto, interview, August 20, 2013, 12–13.

29. Bob and David Toronto, interview, August 20, 2013, 14.

it to everyone. The teacher looked at him and said, “Okay.” “It scared the bajeebers out of me.”[30]

Toronto family, ca. 1950. Courtesy of Church History Library.

Like all children, Bob wanted to be included, so one day he joined a group called the Pioneers. As a Mormon boy, he thought he would know about them. However, they were nothing like the Mormon Pioneers he had grown up learning about. Instead, the Pioneers he joined were a Communist youth group. They would cut the cornstalks and clean the cornfields, even though there was not actually any corn to pick. When Bob told his father that he had joined such a group, Wally said, “Well, I don’t think you need to do that,” explaining its true nature.[31]

30. Bob and David Toronto, interview, August 20, 2013, 14.
31. Bob and David Toronto, interview, August 20, 2013, 14–15.

Bob later told his teacher that he did not want to be a part of the Pioneers anymore. Much to his surprise, one of his friends then stood up and said he did not want to be one anymore either.[32]

Bob recalled learning very little in Czechoslovakia. "I don't remember ever opening a book for three years except those early experiences with my dad." He did, however, remember having to buy his own books, which surprised him because the schools in America provided all the books for their students. He learned the language instead by talking to other children but "pretty much did not understand what was going on in the classroom." It impacted his intellectual development for ten years. When the Torontos returned to America, Bob did not know how to do arithmetic or grammar or how to diagram sentences in the English language. For him, the deficiency affected him through college and even graduate school.[33]

The toys that the Toronto children played with were different from those they would have had growing up in Salt Lake City. In a big World War II dump, they found some very interesting things to play with such as shotguns. The dump was located just over the hill by the mission home. Bob "found on the ground thousands of .30 caliber cartridges, so [he would] just sweep them up and take them home." He built a bunch of pretend villages and bombed them from the balcony for entertainment. Over the years, he realized that such activities had more of an effect on him than he had thought. In Czechoslovakia, he had actually experienced great fear. Because his mother had been so afraid, he felt like it was his job to take care of her. So he grew up in what he called an "envelope of anxiety and utter fear."[34]

While Martha exhibited some well-founded fears, she was not necessarily a doting mother. Sister-in-law Carma Toronto remembered that she was a "competent mother" in that the children were always well clothed, fed, and taken care of physically; however, there was never "any outward show of affection." Martha did not put her arms

32. Bob and David Toronto, interview, August 20, 2013, 14–15.

33. Bob and David Toronto, interview, August 20, 2013, 15.

34. Bob and David Toronto, interview, August 20, 2013, 7.

around her children. It was obvious that she was proud of them and of what they did, but it was just not "in her nature to be demonstrative." She never put her arms around Wally in public either, but as Carma explained, "People in that day didn't do that. . . . Public show of affection was frowned on."[35] Regardless, there was always laughing and teasing. Wally, of course, found a way around such norms. When he greeted a female, he would grab her hand as if he were going to kiss it. Instead, he would kiss his thumb.[36] And when his future son-in-law, Vern Miller, asked for Marion's hand in marriage, Wally asked him to crawl across the floor and kiss his feet to ask.[37]

In Prague, setting up a household was "no small task as necessities were scarce. Rationing severely limited available foodstuffs, and the family could not afford to buy on the thriving black market . . . [Martha] shopped daily, going from the butcher to the vegetable market, to the baker and then to the dairy for the children's small ration of milk."[38] There were sacrifices that the Torontos had to make as a mission family. Because they had six children, the Torontos were able to get ration stamps for a quarter liter of milk a day per child, which equaled about one glassful a day. It was not a lot, but it was certainly more than most Czechs were receiving. "Each person was allowed two eggs per month, about one pound of meat, and a quarter pound of sugar." Feeding a family of that size was problem enough, but the Torontos often had sixteen missionaries to feed at the mission home as well. "Housing was critical and . . . [it was] almost impossible for the young men who came to our mission" to find lodging. The missionaries were often housed and fed in the mission home while they were learning how to speak the language, to teach the gospel, and use good proselyting methods. Because the missionaries had to stay at the mission

35. Carma Toronto, interview, February 26, 2004, 10.
36. David Toronto, interview by Daniel Toronto, 2010, 8.
37. Bob and David Toronto, interview, August 20, 2013, 24.
38. Mehr, *Mormon Missionaries Enter Eastern Europe*, 82.

home for several months before they were sent out into the branches with senior companions, rationing was always a juggling act.[39]

The rationing of commodities often caused problems for the Torontos. To begin with, people could only purchase certain kinds of food as they were available, even if they had the necessary stamps. And to find out if something was going to be offered, they had to listen to the radio, which notified everyone about what items would be in the market. One thing that was never available was peanut butter. One time, someone had sent Wally some peanut butter from home, knowing how much he loved it. He only shared it with his children. Elder Mel Maybe remembered one particular occasion when Martha and Sister Krejčy, the cook, were going to bake a cake. The recipe that they used required two eggs, which was all they had at the time. They added the rationed ingredients—flour, fat, sugar, eggs—in the bowl. But when Martha cracked the second egg, she realized it was rotten. She and her cook debated back and forth about what to do. Finally, Martha said, "Let's cook it. That will probably kill all the bacteria that's in it."[40] So they did. The cake was passed around to everyone at the table. Martha, however, chose not take a piece. Sister Krejčy followed suit. But Wally did. When he took a bite, he supposed, "You've used my peanut butter!" He was rather upset to think they would use his peanut butter in a cake. But Martha and Sister Krejčy were taken by surprise by the egg's unexpected flavor.[41] That, Elder Maybe said, was the only time he saw his mission president angry.[42]

Marion saw the mission home "as a place of refuge . . . , a place where [she] could escape from the merciless teasing of [her] Czech classmates who thought [she] was a spoiled, stupid, rich American girl who couldn't even speak their language."[43] While in Czechoslovakia, Marion gained a lifelong love and appreciation for music as she

---

39. Anderson, *Cherry Tree*, 43.

40. Mel Mabey, interview, August 13, 2013, 8.

41. Mel Mabey, interview, August 13, 2013, 8.

42. Mel Mabey, interview, August 13, 2013, 8.

43. Miller, "My Story: The Dream," 6.

took piano lessons. At the time that they were forced to leave, she had been taking lessons from a man who planned on putting her in the Prague Conservatory of Music.[44] She continued piano lessons when she returned to America. Because she was the eldest child of the mission president, she believed that she "was expected to be an example to my siblings, to [Church members], and to the Czech people in general. In short, I felt my father expected me to be no less than perfect. However, perfection was different in his eyes than in mine," she remembered.

Marion knew that her father liked women with dark hair, dark eyebrows, and dark eyelashes. As she explained, "Along with my red hair came freckles, fair skin, and desperately blond eyebrows and eyelashes. . . . Bright lipstick helped a lot, [but] that was often the source of painful teasing from my father." Because of her desire to look better, she got herself in a predicament that was particularly traumatic for her. When she was fourteen years old, Wally and Martha allowed her to take the tram down to the middle of Prague to get her hair cut.[45] After cutting her hair, the beautician said, "You have such long eyelashes, but they're so white. Wouldn't you like to put some color on them?" "Oh, no, no. My father wouldn't like that," Marion replied. The beautician assured, "They'd look just like mine." She showed Marion her nice, light brown eyelashes. So Marion agreed to let her go ahead and color her eyelashes.[46] The beautician dabbed cotton around Marion's eyes, and after a little while, she took the cotton away. "Now, look." When Marion looked in the mirror, she was horrified. It looked like she had huge black brooms on the top of her eyes, and she had no idea what to do.

When she got home, she went inside through back door and wanted to go straight to her room. But it was dinnertime. Everyone was seating themselves at the dinner table. The only empty chair was for her. Wally called for her to join them, but she told him she wanted to go upstairs. He was insistent, and when she finally walked into the room, every-

44. Miller and Richards, interview, May 3, 2013.

45. Miller, "My Story: The Dream," 7–9.

46. Miller and Richards, interview, May 3, 2013.

body burst out laughing, including Wally. Despite her humiliation, she handled the situation well and laughed alongside everyone else. Everyone started calling her "Brooms." She described, "A fun comedy hour played itself out during dinner . . . 'Brooms, please pass the salt,' or 'Did you enjoy your dessert, Brooms?' 'Brooms, you wash the dishes and we'll dry.' 'Flutter your eyes at us, Brooms. It's so thrilling!'"[47]

After the dishes were done, Wally decided to figure out what to do about Marion's eyelashes. She told him the color was permanent, but he was determined. She felt bad and began to cry.[48] "Sit down, let's do something." She tried to explain, "Dad, they're dyed." There was nothing they could do. But he was adamant. He tried soap and water, and then nail polish. When nothing worked, she cried even harder. He grew more and more angry at the situation. He even tried using a rag with some turpentine on it, but that didn't work either. He declared in disgust, "Okay, we're going to take care of this." He went into another room, got some nail scissors, and cut off all her eyelashes. Surprisingly, they still stayed black on the ends when they grew out again.[49]

Because of that incident—and others—Marion felt that her father was really hard on his children, particularly on her because she was the oldest. She explained that she was uprooted from a place she was used to—a place where she had grown up—and from her friends. She and her family were plopped into an entirely new situation, a new country. For her, the adjustments were awful. Wally did not want her to grow up, but unfortunately, she grew up fairly quickly. She was growing up in a situation that made her far more mature than most people of her age,[50] including those Marion called "beautiful young missionaries" that were in the mission home constantly. As nature would have it, she fell in love with them. Wally and Martha had been concerned that Marion might find a missionary, and she did.

---

47. Miller, "My Story: The Dream," 7–9.
48. Miller, "My Story: The Dream," 7–9.
49. Miller and Richards, interview, May 3, 2013.
50. Miller and Richards, interview, May 3, 2013.

Marion had her favorites among the missionaries. "Some were tall and handsome; others were full of fun and teasing." But there was one man who would make a bigger impression on her than all the others: Vern Miller. When she developed feelings for Elder Miller, she could hardly wait to tell her mother about her new love. Martha "seemed to know that this was more than a girlish fantasy," even though Marion was only fourteen. "She was more concerned than ever when [Marion] told her of a goodbye kiss" that had taken place when Elder Miller left the mission field. Marion knew she had broken the rules. She begged her mother not to tell Wally. She was afraid that Vern would receive a dishonorable release. But despite Marion's wishes, Martha did tell Wally.[51]

The following morning, Wally ushered Marion into his office. She vividly remembered that moment in her father's office: "My father was very stern and furious. I was told that Vern would not be dishonorably released, but that I was not to write or hear from him. It was absolutely folly to think that Vern would wait for me to grow up. After all, when he returned home, he would be going to BYU. Who would remember a funny teenager in the midst of a bevy of beautiful coeds? But I stood my ground and with tears streaming down my cheeks, I told my father that if Vern would have me when I was old enough, I would marry him! In utter frustration, he angrily dismissed me and told me to stay in my room."[52] Marion's words were prophetic, for later, when they returned from Czechoslovakia, she married Vern Miller.

For all the Toronto children, not just Marion, the years spent in Czechoslovakia left a lifelong impression and changed their lives forever.

---

51. Miller, "My Story: The Dream," 15–16.

52. Miller, "My Story: The Dream," 15–16.

13 "SATAN'S WORKERS"

As soon as Martha returned to Prague, she adjusted quickly back into her role as mission mother. Her duties, along with taking care of her own family, included other Church callings such as overseeing the Relief Society in each of the larger branches. She tried to execute several programs as outlined in the *Relief Society Magazine* and supervised the translation of Relief Society lesson materials into Czech. In addition to those responsibilities, she managed the mission home. Because of a housing shortage, many missionaries ended up staying at the mission home for several months instead of weeks. The Mutual Improvement Association also held their meetings at the mission home. Many of the Church's new converts were young adults. Kahlile Mehr explained that the Church in Czechoslovakia was constantly getting younger: "The average age dropped from thirty-six in the prewar period to twenty-nine after the war."[1]

1. Mehr, *Mormon Missionaries Enter Eastern Europe*, 83.

The Latter-day Saint young adults tried to seek converts in various ways, including through sports, especially volleyball and basketball.[2] LDS young adults revitalized the tradition that Wally started years earlier. As a result, member friendships strengthened, and the Church increased as a family of brothers and sisters. The focus of the activities was first on friendship, brotherhood, and sisterhood. "Then the way to the Church was open [in] a matter of time."[3]

Missionary Dale Tingey talked about how well Wally worked with the young Czech Church. "He [was] organized. It was more than just church. He wanted the people to work together." Wally wanted his missionaries to help the members be better Saints, to be better in their families. He wanted to protect them against the coming onslaught. He told them that they would surely "be in very difficult circumstances." As a result, "all of his programs were designed to try and strengthen them in small groups so they could carry on after [the missionaries] left."[4]

Wally visited members in their homes to build friendships. He attended every baptism when possible. "Everyone knew him well and viewed him as their father."[5] Bob Toronto remembered going with his father to baptisms, which often took place in a spa or a pool.[6] Wally organized public discussions where he again presented movies and spoke about "Utah—majestic land of America," followed by a discussion on religion and the people.[7] He shared his messages wherever he could: at the YMCA, the British-American club, Scouts meetings, and at other organizations. He also utilized the media. He started the Church magazine *Nový Hlas* (New Voice), a monthly religious and cultural magazine for both members and nonmembers, which made

2. Miller and Richards, interview, May 3, 2013.
3. Vojkůvka, "Memories of President Wallace Felt Toronto," November 9, 2013, 6–7.
4. Dale Tingey, interview, 2.
5. Vojkůvka, "Memories of President Wallace Felt Toronto," November 9, 2013, 6.
6. Bob and David Toronto, interview, August 20, 2013, 18.
7. Vojkůvka, "Memories of President Wallace Felt Toronto," November 9, 2013, 6.

Church doctrine available to people who were not very interested but who still had questions.[8]

Wally wanted his missionaries to listen to the Spirit when it came to teaching investigators. He did not want the missionaries to go too far too soon and leave their investigators confused and overwhelmed. "When you teach the gospel, teach them so they want to know more not because they're saturated." Using an object lesson to explain the concept, he had someone bake two little cakes and decorate them beautifully. He asked the elders, "Does this look good to you?" The missionaries, who were all famished as usual, responded, "Yes! Yes!" He then asked, "Who would like to be the first one to have a piece?" When the missionaries all raised their hands, he took the cake and shoved it in one of their faces.[9] The lesson proved his point most effectively. From then on, they did their best not to bombard investigators with too much information.

On every July 24, Wally continued to have members and their families commemorate both the Mormon pioneers entering the Salt Lake Valley and the dedication of Czechoslovakia for preaching the gospel. He used the event as an opportunity to invite nonmembers and their families to hear interesting and positive things about the Church for the first time.[10] He also planned a pageant around that day each year "to demonstrate by historical presentation how the Czechoslovak lands were prepared 'line upon line, and precept upon precept' for the advent of Christianity and the later restoration of the Gospel of Jesus Christ, with the subtheme of 'Peace and prosperity are complimentary with righteous living.'"[11]

Elder Ezra Taft Benson of the Quorum of the Twelve had been sent to Europe as the administrator of Church humanitarian aid. He arrived

8. Vojkůvka, "Memories of President Wallace Felt Toronto," November 9, 2013, 7.

9. Mel Mabey, interview, August 13, 2013, 16.

10. Vojkůvka, "Memories of President Wallace Felt Toronto," November 9, 2013, 7.

11. Papers found in Jiří Šnederfler papers, Europe Church History Center, Bad Homburg, Germany, copy in author's possession.

in Czechoslovakia in 1948 and worked closely with Wally. Wally arranged for him to speak in Prague and as well as in Brno, which at the time was the capital of Moravia. Almost 1,500 people gathered in a large auditorium to hear Elder Benson. There were even Communists in attendance who were "very interested in learning more about the Church. They exhibited more interest than a lot of the other people."[12] Wally made the arrangements for the meeting and gave his own comments, speaking excellent Czech and German.[13] "A steady stream of missionaries began to swell the mission forces. In August 1947, six missionaries joined the four that had come with the Toronto family in June 1947. In October 1948, the proselytizing force totaled thirty-nine, the largest group of U.S. citizens in Czechoslovakia except for the U.S. embassy staff. . . . Attendance at Church meetings reached unprecedented levels. Tithes and offerings increased, . . . [and] Toronto's lectures typically drew crowds from seventy to nine hundred." At one particular lecture, "two hundred people had to be turned away due to lack of space. Opposition engendered a greater commitment among members and increased interest among those not yet of the faith."[14]

A total of thirty-six missionaries served in the Czechoslovakian Branch after the war. Years later, missionary Ed Morrell went into the archives of Czechoslovakia and looked at the government records to find what was written about the Mormons at the time. There he found names, addresses, photographs, and information about Wally's role. Additionally, missionaries serving in Brno from 1946 to December 1947 were listed with their backgrounds, especially if they had been in the U.S. military. "Another two sheets (dated March 16) counted twenty-eight Mormon missionaries, former American army officers and non-coms" (noncommunists). Two descriptions of missionaries humorously listed, "he washes and dries his own laundry." A very large file, dated February 4, 1948, discussed "meetings in Mladá Boleslav and five 'preachers of Jehovah' led by Toronto," driving a Ford vehicle

12. Don Whipperman, interview, October 9, 2013, 2.

13. Don Whipperman, interview, October 9, 2013, 2.

14. Mehr, *Mormon Missionaries Enter Eastern Europe*, 83–84.

with the Utah license plate H 9260. They also documented a particular meeting that Wally had led in Olomouc in March 1948, which 250 individuals attended. Six elders were listed in Brno and one in Olomouc. Nine of fourteen were thought to be in Prague, and the other five in Mladá Boleslav. An account dated April 1948 concluded that the missionaries were "masked agents of the American intelligence service." Then there was something written about how "this Church should be forbidden in the CSR, or at least the number of missionaries appropriately reduced."[15]

Free Czechoslovakia survived less than three years after World War II. "Soviet leaders pressured the Czechoslovak government to appoint high-ranking officials of Communist persuasion."[16] Noncommunist leaders in the government were fighting hard against those of the Communist Party. Among the lovers of democracy were Edvard Beneš, the president of Czechoslovakia elected in 1935, and Prokop Drtina, the Minister of Justice. "Under Interior Minister Václav Nosek, the security forces, the National Security Corps (SNB) and State Security (StB), became weapons that the Communists could use against their political enemies." Drtina managed to expose the conspiracy before any further action could be taken, but damage had already been done. "The policies of Nosek and the police led to the arrest of some 400 people."[17]

Despite their high ranks in the government, they were unable to hinder the unstoppable progress of the Communists. In mid-February, Drtina reported an incident to the cabinet in which "the remaining eight noncommunist district police chiefs [were to be] transferred out of Prague." Nosek had supported the transfers. The other noncommunist members of the Cabinet ordered Nosek to "reverse his position

15. Ed Morrell, "Summary of Czechoslovak Archive Documents, dated in the 1940s and 1950, turned over to the Torontos in 2007," in author's possession, 1.

16. Mehr, *Mormon Missionaries Enter Eastern Europe*, 83.

17. William M. Mahoney, *The History of the Czech Republic and Slovakia* (Santa Barbara, CA: Greenwood, 2011), 198.

Missionaries who reopened the Czechoslovak Mission, 1947. Courtesy of Church History Library.

and prevent the transfers." Furthermore, if Nosek refused to oblige, "the noncommunist ministers, with the hoped-for participation of the Social Democrats, would submit their resignations and bring down the government." Their intention was for President Beneš to either "appoint a short-term government and schedule new elections or refuse to accept the resignations and force the Communists either to negotiate with the other coalition parties or accept responsibility for the government's dissolution."[18]

The support of the Social Democrats "failed to materialize." Their plan had entirely backfired.

18. Mahoney, *The History of the Czech Republic and Slovakia*, 199–200.

Instead of the Communist Party bowing in submission, Beneš and Drtina along with their allies were forced out of the government. The prime minister and leader of the Communist Party, Klement Gottwald, gladly advised Beneš to accept the resignations. Beneš tried to find a way out of the mess, but he was defenseless. "Exhausted, in poor health, and believing he was without any viable options, Beneš conceded." The formidable events of the month became known as the Communist *coup d'état* of February 1948.[19]

Some of the events that transpired in the aftermath shocked everyone. After Drtina was stripped of his position as Minister of Justice, he "allegedly chose to end his own life by throwing himself from a third-story window on February 26. In the early morning hours of March 10, Jan Masaryk became another victim . . . as his body was discovered dressed in pajamas below the window of his apartment at Čzernín Palace, the home of the Ministry of Foreign Affairs. The Communists quickly announced to the nation that Masaryk's death had come at his own hand, but friends and colleagues responded by accusing the Communists of covering up a murder." Masaryk's death remained a source of controversy for many years. He was, after all, the well-liked son of the beloved "George Washington of Czechoslovakia," Tomás Masaryk. An investigation conducted in the early 1990s pointed to suicide, but "forensic research by the police in Prague in 2004 [supported] the accusation of murder." Edvard Beneš resigned from his office of president on June 7, 1948. "On September 3, he died a defeated man at his villa in Sezimovo Ústí."[20]

As Martha put it, "We found ourselves shackled to the Communist regime. The Iron Curtain had fallen, and this fact changed our lives and our religious work considerably."[21] After the Communist coup, "the government began controlling all businesses, industries, churches, and schools. Mormon missionaries came under secret police surveillance. The police ordered publication of the mission magazine,

19. Mahoney, *The History of the Czech Republic and Slovakia*, 200.
20. Mahoney, *The History of the Czech Republic and Slovakia*, 200–201.
21. Anderson, *Cherry Tree*, 48.

Nový Hlas (New Voice), to cease, ending its influence [on] over three thousand readers, mostly members of other faiths."[22] The Communists seemed determined to make things as difficult as possible for the Torontos in the hopes that they would simply go away. Their efforts, however, made the Torontos only more determined to succeed under such difficult odds. Police officers threatened the members for going to Church meetings.[23]

The Communist coup of February 1948 changed everything. Many elders watched in horror as they witnessed the police shoot people right in the center of town in Brno. Some people who opposed the regime just disappeared. But President Toronto always did what he could to help people understand that the gospel was the greatest strength that they could possibly have to fight their fear. To ensure their safety, the elders always worked through Wally. "If we had anything that we wanted to do, we would have to get permission from Prague and President Toronto . . . to pass out certain tracts . . . to people informing them of the Church. He, of course, would require that we say it in his way so that we didn't offend anyone."[24]

Wally persistently reminded the missionaries to "be careful." In an effort to heed his warning, they started getting creative in their strategies while tracting apartment buildings. They started at the top of the buildings instead of at the bottom. If the Czech people did not like them, they would call the police. So, if the elders started at the top, "[they] could get out of the building, but if [they] started at the bottom and worked up, the police could catch [them]."[25]

The mission was once again approaching peril. It was a well-known fact that the Mormon missionaries were only interested in spreading the beliefs of the Church, for they had been proselytizing

---

22. Mehr, *Mormon Missionaries Enter Eastern Europe*, 83.
23. Anderson, *Cherry Tree*, 50.
24. Don Whipperman, interview, October 9, 2013, 4.
25. Mel Mabey, interview, August 13, 2013, 16.

for many years without unrest.[26] Nevertheless, the new government became increasingly suspicious of the LDS missionaries and believed they were spies for the U.S. government. When the missionaries told them about the Book of Mormon, it "seemed to scratch a scab on their nose." Missionaries had to be very careful when teaching the Book of Mormon in a way that would not be offensive. There were always Communists present in their meetings, especially those held in Brno and Prosteel.[27]

Missionary work was "being hampered more and more by the new regime," which had ironically promised "greater freedom, equality, job opportunities, more food, greater luxuries, and so on." All of it turned out to be what Martha called a "great joke. Job opportunities turned out to be a form of forced labor."[28] Missionaries were repeatedly "accused falsely of espionage and were threatened with expulsion for being a menace to the peace." Wally encountered "new and terrible problems" as time went on. The secret police began following many Latter-day Saints, including the Toronto children. Marion remembered being followed home from school on a few occasions, which naturally made her parents very nervous. "It was necessary to pass a Jewish cemetery on my way from the tram to the mission home. The street had huge trees on one side and the cemetery wall on the other. It was frightening to see grown men stepping behind a tree to avoid being seen," she remembered.[29] Martha also found it very difficult to endure the paranoia of being watched constantly. It took her a while to lose the feeling of uneasiness. "If you live with it long enough, you do get used to it," she wrote.[30]

26. "U.S. Requests Data on Missing Mormons" *New York Times*, February 10, 1950, 14,.

27. Don Whipperman, interview, October 9, 2013, 1–2.

28. Anderson, *Cherry Tree*, 55.

29. Miller, "My Story: The Dream," 14.

30. Anderson, *Cherry Tree*, 50.

Unidentified missionary with Wallace Toronto in Brno, 1947. Courtesy of Church History Library.

It appeared as if the government was waiting for someone to slip or make a mistake that would incriminate the Church. "God and religion were suddenly frowned upon. People mysteriously disappeared from the streets, never to be heard from again. Everyone walked in fear. Even mothers and sons could not trust each other."[31] Because Communism was "an atheist organization at its core, it focused on repression of all forms of religion," although it eventually accepted eighteen churches and religious organizations.[32] However, The Church of Jesus Christ of Latter-day Saints was not one of them.

When the Communists came into power, Martha explained, "Suddenly we found ourselves restricted in missionary activities. We all had to report to the secret police office and register there as aliens, giving reasons for our being in the country. We had to abide by rules and regulations that seemed very stupid to us." They even had to submit any speech that they had written to the authorities so it could be censored. Then, if they were unsatisfied, they had to rewrite the speech. Eventually, after the authorities were satisfied, they could present the speech. Nevertheless, agents always attended the meetings "to see if everything went along as it should. We got used to seeing these strangers in our midst, and we welcomed them along with all our members and friends," Martha recalled.[33]

Just as the Church faced much adversity because of the antireligious government, other denominations suffered similar repercussions. The Communists felt animosity toward the Mormons and the Catholic Church. In fact, the government probably saw the Catholics as an even greater threat. The Church of Jesus Christ of Latter-day Saints had the advantage of being "American." And as such, they were protected to a degree. The Catholic leaders, on the other hand, were involved in politics. "Efforts to silence the Catholic Church in Czechoslovakia and to sever diplomatic connections with the Vatican led to the imprisonment of priests and nuns, the elimination of religious orders, the closing of monasteries and convents, the subordination of clergy to state authority, and the institution of legal proceedings against bishops and Church leaders."[34]

31. Miller, "My Story: The Dream," 14.

32. Vojkůvka, "Memories of President Wallace Felt Toronto," November 9, 2013, 2.

33. Anderson, *Cherry Tree*, 49.

34. Mahoney, *The History of the Czech Republic and Slovakia*, 203.

Under Communist control, "everyone was afraid to even speak to others." Wally made it a priority to visit the missionaries personally and keep track of them to make sure that nothing bad had happened to them. While he was a little worried, he was also "very brave and very outspoken" against the Communists. Wally once said the citizens were "kind of bootlickers . . . because they've been always under someone's rule. They just got out from under the German rule, and now they're in the Communist rule. Before that they were under the Prussian rule." Nevertheless, "[Wally] dearly loved the people and wanted to help them in every way possible."[35]

The Communists abused and beat the people, but they were careful not to hurt the Americans, of course, because they did not want to raise any suspicion. Wally spoke bravely against the government to Church members. "They're all Satan's workers. You just have to hold on and keep the faith. They're wicked; they're cruel."[36] He refused to back down. In July 1948, he organized a meeting for the president of the European missions, Elder Alma Sonne. Branch President Vojkůvka in Brno threw out airplane leaflets with an invitation to go to the meeting. Elder Sonne spoke to the thirty-nine missionaries on that occasion. "[It] was the largest meeting in European Church history, with 1,800 people attending."[37]

In February of 1949, the mission held another conference. One Czech member expressed the heartache of many as he mentioned that the members sometimes felt like they had no reason to smile. Wally replied:

> We members of our Church of Jesus Christ belong to the Kingdom of God. The Church of Jesus Christ isn't an American church, nor an English church, nor a Czech church; it is for all people. The plan of life set forth in this gospel includes not just this short temporal lifetime; it protrudes into the eternity. We, as members of the Church, have a passport to that eternal afterlife. No matter where we live now

---

35. Dale Tingey, interview, 1–2.
36. Dale Tingey, interview, 5.
37. Vojkůvka, "Memories of President Wallace Felt Toronto," November 9, 2013, 2–3.

> while on the earth—in America or Czechoslovakia or Russia—it will last only a short while. . . . If for some reason I wasn't permitted to go back to America I could be happy with the blessings here. I could smile.[38]

Ironically, during that tense period, the number of baptisms rose from twenty-eight in 1948, to seventy in 1949, and then to thirty-seven in the first three months of 1950. Among the new converts, one was of most importance, a seventeen-year-old named Jiří Šnederfler, who would later become a major Church leader in Czechoslovakia.[39]

Two-thirds of the converts in 1949 were young people below the age of thirty. Mehr explained why the gospel resonated more with the younger generation:

> Youth, stirred from the long-accepted traditions [and] finding little in Communist doctrine to sustain belief, may have found meaning in the Church's message. Only five converts belonged to the thirty–forty age group and ten in the forty–fifty age group. Middle-aged people, stable in their traditional belief, established in their professions, and worried about supporting families, may have been less disposed to take chances by adopting a new religion. Twelve converts fell into the fifty–seventy age group. One would assume this group might be beyond the age of questioning their beliefs, so the reason for their conversion is unclear. However, more than half of these were single adults, suggesting that the Church provided comfort in their partners' absence.[40]

In the same year, Wally used one missionary tool that particularly attracted young people. Through his efforts, the government permitted the British Mission's basketball team, national champions in England, to tour Czechoslovakia in February and March. "In four weeks, the team played . . . games in seventeen cities. . . . The missionaries in Czechoslovakia passed out tracts during half-time, gave short talks in connection with the game, and held special meetings to explain the players' religion. The visit generated more than a hundred articles in

38. Ed and Norma Morrell, interview, May 8, 2013, 8.

39. Mehr, *Mormon Missionaries Enter Eastern Europe*, 84.

40. Mehr, *Mormon Missionaries Enter Eastern Europe*, 84–85.

the press."[41] The *New York Times* published an article on March 1, 1949, reporting the games' success. "Basketball prowess and preaching skill have been successfully combined by a team of Latter-Day Saints (Mormons) who are returning to missionary duties in England after a three weeks' tour of Czechoslovakia. The team was pitted against Czechoslovak players. . . . The Mormons reported they had won sixteen of seventeen games, and said they had scored 'just about as well' in their preaching sessions."[42]

While 1949 was a year filled with blessings, it did yield some difficult and unfortunate setbacks. All churches had to request official permission to operate from the Department of State. The government did not grant permission to The Church of Jesus Christ of Latter-day Saints, nor to the Methodists, the Seventh-day Adventists, the Protestants, or the other smaller churches. Of those, only the Seventh-day Adventists were eventually given permission to operate fairly soon thereafter because they were able to produce twenty-three thousand signatures of local miners. The members of the sect were easy to find due to the religion's refusal to serve in armed forces; they had opted to work in coal mines instead to increase the industry.[43]

Mehr traced what happened in 1949: "The Communist government soon ceased to grant or renew resident permits for the missionaries, making their presence in the country illegal. In May 1949, officials expelled three missionaries, claiming they were a danger to the nation's safety and security. By October 1949, the number of missionaries had been reduced to half that of the previous October, leaving only about twenty. Local authorities ordered expulsions. . . . Toronto protested these orders but had no basis on which to reverse them.

41. Mehr, *Mormon Missionaries Enter Eastern Europe*, 84.

42. Religious News Service, "Mormon Missionaries Mix Basketball and Preaching," *New York Times*, March 1, 1949: 16.

43. Vojkůvka, "Memories of President Wallace Felt Toronto," November 9, 2013, 2.

Though disappointed, the missionaries realized the futility of refusing to leave."[44]

Martha recorded the events of the second exodus of the Mormons from Czechoslovakia. "By twos and fours our most valuable missionaries and their younger companions were expelled from the country. Younger elders finished their missions in England or the United States where they wouldn't have to learn another language. The older ones went home with an honorable release. [After] a year had gone by, our missionary force was down to less than half. This process continued until the expulsions were coming quite often, and instead of giving a time limit of two weeks, it gradually got down to three days, and finally 24 hours."[45]

Elder Mel Mabey encountered many trying obstacles near the forced end of his mission. On several occasions, some members who worked at the American Embassy invited him and his companion to dinner. Mabey and his companion tried to invite them to go to Church, but they feared the consequences of being questioned by the authorities, which would surely follow if they chose to attend. In January 1950, Wally asked Elder Mabey if he would stay behind with his companion as long as they could, but Mabey was immediately expelled as a spy. His mission was then over.[46] Wally stated, "Then finally . . . they expelled me as the last Mormon missionary, and upon being, as they charged me with, a spy against the Communist government."[47]

Members of the Church suffered greatly throughout the period of Communist power. Gad Vojkůvka's father was taken into police custody and his factory, and all his property, confiscated. He was sent to Tabor, a camp of forced labor where the prisoners built a metal works factory. "The judge stated, 'Mr. Vojkůvka, you have to understand. We know you are innocent, but there is nothing we can do!'" He was

44. Mehr, *Mormon Missionaries Enter Eastern Europe*, 84.

45. Anderson, *Cherry Tree*, 57.

46. Mel Mabey, interview, August 13, 2013, 1, 4.

47. Wallace Toronto, fireside in Nashville, Tennessee, 1965, transcript in author's possession, 2.

always an optimist. Instead of letting negative feelings toward the government get the best of him, he simply compared politics to the weather. He was incarcerated when he was ill, so he was re-assigned to an office. There, he noticed that the officials had a folder of a particular color for every individual in the camp. True criminals had green folders; "political prisoners had red folders; priests, bishops, and religious workers had white folders." His folder was white, so he knew then why he had been imprisoned: he was a religious worker. By the time he was released, which was soon after Wally's departure, the Church became illegal. While he was still incarcerated, he infused his fellow prisoners with his positive attitude. As a result, nobody committed suicide while Vojkůvka was there, though suicide was sadly very common. But tragically, three people he knew took their own lives after he left the camp.[48]

Like Brother Vojkůvka, every Latter-day Saint was identified by the government and was, therefore, constantly watched by the secret police. They had to be very careful to meet only on Sundays. Even then, they had to hold their meetings in private to avoid alarming the officers. Many members had to stop going every Sunday because someone would follow them on their way to Church.[49] And worse, in only a few short months, the missionaries went from being watched and followed to being arrested. For instance, Elders Stanley Abbott and Alden Johnson disappeared in a remote area near Olomouc while attempting to visit a member. They were charged with entering a restricted border zone and accused of spying. For eleven days, nobody heard from them.[50]

When Church members phoned Wally to inform him of what had happened, he immediately drove out to the branch, which was very close to the Polish border. He found the elders' apartment sealed up around the doors and windows with some official tape that the secret

---

48. Vojkůvka, "Memories of President Wallace Felt Toronto," November 9, 2013, 3.

49. Olga Kovářová Campora, *Saint Behind Enemy Lines* (Salt Lake City: Deseret Book, 1997), 89.

50. Mehr, *Mormon Missionaries Enter Eastern Europe*, 85; Mehr, "Czech Saints: A Brighter Day," 51.

police used. He chose not to enter, knowing it was a felony to remove the tape and break the seal. The only thing he could learn about the situation was that his missionaries were being held in a Communist prison somewhere. By devious means still unknown, he eventually learned where they were being held. Finding that he could do nothing in the countryseat, Olomouc, he returned to Prague to alert the American Embassy of their arrests. One Church member in particular, who was a lawyer, worked with him to secure the release of the elders. He told Wally, "I know these people and how they function. They would be very happy if you made an international incident out of this. That is what they want. My advice to you is to let this thing lie. If you leave it alone they will release them much sooner. If you bring the U.S. Embassy into it, they will demand ransom or some other form of blackmail." Taking the lawyer's advice, Wally did nothing.[51]

With the Abbott and Johnson case pending, authorities promulgated a new law that required all clergy to be native Czechs. They informed the U.S. State Department that the two prisoners would be released only if the other Mormon missionaries were evacuated. Seeing no alternative, Wally told the remaining missionaries to start packing.

> Abbott and Johnson . . . languished in prison for twenty-seven days without a change of clothing or a bath. They were interrogated, not brutally but severely, during the first three days. Thereafter, they suffered long hours of loneliness and uncertainty, isolated from the outside world, each other, and the mission. They subsisted on a diet of Postum and black bread in the morning, and soup with a floating meatball in the evening. Eleven missionaries had already departed when word came that the imprisoned missionaries would be released if Toronto could get them passage within two hours. The president raced to the airport and purchased tickets. Plainclothes guards escorted the prisoners by train from Olomouc to the Prague airport, where Toronto gave them their tickets and they boarded a flight to Switzerland. Sister Toronto arrived in time to watch the meeting from a distance and wave good-bye.[52]

51. Anderson, *Cherry Tree*, 57–58.

52. Mehr, *Mormon Missionaries Enter Eastern Europe*, 85.

Wally was never allowed to see the incarcerated missionaries. The biggest problem for him thereafter was trying to keep the missionaries in the country. "Eventually the accusations of espionage became intolerable." One by one, the missionaries received notices of expulsion—orders to leave the country within a certain period of time. Wally spent most of his time in police stations asking them to extend the time.[53]

Eventually, as the mission president, Wally advised all the elders working in the branches to close their activities and gather in Prague. Apart from two elders who were working in the office, Wally sent the remaining eleven either to other assignments in the United States or home. As a result, the mission staff consisted only of the president, his family, and two missionaries. The secret police then focused on getting rid of them. Wally began making preparations for his family to leave. "It isn't easy, even for Americans, to leave an Iron Curtain country. There were so many details—visas accompanied by photos, permission for money, written permission for luggage, even after thorough inspection by custom officials. Visas were also required to travel over all the occupied zones."[54]

On February 28, 1950, the police arrived at the mission home.[55] Martha grew very suspicious when she noticed a black car and a police escort standing in front of the gate. Two strangers approached the mission home door and asked for Mr. Toronto when Martha answered it. The police also told her that she and her family, and the two missionaries, had forty-eight hours to leave. Packing everything for a single person in that amount of time was hard enough. She had to pack up everything for six children too. Anxiety gripped her as she made her way to her room, expecting the worst of the situation. Wally went to her and explained that he had to leave with them.[56] "I'm sure they want to question me about the two elders who were flown out to Switzerland. . . . I have everything here for you. Your tickets for trains and

53. Anderson, *Cherry Tree*, 56.

54. Anderson, *Cherry Tree*, 58.

55. Mehr, *Mormon Missionaries Enter Eastern Europe*, 85–86.

56. Miller, "My Story: The Dream," 16.

the ship are here, and the reservations are all made. Here is the money you'll need—crowns, dollars, and French francs. Take the children as planned tomorrow morning and get them home."[57] He told her gently, "If I don't come back, go without me."[58] She "was brave and outwardly she was calm, but her eyes were full of apprehension."[59] She wondered at that moment if she would ever see her husband again.

Wally left as Martha watched anxiously for a last glimpse of her husband from the bedroom window. "I saw below me two other men waiting outside. They encircled Wally as he emerged from the house and marched him past our cherry tree that was barely beginning to bud to an official car that stood waiting beyond the gate."[60] For the next seven excruciating hours, she did not know where he was, but he finally returned.

Much to Wally's surprise, the Communist government granted him alone seven more days. On March 1, 1950, Wally took his family to the train station, where they were greeted by a throng of Czech members who wanted to see them off. Each member presented the Torontos with a little gift of food to eat along the way after they boarded the train. There was no luxury dining car on the train, so the Torontos were delighted by the members' generosity.[61] Food was still severely rationed. Mel Mabey remembered losing twenty pounds during the first month and a half that he was there. He was always hungry.[62] For the Czech Saints to bring food was a real sacrifice. As the train pulled out, they cried as they sang "God Be with You Till We Meet Again," thinking they would never see them again.[63] "As the train departed,

57. Anderson, *Cherry Tree*, 61.
58. Miller and Richards, interview, May 3, 2013.
59. Miller, "My Story: The Dream," 16.
60. Anderson, *Cherry Tree*, 61.
61. Anderson, *Cherry Tree*, 61.
62. Mel Mabey, interview, August 13, 2013, 4.
63. Miller and Richards, interview, May 3, 2013.

some members ran alongside [it], expressing their farewells in . . . kisses and tears."[64]

Much to Martha's surprise, a few railroad officials and a customs agent entered their compartment on the train. They checked their train tickets and passports and then went through every little package they had been given by the members. "[They] broke open each sandwich, roll, cake or cookie to see if anyone had handed [the Torontos] some contraband. Even the apples were cut up, and all those beautiful gifts that were so lovingly prepared for [them] were left lying in a big mess on the opposite seat in the compartment."[65] Consequently, the children were traumatized and felt violated.[66] It seemed ridiculous to accuse little children of being spies as if they could do any real damage. The officers even checked to see if anybody had hid "microfilm in the [baby's] diaper."[67] It was ridiculous, to say the least.

Bob Toronto was particularly upset when they took everything out of his trunk, including two big stamp books that were about two inches thick. He had spent three years trading and collecting stamps with his friends. The officers would not let him take the stamp books with him. He shouted, "You're not going to take my stamps!" The officers threw the stamp books away. When they turned away for a moment, Bob went over to the trash and quietly picked up his books and dropped them behind the garments and suits. The officers strapped up the trunk, and Bob found satisfaction in his success at saving his stamps.[68]

After securing his family on the train, Wally returned to the mission home to put things in order. The first thing he needed to do was make sure that the last two missionaries got out. He also needed to finish a mission history and report to send to the First Presidency. The history was somewhat bulky, about three-quarters of an inch thick. He asked Elder Mabey to mail the history to Church headquarters when

64. Mehr, *Mormon Missionaries Enter Eastern Europe*, 85–86.

65. Anderson, *Cherry Tree*, 62.

66. Miller and Richards, interview, May 3, 2013.

67. Bob and David Toronto, interview, August 20, 2013, 28.

68. Bob and David Toronto, interview, August 20, 2013, 12.

he got to Germany. Mabey asked him how he was supposed to carry it out. "Put it under your sweater." But just before Mabey left the mission home, Wally received an interesting prompting. "Brother Mel, will you give that mission history and report to the First Presidency to your companion to carry." Mabey thought the request was strange, but he did it gratefully since he felt like he "looked pregnant" with the papers in his sweater. When the two elders got to the railroad station, they inspected Mabey very carefully but never looked at his companion. The mission history and record arrived safely.[69]

After the last two missionaries departed, Wally concluded mission affairs as best as he could. He set Rudolf Kubiska apart as the acting mission president and the branch president in Prague, with Miroslav Děkanovský and Jiří Veselý as his counselors.[70] Wally planned to lead the mission from abroad. He was relieved that there was sufficient priesthood in Praha, Brno, and Plzeň to carry out what Wally would describe as their "underground plan," which the Czech Saints would carry on for fifteen years. This plan was put in action when Wally's seven days of extension concluded and Brother Kubiska was given the leadership of the Czechoslovak Mission in Wally's absence. Despite the Communist restrictions on religion, the plan was to "help carry [the Church] on, and the way they [did] it is by what's very comparable to the home teaching program of the Church at the present time. Once a week, usually on Sunday, two of the local elders go from home to home as though making a friendly visit. While somebody watches at the front door or at the window to ward off any unwanted visitor, they prepare and bless the sacrament, pass it to the members of the family who are present, teach them, . . . and then move on to the next place."[71] With the plan and priesthood leadership in place, Wally drove his '47 Ford out of Czechoslovakia on March 30, 1950.

69. Mel Mabey, interview, August 13, 2013, 3–5.

70. Mehr, *Mormon Missionaries Enter Eastern Europe*, 86.

71. Toronto, fireside, 1965, 2.

When Wally left his cherished country, the border patrolman said to him, "We're red on the outside and white on the in."[72] The words likely comforted him greatly, recognizing the country's unquenched patriotism. He arrived in Basel, Switzerland, where he stayed for a month as he tried to keep in touch constantly with the local leaders left in Prague either by phone or by telegram. On the date of April 6, 1950, the government declared that all public and private activities of the Church cease, possibly out of spite because it was the anniversary of the organization of the Church.[73] The Czech Communists liquidated all assets of the LDS Church in Czechoslovakia. Wally stayed on in Basel, hoping that he could run things from there, but he soon realized that he could manage just as well in Salt Lake City, so he finally went home.[74]

The decree of April 6 "eliminated the public Church, but not the one that persisted privately in the hearts and minds of its members. . . . The circumstance did little to erase the hopes of those who gathered at the Czech Mission reunion held April 7, 1950, in Salt Lake City. The group included Elders John A. Widtsoe and Ezra Taft Benson and President Arthur Gaeth, among others. These leaders knew the decree was only a delay, though it turned out to last much longer than they might have hoped."[75]

The Communists did not stick to eliminating just their religious enemies. They continued to sift out their foes within the confines of their own offices and ministries and turned on their own whenever the situation benefitted their goals. The leader of the National Socialist Party, Milada Horáková, "was sentenced to execution by hanging on the charges of treason and conspiracy at the conclusion of a show trial in which she defended her position in spite of the scripted legal proceedings. The show trials continued as members of the government, security offices, and eventually even the general secretary of the

72. Ed and Norma Morrell, interview, May 8, 2013, 21.

73. Vojkůvka, "Memories of President Wallace Felt Toronto," November 9, 2013, 4; Toronto, fireside, 1965, 2.

74. Anderson, *Cherry Tree*, 66.

75. Mehr, *Mormon Missionaries Enter Eastern Europe*, 86.

Communist Party, Rudolf Slánský, fell victim to the purges." The government felt that they needed "a more highly visible and powerful scapegoat to increase the political and psychological impact of the purges." Prime Minister "Gottwald and other party leaders had Slánský arrested in November 1951." They proceeded to torture and abuse the general secretary, both physically and psychologically, for a year. He was placed on trial with thirteen other codefendants, most of them Jews, on November 20, 1952. "Ironically, Slánský had sanctioned the purge trials in Czechoslovakia and even drafted the letter requesting that Stalin send Soviet experts, who now acted against him."[76]

Wally's expulsion, as well as those of his missionaries, had drawn "national headlines, chiefly because of his successful efforts to win the release of several missionaries who had been imprisoned by the Communists."[77] The papers kept up with Wally's grim situation as it unfolded. One headline read, "Eleven United States Mormon missionaries have been ordered expelled from Czechoslovakia, apparently in a Government drive to reduce the number of foreigners in the country."[78] It made sense that the government was trying to eliminate foreigners. "This has been developed progressively in the last six months by continuous propaganda related to a series of arrests, trials, executions and expulsions. The Czech people are given to understand that almost all foreigners in their midst are spies and that to give them anything more than the most banal information is to risk committing treason. The facts of the country's economic life are guarded like military secrets."[79] When the twelfth missionary was expelled, the reason was that he represented "a threat to the peace and security of the state."[80] This, of

76. Mahoney, *The History of the Czech Republic and Slovakia*, 204.

77. "W. F. Toronto Dies In S.L.," *Deseret News*, January 10, 1968.

78. "Czechs Oust 11 Mormons: Order Affects Missionaries of U. S. Church Group," *New York Times*, November 17, 1949: 17.

79. Dana Adams Schmidt, "Czech Police Said to Hold Mormons," *New York Times*, February 11, 1950, 3.

80. "Czechs Expel Twelfth Mormon," *New York Times*, December 19, 1949, 19.

course, was an issue that Wally faced for years, first with the Catholics, and last with the Communists.

After Wally's departure in 1950, many Church members were interrogated by the secret police, including Sister Zdenka Kučerová "concerning her genealogical activity, saying such information could be used to establish covers for Western spies coming into the country. Undaunted, she responded there was nothing in Czechoslovakia worth the attention of spies. Ljuba Durd'áková was interrogated with a light glaring in her eyes and was denied access to restroom facilities. While there was an inevitable attrition [in Church membership], the faithful bonded together with a sense of spiritual unity that toughened under testing."[81]

81. Mehr, *Mormon Missionaries Enter Eastern Europe*, 87.

14 "LEADER OF A SPY RING"

The situation in Czechoslovakia was, in a word, precarious when the Torontos returned home to Salt Lake City. Their experiences with Nazis and Communists had especially affected Martha for the worse. Even when crossing the ocean, she was "strongly sea sick" and could not even get out of bed.[1] When Martha and the children anchored in New York City, they were greeted by crowds of people, including reporters, all eager to know what was going on. The same thing happened when they arrived in Salt Lake City. Everyone seemed to want to get the story and a photograph of the "broken down" wife of President Toronto.[2] Arriving home, Martha was in shock after encountering so many horrifying experiences with six children. She would not get out of bed, and the children were told to not disturb her. In spite of how brave she had appeared and how

1. Miller and Richards, interview, May 3, 2013.
2. Martha Sharp Anderson to Wallace Toronto. April 4, 1952, 1, Church History Library.

blessed they all had been, she had become a very sensitive and delicate soul.[3]

On arriving home, she and the children went directly to her mother-in-law, Etta Toronto's, home, and Martha immediately went to the attic to lie down. The pressure she felt on her mission was too much for her to handle.[4] And the possibility that she would never see her husband again terrified her immensely.[5] The family called in Dr. Louis Moench to examine her. When he asked her how long it had been since she had managed to sleep, she could not remember. She had suffered a nervous breakdown. She could barely even talk. He gave her a shot, and she slept for practically three straight weeks. Only when no one was around, she crept down the stairs to get food.[6]

After three weeks, she still seemed "semi-distant. She did not really get involved with other people, at least with the family."[7] Martha wrote that she had recovered by the time Wally had arrived home two months later.[8] However, the children remembered her illness differently. She had, in their minds, remained bedridden for nearly a year.[9] At fifteen, Marion became a mother to her siblings in many ways. To David, "Marion was more of [his] mother in those motherly ways" than Martha was in many respects.[10] By the time he had any recollection of that year, his mother had fully recovered. His chief memory of her was when she would "lovingly [put] . . . lunches together" for him. Years later, he realized that Marion really had been the one taking care of him then.[11]

3. Miller and Richards, interview, May 3, 2013.
4. Judy Richards, interview, 2.
5. Bob and David Toronto, interview, August 20, 2013, 7.
6. Carma Toronto, interview, February 26, 2004, 7, 11.
7. Carma Toronto, interview, February 26, 2004, 7.
8. Anderson, *Cherry Tree*, 67.
9. Miller and Richards, interview, May 3, 2013.
10. Bob and David Toronto, interview, August 20, 2013, 7.
11. David Toronto, interview by Daniel Toronto, 2010, transcript in author's possession, 8.

For the most part, the younger children were somewhat oblivious to what was going on. Bob, who turned fourteen when they returned to America, had not truly recognized the extent of the danger he had been in. He had no idea that they were throwing the missionaries out, that his father was targeted as a spy, or that his mother was stressed to the point of emotional and physical absence. She was not really in his picture in particular while they were in Prague anyway "because she had 50 missionaries that she had to take care of, and at the end, two . . . were in some prison somewhere." At the end of it all, "the thing that I recall is that when we did get home . . . she [looked] like she'd been dragged through a wringer."[12]

Even though Martha gradually began to recover, she was never completely the same. Her children remembered that a lot of people in their ward thought she was "really snooty and stuck up." Whenever they said such things to Carma, she defended her sister-in-law immediately. "Cut her some slack. You don't know what she's been through." Carma observed, "I think she was just absentminded; she just wasn't tuned in to other people. It wasn't that she ignored them on purpose." When she walked down the aisles at church, she looked neither to right nor to the left. She walked around everyone. "And that was just Martha."[13]

Eventually, Wally and Martha began to share their experiences. They participated in firesides and discussed World War II and Communism, relating the many incidents they endured. When Martha took on such speaking engagements, it took her days after retelling the story to recover from the flood of apprehension and discomfort that rushed back to her. Occasionally, she ended up in bed yet again for days before she could erase all her fears and anxieties.[14]

When Wally returned home, he started looking for a job immediately. Subsequently, he ran for the Salt Lake City school board and served there for thirteen years. He became president of the Utah

12. Bob and David Toronto, interview, August 20, 2013, 6.

13. Carma Toronto, interview, February 26, 2004, 8.

14. Bob and David Toronto, interview, August 20, 2013, 8.

School Board Association and served as the chair of the board's legislative committee. He was also president of the board of control of the Salt Lake Area Vocational School. Most importantly, however, he eventually became the director of the American Cancer Society, after which he rejoined the Salt Lake Kiwanis Club.[15] He also worked with Toronto and Company, the family business that his father and brothers ran. He helped out every once in a while with his brothers in constructing homes during the summer. He even sold houses and helped in the office as well.[16]

The brethren never released Wally as the mission president over Czechoslovakia. Instead, they asked him to remain as president in liaison with those he had left behind. The calling posed its own difficulty. The branch president in Prague was a member of the Communist Party and had not been a member of the Church for very long. Consequently, Wally struggled just to keep in contact with him and fulfill his duties as a liaison to the best of his ability.[17] He did, however, find it easy to faithfully keep in touch with his returned missionaries. He was adamant that none of them go inactive. He attended their homecomings and their marriages. "He was an eternal friend, not just a mission president."[18] One of his missionaries was of particular interest—Ed Morrell. Wally and Martha pushed for Wally's sister, Norma, to get together with Elder Morrell. The two had known each other but had never dated. For their first date, the Torontos had the two of them to dinner one Sunday. They "decided to marry on [their] second date, were engaged privately for two months, and wedded a month after."[19]

Wally gathered his former missionaries every month or two. As many as could would meet with him. They held mission reunions in Salt Lake City during every general conference until Wally died. For a while, even some of the pre–World War II missionaries attended. The

15. "W. F. Toronto Dies in S.L.," *Deseret News*, January 10, 1968.

16. Albert Toronto Family Organization, "Story of Albert and Etta Toronto," 2.

17. Ed and Norma Morrell interview, May 8, 2013, 14.

18. Mel Mabey interview, August 13, 2013, 16.

19. Morrell, "Summary of Czechoslovak Archive Documents," 2.

elders "formed a kind of compact together. . . . [Wally] helped us to love each other."[20]

At Christmastime, Wally and Martha gathered the children around the dining room table to stuff envelopes with Christmas messages for the Church members in Czechoslovakia. The messages were "pretty innocuous. There was no real talk of Christ. There was no real talk about religion" in general.[21] David remembered, "Those Christmas letters . . . were very generic, just enough to let them know we were thinking about them." The Torontos simply conceded to wishing the Saints, "Happy Holidays." The members addressed their return letters to Martha Sharp (Martha's maiden name), rather than Wally or Martha Toronto, to keep their letters from being confiscated by the Communists. The members in Czechoslovakia used all kinds of codes in the letters so they could communicate to the Torontos what was happening. The members included stories like, "Kilroy was here," or, "Uncle Kilroy came and . . . they had some good discussion." It really meant that a Church member was interrogated severely, but everything turned out okay.[22]

Because stuffing envelopes took so long, the Torontos started the process in November of each year. Though it was not much, it did provide one way for Wally to stay in touch with the members. Along with the letters, they sent care packages with food and chocolate; however, those items never arrived. In fact, the Communists frequently confiscated both the packages and letters. Wally had to be very careful about what he wrote and sent. Fortunately, the Church eventually began to supply funds for coupons that the members of Czechoslovakia could use in the export store in Wenceslas to buy shoes, clothes, and other items that were unavailable in any other store.[23]

Life eventually began to take on some vestige of normalcy. Wally was always "very curricular. He loved being with people." On the

20. Mel Mabey interview, August 13, 2013, 16.

21. David Toronto interview, Daniel Toronto, 2010, 1.

22. Bob and David Toronto, interview, August 20, 2013, 28.

23. Bob and David Toronto, interview, August 20, 2013, 9.

other hand, Martha just needed to "have a chance to dress up." She was not a shallow person, according to Carma. She just became "tired of people . . . and wanted to do what she wanted to do." She "loved the symphony, she loved ballet, she loved going out to dinner." In fact, she and Wally joined what seemed like "a hundred thousand dinner groups."[24]

During the 1950s, visitors from Czechoslovakia began trickling to the Toronto home. Some were people who had escaped the Communists. Others were Czechoslovakian dignitaries visiting Salt Lake City. Because Wally knew the Czech language and people so well, he was always asked by the Church to be their escort, and Czechoslovakian people often contacted him when they were in town. David remembered going with his dad to the Bingham Copper Mine one time and showing a Czech government official around the city.[25]

Even though he was in Salt Lake City, Wally Toronto held the Czechoslovak Mission together from thousands of miles away.[26] "For nearly fourteen years, the Czech membership kept their faith in silence, unable to worship publicly or to enjoy any type of regular contact with the Church beyond the Czech borders."[27] From his home in Utah, Wally provided whatever assistance he could. He sent financial aid, clothing, medicine, and Church publications. And though the Saints were isolated, they continued to save their tithing. Wally was certain that such a sacrifice played a role in preventing apostasy.[28]

Apart from being the de facto mission president of Czechoslovakia, Wally served in other Church callings in his home ward and stake. His assignments included membership in several committees, such as the M Men, Special Interest, and *Ensign* committees. He served in the leadership of the Parleys Stake high priests quorum. He was a Gospel Doctrine teacher in the Parleys Fourth Ward, an Aaronic Priesthood

24. Carma Toronto, interview, February 26, 2004, 9.
25. Bob and David Toronto, interview, August 20, 2013, 9–10.
26. Bob and David Toronto, interview, August 20, 2013, 15–16.
27. Mehr, "Czech Saints: A Brighter Day," 51.
28. Ed and Norma Morrell interview, May 8, 2013, 16.

adult general secretary, and a priests quorum adviser.[29] He participated on the general board of the Young Men's Mutual Improvement Association in 1950 and served in that capacity until 1964, traveling extensively. In the same year, "the General Board of the Mutual Improvement Association appointed Wallace Toronto to visit Switzerland. . . . [Wally] sent his passport to Swiss Mission President John Russon in advance, hoping that Russon might get a visa for him to cross the border into Czechoslovakia. Permission was denied." That same year, the country granted permission for Czech Latter-day Saint Marie Vesela to visit the United States.[30]

It would be Marie's visit that would bring about Wally and Martha's return to Czechoslovakia. Marie Vesela, who had served as Wally's personal secretary in Prague, came to Salt Lake City at the invitation of her sister for three months. Her sister had married Joe Roubíček, "a young man who had acted as mission president during the war years [keeping] the mission together as much as possible." He later moved to Midvale, Utah, in 1949. "He and his family were some of the very few who had ever left a Communist country legally. They waited a long time, two years, for permission and visas." When they had settled in Midvale, they sent a letter asking if Marie could visit them in America. "The new regime was reluctant to let young and strong people leave" Czechoslovakia. In fact, they "avoided it at all costs." But "the Lord was on their side," and somehow permission was granted.[31]

One of Marie's requests while she was in Utah was to meet President David O. McKay. Wally arranged the meeting, which Vesela said was "the highlight of [her] life."[32] The discussion that ensued shaped the future of the journey that the Toronto family had yet to commence. President McKay asked Wally, "How is it that this woman can get out of the country and visit here for three months?" Wally explained that

29. "W. F. Toronto Dies in S.L.," *Deseret News*, January 10, 1968.

30. Mehr, *Mormon Missionaries Enter Eastern Europe*, 88.

31. Anderson, *Cherry Tree*, 75–76.

32. Anderson, *Cherry Tree*, 75–76.

> Czechoslovakia at this particular time was on the brink of economic ruin. "They will do anything to get foreign exchange. Their whole economy at this time depends on money from other countries. English pounds and American dollars are particularly sought after because of their stability on the economic market. This woman's fare was paid, in dollars, to the travel bureau in Prague, not only one way, but her return fare also. They haven't softened their hearts any—they just want money, and at this particular time they are encouraging tourists from anywhere to come and spend money in their country."[33]

President McKay then questioned, "Brother Toronto! If this is the case, why would they refuse you a visa into that country?" Wally replied, "President McKay, I am still considered a threat to the peace and security of that nation, and money or not, I don't think they would let me in, not with my record. In their eyes I am still the leader of a spy ring, and they are not about to let me do it again." To this, President McKay countered, "Our members need you at this time. They have been carrying on underground long enough. They need the authority of their mission president. I advise that you and Sister Toronto go home, make application again, and if it's the Lord's will, He will open the way. If you get a visa, we will send you as soon as you can get ready."[34]

The Torontos were stunned with President McKay's instructions. For a decade and a half, they had been on American soil. "Ever persisting during the next fifteen years, [Wally] applied nine times and received nine refusals for a Czech visa."[35] After nine failed attempts, they were to try once again. Halfheartedly, they went through the same routine of obtaining passports and sending them through the proper channels to the Czech Embassy for their visas. They "made no plans, nor did [they] anticipate any journey. [They] had done this too many times to get excited." Much to their surprise, the passports came after just one week of waiting, granting them a visa for fifteen days in Czechoslovakia. As Martha put it, they "nearly exploded with excitement,"

---

33. Anderson, *Cherry Tree*, 76.

34. Anderson, *Cherry Tree*, 76–77.

35. Mehr, "Czech Saints: A Brighter Day," 51.

but they also had "mixed feelings" at the possibility of jail time or being held at the border.[36]

The Torontos paid for all their reservations for hotels and planes in advance, as required by the Czech government. Wally and Martha were both very excited at the prospect of seeing their people again. They could barely sleep at night from "the excitement and anticipation."[37]

Before the Torontos departed, President McKay placed his hands upon Wally's head and gave him a blessing. In it, he promised that Wally would be inspired by the Lord to accomplish what was necessary "for the good of the mission and necessary for the morale of our members, who were by this time feeling the oppression and discouragement of a downtrodden people." He blessed him that we would go safely into the country and come back out without bodily harm or undue detention. He set him apart once again as president of the Czechoslovakian Mission and told him that we would travel safely by land, sea, and air to accomplish the desires of his heart. "Satan, himself, is at the head of the vicious men who banished you from Czechoslovakia," President McKay stated in the blessing.[38]

President Hugh B. Brown of the First Presidency then blessed Martha, saying, "We seal upon you the blessing of peace, tranquility and confidence. May you both be wise under the inspiration of the Holy Ghost. Take no action that would bring any condemnation or criticism from government officials, but go quietly about your work and, without stirring up any ill feeling or turmoil, leave a blessing with those people."[39]

The Torontos flew to Vienna on December 30, 1964. They rented a car and began driving first to the embassy to report their visit. The drive was "picturesque" as they traveled the countryside. However, "the tranquility of the scene soon changed as [they] left the Austrian border station and approached the Czech station nearly a half mile

36. Anderson, *Cherry Tree*, 77.

37. Anderson, *Cherry Tree*, 70.

38. Anderson, *Cherry Tree*, 79.

39. Anderson, *Cherry Tree*, 82.

ahead." Wally asked Martha to pray for the Lord's blessing as they drove down the "narrow strip."[40] She prayed that God would "soften the hearts of those men at the gates who were all armed with machine guns, and especially those in the border station who would be the final decision makers about [them] entering [the] country."[41]

The guards hesitated for quite some time as they examined the passports. But in the end, they let them through, and the Torontos passed through three separate gates, parked the car, and went into the border station building. When they left, Martha noticed, "On either side of [the] clearing were high entanglements of barbed wire, high enough and thick enough that an escapee could not possibly get through. If he did, he took the chance of being attacked by a vicious dog or shot by one of the guards before he crossed the clearing. The whole country of Czechoslovakia was surrounded by this barrier—not to keep people out but to keep them in, as it formed an immense concentration camp."[42]

A "new wave of fright" washed over Martha as they entered the building. They were met by uniformed officers, who spoke to them in English. The Torontos declared their valuables, cameras, typewriter, and money. The guards were naturally interested mostly in the large amount of money that Wally received from the First Presidency not only to impress the guards, but also to help the people in the Czech Mission. While Wally and Martha waited on a bench, the guards took their passports into the inner office. The Torontos were "holding hands and praying inwardly that they wouldn't open the 'black book' and see Wally's name on the top line of 'undesirable characters.'"[43]

Though Wally had been expelled from the country and had been gone for nearly fifteen years, he was still considered a leader of a spy ring. His picture was "flashed on the movie screens, and it was posted

---

40. Bob and David Toronto, interview, August 20, 2013, 10; Anderson, *Cherry Tree*, 82–83.

41. Anderson, *Cherry Tree*, 83.

42. Anderson, *Cherry Tree*, 83.

43. Anderson, *Cherry Tree*, 84.

up in the post offices as being one of the dangerous capitalistic spies within Czechoslovakia."[44] Martha recorded:

> If [the guards] did look in the "black book," they passed it over or the Lord blinded them as they looked. Perhaps the thoughts of us spending all that money was too much to let them refuse our entry. President McKay had said, "If dollars will get you in, and it is obvious that is what they want, we will give you plenty to show them." They gave the permission, looked in the trunk of the car, but didn't open any suitcases. We had made sure there would be no printed matter, list of names, or church literature that would incriminate us in our attempt to enter the country. As we drove off, leaving the reminders of a police state behind us, the feelings of fear or apprehension that had been so constantly with me melted away.[45]

Wally added that before they reentered Czechoslovakia, they had received a blessing from "President McKay [which said] 'you will cross the border without difficulty, you will go in and you will do your work, and you shall have influence with the leaders . . . you shall come out without difficulty,' we crossed the borders in just 20 minutes." Other tourists were held in customs for many hours, and Wally was reminded again "of the great concentration camp Czechoslovakia [had become]."[46]

With gratitude in their hearts, the Torontos drove to Brno. They were sure that Sister Vesela had told other Church members that they had secured visas and were going to be there. Word of mouth was the only way they could inform members about their visit ahead of time. The Torontos expected to find Brother and Sister Vesela but were not expecting the crowd that greeted them. There was a law in place requiring that no more than five people could meet in one place at the same time. But the Czech Saints in Brno "had learned to be very clever in skirting the law if they wanted something bad enough, and [the Torontos'] visit was important to them."[47]

44. Toronto, fireside, 1965, 3.
45. Anderson, *Cherry Tree*, 84.
46. Toronto, fireside, 1965, 3.
47. Anderson, *Cherry Tree*, 86–87.

That evening, Brno members shared their experiences "of the fourteen years that had intervened since their last acquaintance."[48] As they were serving the Torontos a delicious Czech meal they had prepared, the doorbell rang. Everybody feared that it might be the police. The Torontos had parked their car far away from the house as a precaution, but they were still apprehensive. When they opened the door, they were relieved to see an older woman who had made a habit of visiting the branch president, Brother Vrba, regularly. The branch president said nothing to the woman as she entered his house. He let her figure out what was going on by herself. When she saw Wally and Martha sitting there, she turned white as a ghost and began trembling, overcome by emotion. She pointed to them and asked Brother Vrba, "Is that Brother Toronto?" His reply was music to her ears as he affirmed that it was indeed. Wally put his arm around her shoulder, and she burst into a flood of joyful tears as she embraced him. Still trembling, she moved to Martha, who stood to greet her as the sister kissed her cheeks. Over and over, she repeated, "I never thought I'd ever see you again. How is this possible?"[49]

The next fifteen days were filled with similar experiences as the Torontos traveled from home to home, taking local priesthood leadership whenever possible.[50] The only warning members would receive was a phone call an hour before the Torontos arrived. At the sight of their beloved mission president and his wife, tears came freely and the Saints cried with joy. Martha remembered that they all went up to them "at once to kiss and embrace [them]."[51] As they went from home to home, "Wally's main concern was to bless those who were in need of the Lord's blessing. Many were sick and found great comfort in their president being able to administer to them."[52] Some members would look at him with tears in their eyes and ask, "Why are we going

48. Mehr, *Mormon Missionaries Enter Eastern Europe*, 90–92.

49. Anderson, *Cherry Tree*, 89.

50. Toronto, fireside, 1965, 4.

51. Anderson, *Cherry Tree*, 87.

52. Anderson, *Cherry Tree*, 93.

through this? Why are we suffering like this?" Wally would answer, "It's because you're going to be witnesses."[53] After each day, the Torontos returned to the same hotel at night, unable to sleep because of their overfilled stomachs from the generosity of the Czech Saints. They visited Martha's Beehive girls, who were by then married, and the young men, some of whom were ready for ordinations to new priesthood offices.[54]

The Torontos learned that the priesthood brethren still operated their underground plan and visited members in their homes on Sunday to deliver the sacrament. They taught the gospel "to one family at a time." In an effort to be extra cautious, they regularly altered visiting assignments and only stayed for twenty or thirty minutes at most to avoid arousing suspicion.[55] They were especially careful when the Torontos were present since "any attention [given] to Americans or Mormons" meant imprisonment or terrible harassment. But it remained a challenge, nevertheless, because they had to work faithfully yet stay undetected. By 1964, the Saints were used to functioning underground in such a way.[56] Wally found that "not more than two percent of our entire membership [had] been lost to apostasy. . . . This is remarkable and certainly shows what a home teaching program can do when the gospel is taught in the home and with regularity."[57]

In large metropolitan areas like Prague and Brno, members lived many miles apart, and the brethren would have to travel by streetcar to reach them. They did not use their own vehicles. The Torontos had to be very careful about where they parked their car on the streets. Czech citizens were required to report to the officials if they saw a car with a foreign license plate. When a visitor went to the border to leave the country, the Communists knew exactly where they had been. It seemed like the government knew everything, "what you spoke, whom you . . .

53. Miller and Richards, interview, May 3, 2013.

54. Mehr, *Mormon Missionaries Enter Eastern Europe*, 90.

55. Mehr, *Mormon Missionaries Enter Eastern Europe*, 90.

56. Miller and Richards, interview, May 3, 2013.

57. Toronto, fireside, 1965, 4.

called in your hotel, everything."[58] If a citizen even spoke with a foreigner, they had to report it. Consequently, the Torontos had to stay in hotels rather than with members so the police would know where they were at all times. If they planned on going to a surrounding town to visit members, they always made sure to be back in Prague by the end of the day, even if that meant traveling a long way very late in the evening. They were also required to leave their passports at the hotel desk at night in order for the secret police to check them as they made their rounds at the hotels and, therefore, keep track of all foreigners.[59]

As soon as they entered the country, Martha found that her ability to speak Czech returned easily, just as promised in the blessing she received from President Brown. He promised that "once she got into the country, she would have the gift of language."[60] Members told her, "You speak as well as you did when you were here fifteen years ago." They said that Wally spoke as well as a native, except that it was not quite right. His accent was a little off. Because meetings were prohibited, they visited members one-on-one. Wally would put his arm around the members as he talked to them. There were only six or seven hundred members at the time in the country.[61]

Czechoslovakian member Olga Kovářová Campora remembered hearing about what had happened during the Toronto visit in December 1964. A number of Czech members and their families had been questioned and persecuted. Many had to leave the country as a result. A lot of members who stayed behind had only pictures of their sons and daughters who lived outside of Czechoslovakia. "These pictures were their entire [treasure], their life and hope. Those photos were often the only connection they had with their families [who had left the country]. Sitting among these old members felt like sitting under a beautiful tree, surrounded by long branches which gave you peace from the sharp world around you. . . . Communist oppression was a fact of their lives

58. Johann Wondra, interview, May 30, 2013, 4.

59. Anderson, *Cherry Tree*, 91.

60. Toronto, fireside, 1965, 7.

61. Bob and David Toronto, interview, August 20, 2013, 10, 16.

that had left certain marks but didn't change their faith a bit. Sometimes it seemed their lives were stopped in the middle, and they were left only with their faith to work through to the end of their lives."[62]

Gad Vojkůvka took Wally and Martha to visit members in Praha, Mladá Boleslav, and Bakov. "This was a wonderful experience. I saw the joy of members, heard their testimonies, and heard the [advice] and support given to them by President Toronto."[63] During Wally's absence, the Saints had rejoiced with every piece of news, every card, and every letter that he sent from Salt Lake City. Those "shards of the Lord's light that came to their houses as a miracle would be cherished." They generated so much joy, not just for weeks but for months and years.[64] And then Wally was actually there in person.

On New Year's Eve the Torontos decided, "The most important thing for us to do would be to see each of our members, if possible. Their morale was very low after fifteen years of servitude and oppression, and a visit from us would be like a shot in the arm for them." Before the country banished him, Wally had appointed several local men to leadership positions to take care of the members in his absence. He assigned, for example, "a brilliant and vibrant man"—Brother Vrba—to be the branch president in his area. Brother Vrba had "run the affairs of this branch in a manner that was most pleasing to Wally."[65] Nevertheless, some members had "become disgruntled with the local leadership," even with the men who Wally had appointed. After some discussion, it was decided that the local leaders would go with the Torontos on their visits. Wally always made it a point to declare to the Saints that the local leaders were appointed by the power of the Lord, that they were to lead them during his absence.[66]

62. Campora, *Saint Behind Enemy Lines*, 78.

63. Vojkůvka, "Memories of President Wallace Felt Toronto," November 9, 2013, 4.

64. Campora, *Saint Behind Enemy Lines*, 79.

65. Anderson, *Cherry Tree*, 88.

66. Anderson, *Cherry Tree*, 91–92.

Wally did, however, make some changes in the branch presidencies while he was there, setting brethren apart to certain positions and calling others to replace those who had died or moved away. However, it was not his main purpose. From the beginning of their journey, both Wally and Martha had a feeling that the Lord had a particular reason that they go back to Czechoslovakia, but they were unsure of what it was initially. As they visited with members, Wally was led to tell many of them a message from the Lord:

> Brethren, your calling in the priesthood is far greater than you can ever imagine. . . . In the providence of the Lord, an iron curtain cannot be rung down on His gospel, cannot be rung down on the Priesthood. You brethren are still His representatives. You still speak for him in spite of the fact that I'm not here and that missionaries are not here and that you don't have direct contact with the President of the Church. . . . And when the time comes, brethren, if you live faithfully from here on out, continue to uphold the principles of the church, keep close to the Lord in prayer, and manifest and exercise your priesthood to the best of your ability, the day will come when you stand before the bar of God and ye shall testify of all the terrible things that have happened to your nation. . . . You'll also testify of, then, the blessings the Lord has given those who have remained faithful to the covenants.[67]

The brethren responded amiably, expressing joy that they finally "realize[d] and recognize[d] what [their] responsibility and part [was]."[68] Through this and other visits with members, Wally and Martha finally realized that one of the Lord's reasons for sending them back to their mission field was, as Martha explained, that "our people needed us, and seeing us in person was a great morale booster for them. And we knew the Lord was protecting us, too, because we were not detained anywhere and were never approached by the police nor were we followed. But we knew that they knew we were there and what we were doing. As long as we were not bothered we just kept going as fast as we could in order to accomplish what the Lord sent us to do."[69]

67. Toronto, fireside, 1965, 6.

68. Toronto, fireside, 1965, 6.

69. Anderson, *Cherry Tree*, 93.

Beyond visiting members, Wally had some other specific visits he intended to make: the Ministry of Interior to push microfilming of Czech genealogical records and the oncological hospital to build strong, goodwill relationships with the doctors there. Wally felt successful on both fronts stating, in regards to their success with the genealogical progress, "We believe that we pushed the door open at least for the microfilming of the genealogical records in Czechoslovakia. This was one of the achievements that we at least got started." As for the hospital visit, Wally discovered that the Czech doctors were far behind the United States in every aspect of cancer control. Wally "promised to send them films and literature and subscriptions to professional cancer magazines."[70] He followed through on his promise, and the Czech doctors expressed much appreciation for his generosity.

As the Torontos prepared to leave Czechoslovakia, Brother Vrba turned to Martha and asked that she tell President McKay something for him. When she replied that she would love to, he said, "I want to thank him for sending you along with your husband." She inquired, "Why is that?" His answer touched her deeply: "Because you have been an example to our women. Our wives are afraid and won't let us go when we have assignments. We know there are dangers, but now they have seen you, and your assignment with your husband has been far more precarious than ours, yet you have gone with him under very trying circumstances, and they have seen how you share in the priesthood." Martha was overcome with his kind words and promised to tell the prophet when she and Wally returned to Salt Lake City.[71]

After they returned home, the Torontos "read over the blessings [that] had been given [them] by the First Presidency and were astonished by the prophetic nature of these promises. Every item mentioned in the blessings had come true."[72]

70. Toronto, fireside, 1965, 5.

71. Anderson, *Cherry Tree*, 94–95.

72. Anderson, *Cherry Tree*, 95.

15 "COMMUNISM ESPOUSES RELIGIOUS FREEDOM!"

Wally and Martha experienced great success in seeing most of the Czech Saints during their fifteen-day stay, and they felt they had accomplished what the Lord desired of them. But Wally could not shake the feeling that he needed to go back one more time. After a few months, he once again went to President McKay to ask his advice on taking another trip to Czechoslovakia. Wally informed the prophet that he did not want to see the members on another visit but rather that he wanted to see government authorities, especially those in high offices of the ministries over religion and education. "He was sure he could talk them into letting him re-establish the mission and get permission for public meetings again. He already knew some of these men in high places because he had visited them in Washington D.C. when they were in the Czech Embassy there. He felt this was a way to open the door."[1]

An opportunity did open up for Wally. Every ten years, Czechoslovakia held a large athletic festival and

1. Anderson, *Cherry Tree*, 100.

exhibition called the "Sokol Slet." Of course, the Communists had given it a Russian name instead: Spartakiad.[2] The events were being held in Prague in 1965. Wally, then, found a perfect excuse to obtain a visa. All nations were invited to attend, making it easier to get one. President McKay agreed to send Wally in an official capacity for his next visit. He also advised him that he should go by himself. Though Wally was discouraged about leaving Martha home alone, he later recognized that it was "a fortunate inspiration on behalf of . . . President [McKay]."[3]

Wally arrived in Prague as planned in July 1965, during the celebration of the Sokol Slet. "As [he] was sitting there in a crowd of 25,000 people, a cameraman spotted him as an American and asked him to stand in front of the camera and tell the nation about his impressions of the 'Spartakiada.'"[4] In a blessing he had received years before, he had been told that he would testify to the nation. At that moment on camera at the Sokol Slet, it seemed that the prophecy was beginning to be fulfilled. But Wally had hoped he would manage getting in and out of the country without any fanfare or attention. His television appearance ruined his plans. Afterward, surely everybody would know he was in Czechoslovakia.[5]

In fact, on that very day, Gad Vojkůvka's mother sent Gad to go shopping. For some reason that not even he could recall, he decided to turn on the television set in the living room before he left. The TV started making a high-pitched noise. Gad returned to the room to check what was wrong. Much to his surprise, he saw the face of his much-loved mission president on the screen. Gad was in shock. He immediately called to his family to join him in the living room to watch as Wally nonchalantly talked about his children and where he lived.[6]

---

2. Toronto, fireside, 1965, 8.

3. Anderson, *Cherry Tree*, 100–101.

4. Spartakiad or Spartakiade is the English spelling of the Czech word *Spartakiáda*.

5. Anderson, *Cherry Tree*, 101–2.

6. Vojkůvka, "Memories of President Wallace Felt Toronto," November 9, 2013, 5.

The following morning, Wally started visiting people at the various offices of the ministries. Many officials recognized him as the man they had seen on television the day before. Naturally, like Gad, some other Church members had also seen him, so they traveled to Prague to visit him, which was exactly what he had wanted to avoid. He feared that any visits from the Saints could jeopardize his mission to speak with the officials of the government. Despite the notoriety, he seemed to make some progress in his discussions with the officials that he had gone to see. Wally was able to speak to officials in the Ministry of Archives regarding the genealogy and microfilm proposal, and he received word that they were still interested in that project. He also visited the Ministry of Health and Welfare and was welcomed with a "a regular spread . . . [of] Lindon tea and all kinds of sandwiches," a reception Wally had never received during official business. The doctors there who had received Wally's magazines and other materials about cancer had accepted Wally as someone who could truly benefit their nation, medically speaking.[7] Overall, he was treated well and believed he was on his way to getting permission "to get the mission 'above ground' and recognized by the Communist regime."[8]

Wally's most important interview was to be with the Minister of Religious Affairs. He was scheduled to be at the Ministry of Interior on July 12. Because securing a meeting with the man was so difficult, the appointment was a little tentative. On July 8, he and Brother Kubiska, the acting mission president, "drove out into the country about 200 kilometers away from Prague" where Brother Kubiska's sister lived in a farmhouse.[9] While Wally was relaxing, two men came to the door, identified themselves as secret police from Prague, and demanded that Wally go back with them to Prague. Bob Toronto remembered his dad describing his experience. It was the only time Bob ever recalled his father saying anything about being afraid. He asked what they wanted with him. They answered, "We can't tell you that. That will be told you

7. Toronto, fireside, 1965, 9.

8. Anderson, *Cherry Tree*, 102.

9. Toronto, fireside, 1965, 9.

back in Prague."[10] Wally soon discovered two more men outside: one to drive his car back, and one to drive the secret police's car. During the car ride, Wally tried to engage in conversation with them over and over, but they gave him nothing.[11]

Once they arrived in Prague, they immediately took Wally to a government building. To his good fortune, that building was where all the ministers were located, including those with whom he had been trying to procure an audience. Previously, he had been denied access to the Ministry of Religion. They would not even give him an audience then. The officials began their questioning. "During the interrogation he was accused of such subversive activities as stirring up the people and inciting them against the regime, trying to establish the Church illegally again in Czechoslovakia, and bringing in missionaries."[12] Denying all these charges, he told them he was actually there to visit the ministries.

With newfound courage, he talked to them about his earlier trip with Martha. He explained that he had told Church members at that time that he could not do anything to help them with open worship. Wally "took occasion to tell them of the splendid work the Mormon Church had done in Czechoslovakia," work that ranged from humanitarian relief efforts in postwar years to saving villages that had been flooded out. He also took the opportunity to bear "testimony to them of the truthfulness of the gospel, of the need for it, [and that it would] bring lasting peace, harmony, and happiness to the world."[13] The interrogator told Wally that they knew about his visit in January and about everything he and Martha had done.[14] And with even greater courage, Wally charged back at their harsh questioning, "Why are you afraid of 500 Mormons? Why are you afraid of that? Why did you pick me up?"

10. Toronto, fireside, 1965, 9.

11. Bob and David Toronto, interview, August 20, 2013, 27.

12. Anderson, *Cherry Tree*, 103–4.

13. Toronto, fireside, 1965, 10.

14. Anderson, *Cherry Tree*, 103–4.

He was surprised when he realized he was not afraid of his interrogators anymore.[15]

What could have been a terrifying experience turned into a blessing. One of Wally's interrogators was the very man he had hoped to meet on July 12. The man was, after all, in charge of all things religious in the country. Therefore, it was only natural for him to be called in on Wally's case. The smug Communist official informed Wally that seventeen other churches had already been granted state recognition, and in anger he slammed his fist on the table to prove his point. "Communism espouses religious freedom!" he claimed. Wally responded, "You proclaim that you have religious freedom here? What about the many people that don't belong to these seventeen churches? Where's your freedom?" Stunned by Wally's argument, the minister warmed up a little bit and said, "Maybe you could come back again and we can culminate our talks about this matter in a more friendly atmosphere." Wally responded resolutely, "I want to put down notice that I will be back. The Mormon Church has not forgotten the people over here in Czechoslovakia."[16]

The questioning was rough and severe, but Wally kept his composure and resisted showing any visual fear or anger, which confused and bothered the officials. He believed that the Lord had given him "the strength and the wisdom he needed to say the things that had to be said." He recited the history of the mission, a mission that he had personally been a part of since its inception in 1929, ending with his expulsion from Czechoslovakia in 1950. He explained his desire that Church members be left alone and allowed at least the privilege of meeting in groups under the direction of local men. The officials told him that they already knew who the local leaders were, a fact that did not surprise him at all.[17] Before ending the conversation, one of the officials said to him, "When the hammer and sickle are emblazoned

15. Bob and David Toronto, interview, August 20, 2013, 27.
16. Toronto, fireside, 1965, 10–11.
17. Anderson, *Cherry Tree*, 103–4.

across all of America, then you will know that the Communist way is the right way."[18]

Wally was again unable to change anything for Czech Latter-day Saints that day. Unfortunately, "mission growth would be suppressed for another twenty-five years before reemerging in a new epoch of freedom."[19] Nevertheless, Wally informed the Ministry of Interior to take notice that he would keep trying to accomplish his purpose later. Even though he was detained as a prisoner, he believed that his visit to "the highest ministry in the land" was successful. After all, had he not been arrested, "he never would have been able to see all [of the] important government officials, and especially all at the same time."[20] But at the conclusion of the interrogation, Wally was told that his presence in Czechoslovakia would no longer be tolerated and that he was to leave the country that night. The secret police would accompany him to the German border. He insisted that he had a plane ticket to Vienna for the next day and asked if he could stay the night. The answer was "absolutely not." They would take him to the border that very night.[21]

The same guards who picked him up in Brno put him in the same car and drove him and his luggage three hours to the Czech border. Wally had no plans to go through Germany, but he also had no choice. "This is as far as we go," the guard said as he dropped Wally off. Wally picked up his bags and walked half a mile to the West German border station. When he arrived at the station, the German guard looked him over suspiciously. After all, it was not common for a man to appear at his station at one o'clock in the morning, especially without a vehicle. Fortunately, Wally could speak German almost as well as he could English. He satisfied the guard's reservations and explained his situation.[22] The two engaged in a gospel conversation, a merciful ending to an unsatisfying journey. Wally remembered, "There I was with this

18. Bob and David Toronto, interview, August 20, 2013, 27.

19. Mehr, "Czech Saints: A Brighter Day," 51.

20. Anderson, *Cherry Tree*, 103–4.

21. Bob and David Toronto, interview, August 20, 2013, 27.

22. Anderson, *Cherry Tree*, 105.

lonely border guard on the German side, but I preached the gospel to him."[23] The next day a taxi picked up Wally and took him to a train station.[24]

As devoted and dedicated as he was to restoring the legality of Church worship, Wally did not have the blessing of returning to Czechoslovakia after his last visit in 1965. He had always planned to go back later and accomplish his purpose, just as he had told the Ministry of Interior. He would have done anything to get the Church above ground again.[25] Unfortunately, it would not be in his lifetime that his plans for Czechoslovakia, the nation he cherished so much, would come to light.

23. Ed and Norma Morrell, interview, May 8, 2013, 7–8.

24. Bob and David Toronto, interview, August 20, 2013, 27.

25. Anderson, *Cherry Tree*, 106.

16 "THE TORONTO MISSION"

In August of 1967, Wally had a kidney stone operation. A few months later, the doctors discovered he had cancer. Everyone felt that a healing miracle was in store for him because of "who he was and what he was."[1] He had known President McKay and all the other General Authorities. He had been on the Mutual Improvement Association and Sunday School general boards for years. "He knew everybody."[2] But even though "he had all these high-powered friends" on his side, "he died anyway."[3] Wally received no miracle. Martha gave her husband shots for pain and tried her best to keep him comfortable as he suffered the last of his mortal days.[4]

After enduring radiation, Wally admitted, "That's it. This is just not working." His health began to decline quickly once he terminated treatment. The family had a hospital bed placed in the front room. Wally stayed

1. David Toronto interview, Daniel Toronto, 2010, 5.
2. Bob and David Toronto, interview, August 20, 2013, 17.
3. David Toronto, interview by Daniel Toronto, 2010, 5.
4. Anderson, *Cherry Tree*, 109.

on that bed until the last several days of his life.[5] Suffering greatly, he asked President Hugh B. Brown of the First Presidency to administer a blessing.[6] In the blessing, he told Wally that he was appointed to death. At just sixty years old, he passed away on January 10, 1968, in a Salt Lake City hospital.[7] He died "of the disease against which he had crusaded for 16 years as director of the Utah Division of the American Cancer Society."[8] President Brown graciously spoke at his funeral.[9]

The Czech Mission was left without their mission president. Wally had served as president since 1936. For thirty-two years, he held that position, most of that time directing the mission from Salt Lake City. "When the presidency of Wallace Toronto ended with his death in 1968, the Church's tenuous contacts with the outside world continued."[10] President Brown asked Martha to carry on as mission president in Wally's place until they could figure out what to do with the mission.[11] President McKay, too, asked her to "run the mission until [they] could get somebody in there."[12] Almost as soon as she was called, she began writing to the Saints in Czechoslovakia, just as her beloved husband had done. She guessed that she was the only female who had ever served as a mission president.[13]

The appointment did not last long, however. Once the Czechoslovak Mission was joined with the Austrian Mission a few months later, she was released.[14] Church officials went to collect the materials from

5. David Toronto interview, 2010, 6.
6. Bob and David Toronto, interview, August 20, 2013, 17.
7. Anderson, *Cherry Tree*, 109.
8. "W. F. Toronto Dies In S.L.," *Deseret News*, January 10, 1968.
9. Funeral Services for Wallace Felt Toronto, January 13, 1968, copy in author's possession.
10. Mehr, "Czech Saints: A Brighter Day," 51.
11. Anderson, *Cherry Tree*, 110.
12. Bob and David Toronto, interview, August 20, 2013, 29.
13. Anderson, *Cherry Tree*, 110.
14. Anderson, *Cherry Tree*, 110.

the mission and place them all in the Church archives. Everything Martha had in relation to the mission was taken after her release—"her letters, their letters, pictures, photos, albums, everything."[15]

Even before his death, Wally prepared the Saints for what they were going to go through. People even regarded him as a fairly visionary man. He seemed to know "that this was all coming, and he did everything he could to fortify it. He, in a way, prophesied that it would get worse." He knew that the missionaries would eventually be expelled from the country and have to leave. "He tried to prepare the people and . . . instill in them that the gospel [was] the most important thing. If they would stay with the Lord and the gospel, then they could survive anything. . . . He had a vision of what was coming, . . . and that there would be a day when they would be free again, and the Church could prosper there." He said, "They have to look forward to that vision. We're going to have dark days now, but there's a vision of what will happen when the Communists are gone."[16]

Missionary Dale Tingey talked about how "[Wally] was able to build up their confidence." It was extremely important to Wally that he organize everything in such a way that "they could carry on alone without him. . . . His greatest contribution was that he was an example of the Church to the people, and example of what we should do with our families, an example of how they should love one another and support one another." Wally inspired the Saints of Czechoslovakia as nobody had before. "He had the big picture of what was coming down the track and [knew] to prepare for disaster. . . . Beyond that there would be hope and faith, and the Lord would be with them if they would just stay with the Lord."[17] Tingey described Wally with the utmost respect:

> I remember him as a very courageous, dedicated person. I was with him when he talked to the Communists. He almost scared me. He'd just say these things [like] "Know the truth, and the truth will make you free. You're trying to take this away from people." . . . He was

15. Bob and David Toronto, interview, August 20, 2013, 29.
16. Dale Tingey, interview, 4.
17. Dale Tingey, interview, 3.

very brave. In his talks in Church, even when there were Communists there, . . . he didn't kowtow to them at all. He'd just tell them what was right. . . . The youth said to us, "You believe in a Christ that's been dead for 2,000 years . . . ?" He'd say, "That's right, and who do you believe in?" And they would say, "We believe in Stalin. He is . . . the rising star of the East. . . . Someday you'll see that rising star, that red star, flying over the capital of the United States.[18]

Even with all the preparations Wally made, the Czech Saints were distraught at his passing. Only a few months later, Czechoslovakia experienced the "Prague Spring" of 1968:

The Czechoslovakia of old surfaced when Alexander Dubček became leader of the Czechoslovak Communist Party and instituted a series of liberal reforms, including more freedom of the press and increased contact with non-Communist countries. Encouraged by these actions, Ceněk Vrba, Jiří Šnederfler, and Miroslav Děkanovský—three stalwarts of the Church—petitioned for religious recognition. However, hopes were dashed when Warsaw pact troops and tanks, under Soviet orders, crushed the progressive regime and quelled any hope of reviving the Church. Despairing at the lack of religious liberty, the Vrba family from Brno and the Kučera and Janoušek families from Prague escaped with what few belongings they could carry, not knowing what to expect in the non-Communist world, but hopeful that their situation could be no worse. That same year (1968) in far-off Salt Lake City, Wallace Toronto died of cancer.[19]

Along with everything else, Wally's death was a bitter blow for the Czech Saints. Jiří Šnedefler wrote a letter to President McKay expressing the despair that they felt:

Prague, July 10, 1968.

Dear President McKay,

I hesitate to write this letter, but we are sincerely concerned about the future of our Mission in Czechoslovakia. Since the untimely death of our dear [President] Toronto, we do not have any contact to receive direction and encouragement from the First Presidency and Church leaders.

18. Dale Tingey, interview, 4.

19. Mehr, *Mormon Missionaries Enter Eastern Europe*, 92–93.

Many churches are receiving permission to conduct meetings and teach [others] their various doctrines, and we would like you to counsel us in regards to making an application to the government for recognition for our church or for permission to meet together.

The present circumstances are much better than years ago. We have more freedom, we receive *The Improvement Era*, we surely will be able to work in genealogy, and we could find people who are interested in our Church.

We realize you are so busy you personally cannot be concerned about us, but would it be possible to designate someone who understands us, who would correspond with us, who could help us enjoy the blessings we so much want and need.

We think of you and pray for you and remain with best wishes for you and all the Church.

Sincerely,
[Jiří Šnedefler][20]

Wally had understood and corresponded with them, helping them to enjoy all the blessings that they had received. But he was gone. Wally had warned them that when the Czech people received their freedom, there would be fewer conversions than in the days when they were under Communist rule. He believed that they would lose converts even faster. That was his exact reason for encouraging the Saints to be more careful and diligent with whom they taught and how they taught them.[21] Nevertheless, the Saints were yearning for religious freedom in their country and inspired guidance from the Church.

Czech historian Johann Wondra expressed, "The Czech government didn't want to have a situation like in Poland. In Poland, there was a strong Catholic church, but this was not only a Church; it was a political position. . . . Therefore, the Czech government . . . [was] very aggressive against every religious [intention] and [activity]." Every second Sunday, the members in Czechoslovakia fasted and prayed

20. Jiří Šnedefler to President David O. McKay, July 10, 1968, as found in Jiri Šnederfler papers, Europe Church History Center, Bad Homburg, Germany, copy in author's possession.

21. Bob and David Toronto, interview, August 20, 2013, 32.

that the Church would somehow be officially recognized in Czechoslovakia. "It was the Toronto mission. . . . [Wally] really knew how the people in Czechoslovakia felt" about the situation.[22]

From the time Wally was evacuated, Jiří Šnedefler served as the district president in Prague and did so for many years. Otakar Vojkůvka served as the priesthood leader in Brno. Both were authorized to perform all of the ordinances—sacrament services, baptisms, confirmations. However, as Johann Wondra (who was the regional representative at the time) reported, Jiří Šnedefler had to be careful not to reveal who had joined the Church. When someone was baptized, he sent Elder Wondra a postcard with a beautiful lake on the front. To signify how many people were baptized, he wrote something to this effect: "Last Sunday we were swimming with eight friends."[23]

The local leaders were careful not to reveal the names of those who had been ordained to the priesthood either. In order to get the names into Church records, Elder Wondra traveled to Austria. However, because he could not risk taking written information across the border, he memorized it all before he began his journey. Once he was safely in Austria, he wrote down names of brethren who had been ordained. If such information fell into the wrong hands, the government would incriminate the Czech Saints, for at the time Czechoslovakia was the most terrible of the Communist countries.[24] The objective of the leaders was to avoid drawing attention or suspicion to themselves, and they were blessed with success.

"The great loss was the children," said the Morrells.[25] Marion Toronto, who later served a mission in Czechoslovakia, expressed, "The Communist regime . . . didn't allow religion—period. It was a totally atheistic country and so that made it very difficult for the children [of Latter-day Saints]." In fact, if the parents "did speak about God or religion in any way, their families were in danger. So if their

22. Johann Wondra interview, May 30, 2013, 2.
23. Johann Wondra interview, May 30, 2013, 18.
24. Johann Wondra interview, May 30, 2013, 18.
25. Ed and Norma Morrell, interview, May 8, 2013, 17–18.

children stayed faithful, they had to do it in terrible secrecy. And a lot of their children just didn't bother."[26] They resented the fact that they were kept out of universities and that they "didn't have much chance" simply because their parents believed the Church was true. Jiří Šnedefler had one son who had gone to Church when he was single. However, he married a woman who was extremely opposed to it. He drew away and "broke the liaison between the father and the son."[27] Marion realized, "It's a hard, hard mission. . . . It's always been a hard, hard mission."[28]

Despite all the difficulties and setbacks that constantly faced them, the Vojkůvka and Šnedefler families held the mission together after Wally died. After the "Prague Spring," Brother Šnedefler quietly began applying for recognition of the Church.[29] Gad Vojkůvka compared Wally and his mission to Moses and ancient Israel. The Israelites wandered in the desert for forty years before they had the privilege of entering the promised land. But Moses could not join them there. Similarly, Wally died before the Church gained legal status again in the Czech Republic. The Saints suffered many years in secret worship. But even though Wally could not visit them, he continually wrote to them and prayed for them.[30]

Wallace Felt Toronto was, in a sense, the Moses of Czechoslovakia. He gave his heart to the Czech people and to the Czech Mission. He was a powerful but humble leader. He invested time in developing love for the one. He learned about the culture and customs of Czechoslovakia. Consequently, he was able to gain the trust of the people and lead them through the most difficult times of despair and hardship. Wally did everything he was asked to do, despite great sorrow. Although he never had the privilege of witnessing the joy of the Czech members

---

26. Miller and Richards, interview, May 3, 2013.
27. Ed and Norma Morrell, interview, May 8, 2013, 17–18.
28. Miller and Richards, interview, May 3, 2013.
29. Ed and Norma Morrell, interview, May 8, 2013, 17–18.
30. Vojkůvka, "Memories of President Wallace Felt Toronto," November 9, 2013, 8.

when the Church was legalized again, he did everything in his power to push the Church in that direction. The response of the Czech Saints at the time of his death encompassed the intensity of love and respect that the Czechoslovakian members had for their compassionate leader. Wallace Toronto's thirty-year contribution to the Czechoslovak Mission was incredible, to say the least. His son David understood that if someone asked his dad what he had accomplished, Wally would simply reply, "I was just doing what I was asked to do." Bob added, "And, in fact, that's exactly what he did."[31]

31. Bob and David Toronto, interview, August 20, 2013, 17.

INDEX

A

Abbott, Stanley, 78, 182–84
Aerial Exposition of the Republic, 81
American fliers, interment of, 139
Anderson, Alden, 139
Articles of Faith (Talmage), 63
Auschwitz, 141

B

baptismal covenants, 98–99
baptisms, 45–46, 107–8, 222
basketball, 179–80
Bäumelburg, Dr., 115–17
bazaars, 38
Beeley, Dr., 129
Bell, Victor, 131–34, 136, 140–41
Beneš, Edvard, 144, 171–72, 173
Benson, Ezra Taft, 136–38, 170, 188
Bernhisel, John M., 5
bird imitations, 36–37
Bishop, Verdell R., 110–17
Book of Mormon, 62–63, 175
Boone, David, 121
Brodil, Frantisek, 20
Brodilová, Františka Vesela, 19–20
Brown, Hugh B., 199, 218
Broz, Jan, 59–60

C

cake
- made with rotten egg, 162
- used as object lesson, 169

car accident, 33
Catholic Church, 46–50, 177
Chadwick, Trevor, 122
Chapman, Mr., 51–52
chickens, 16
children, evacuated from Czechoslovakia, 122–23
Christmas, 15, 40, 195
church meetings and attendance, 42–43
cigarettes, 151
Clark, J. Reuben, Jr., 57, 86
Clayton, William, 4
cleanliness, of missionaries, 76

club meetings, 54–56
Communist Party, 171–73
Communist regime, 173–78, 180–90, 195, 202–5, 209–14, 219–23
concentration camps, 141–42, 144
conversion, of missionaries, 69–70
Curda, Karel, 145
currency exchange, 109–12, 115–16
Czech Kindertransport, 122
Czechoslovakia
approach to missionary work in, 43–50
attitude toward Americans in, 139
children evacuated from, 122–23
Christmas in, 40
Church eliminated in, 188
under Communist regime, 171–78, 180–90, 195, 202–5, 219–20, 221–23
condition of Saints in, 202–5
dedication of, for missionary work, 21, 61, 106–7, 137–38, 169
deportation or imprisonment of Church members in, 139–40
economic situation in, 197–98
German takeover of, 84–85, 92, 99–104
Heber J. Grant visits, 57–60
Joseph Fielding Smith visits, 106–8
Joseph Toronto called to, 23–25
last baptisms in, before WWII, 107–8
marriage in, 64, 98
missionaries evacuated from, 87–89, 91, 107, 117–22, 123–24
missionaries expelled from, 180–81, 183–88, 189–90
missionaries return to, 97–98
Czechoslovakia (*continued*)
Nazi crimes in, 142–47
people of, 42, 178
political situation in, 27, 50–53, 94–97
Prague Spring in, 220–21
press in, 60–61
Relief Society in, 38–39
resistance to Church in, 22–23, 46–50
Toronto children's experiences in, 155–60, 162–64
Torontos host visitors from, 196
Torontos visit, 198–207, 209
Wally as Moses of, 223–24
Wally expelled from, 214–15
Wally returns to, following evacuation, 92–93
Wally returns to, following WWII, 132–36
Wally's efforts in, 25–26
Wally's last visit to, 209–15
Wally visits government officials in, 209–14
World War II's impact on, 138–39
Czechoslovak Mission
advice for missionaries in, 75–76, 78–79
basketball game in, 179–80
under Communist regime, 173–78
conferences in, 178–79
discouragement in, 93–94
economic difficulties in, 161–62
Ezra Taft Benson visits, 136–38
following WWII, 152–53
government records concerning, 170–71
history and record for, 186–87
increase in missionaries in, 170
and Karlstejn monument, 137–38

Czechoslovak Mission (*continued*)
Martha called as president of, 218–19
Martha returns to, 151–52
Martha's delayed arrival in, 148–50
Martha's responsibilities in, 38–39, 167
during missionaries' absence, 91–92
missionaries called to, 147–48
mission home in, 22, 131, 139, 150, 154
Nazi soldier communes with, 103–4
opening of, 20–22
problems with missionaries in, 71–75
proselytizing process in, 43–50, 152–54, 168–69, 174–75, 177–78, 203
reminded of baptismal covenants, 98–99
saved from closure, 104–6
success in, 26–27, 45–46, 65–67, 69–70, 179
Wally called back to, 131–32
Wally called to, 19, 20
Wally called to preside over, 33–35
Wally prepares Saints in, 219–20
Wally released from, 27, 124–25
Wally remains president of, 194–96
Wally's authority in, 77–78
Wally's spiritual experience in, 129
welfare supplies for members in, 140–41, 195
World War II's impact on, 82–83, 86, 99–100, 102
young adults in, 167–68, 179

D

Dees, Elder, 107, 124
Děkanovský, Miroslav, 220
Depression, 23–24
discouragement
of Czechoslovakian Saints, 199, 202–3
in Czechoslovak Mission, 69–70, 93–94
in missionaries, 59, 71–72
dollars, possession and exchange of, 109–12, 115, 116
Dolores (girlfriend), 17, 25, 29
dream, of Giuseppe Taranto, 2
Drtina, Prokop, 171–72, 173
Dubček, Alexander, 220
Durd'áková, Ljuba, 190

E

Eden, Sir Robert Anthony, 83
English clubs, 54–55
Eyring, Henry B., 129

F

family history records, 207, 211
family history work, 67
fasting, 61–62, 77
fellowshipping, 130
Felt, Etta, 7–9, 11, 12, 13–15, 24
Ferrin, Josiah, 30
Ferrin, Martha Bronson, 30

G

Gabcik, Josef, 144–45
Gaeth, Arthur, 20–21, 41, 188
Garff, Mark, 123–24

genealogical records, 207, 211
genealogy work, 67
Germans, deported from Czechoslovakia, 139–40
Germany
  Albert serves in, 6–7
  Wally serves in, 17–19
Gestapo, missionaries arrested by, 109–17, 119–20
girls, as mission distraction, 72–74
Glasnerová Veněčková, Elfieda (Frieda), 141
Goering, Hermann, 82
gossip, 39
Gottwald, Klement, 173
government officials, Wally visits, in Czechoslovakia, 209–14
Grant, Heber J., 19–20, 24, 57–60

H

Heydrich, Reinhard, 143–45
Hitler, Adolf, 81, 83–84, 144–46
homosexual temptations, 74–75
Horáková, Milada, 188
humor, 16, 36–37, 53, 114

I

Indians, 30

J

Jacobs, Alexander, 95
Jacobs, Heber, 131–34, 136
Jews
  evacuated from Czechoslovakia, 122–23
  persecution of, 94–97
Jews (*continued*)
  treatment of, during WWII, 141–42
Johansson, Anna Catharina, 6
Johnson, Alden, 182–84
Jones, Eleanor, 5–6

K

Karel Boromaeus Greek Orthodox Church, 145
Karlstejn, 61, 107, 137–38
Kimball, Edward P., 20
kitchen appliances, 14–15
Kiwanis Club, 130
Klopfer, Elder, 123
Kotulán, Jaroslav, 92
Kovářová Campora, Olga, 204–5
Kralickova, Martha, 22
Krejčy, Sister, 162
Kubis, Jan, 144–45
Kubiska, Rudolf, 119, 187, 211
Kučerová, Zdenka, 190

L

Lee, Robert E., 109–17, 124
Le Havre, 132–34, 151
Ležáky, 144–46
Lidice, 142–47
Lorek, Jar, 55
Lyman, Richard R., 63, 128
Lyon, Ed, 148

M

Mabey, Mel, 74–75, 77, 162, 181, 185, 186–87
magazine and newspaper articles, 60–61. *See also* newsletters

Marková, Sister, 157
marriage, 64–65, 98
Masaryk, Alice, 62
Masaryk, Jan, 173
Masaryk, Tomás, 173
masquerade ball, 53
McKay, David O., 33–35, 54, 131, 197–98, 199, 201, 207, 209–10
McKay, Thomas E., 86, 92, 118–19
media, in missionary work, 66. *See also* magazine and newspaper articles; newsletters
Mehr, Kahlile B., 79, 87, 124–25, 167, 179, 180–81
"Melody Boys," 53, 54
Merrell, Brother, 72–73
Middleton, Tony, 25
Miller, Vern, 161, 165
Ministry of Health and Welfare, 211
Ministry of Interior, 207, 211–14
Ministry of Religious Affairs, 211–14
missionary conversion, 69–70
missionary training, 69–70
Moench, Louis, 192
Mohl, Dr., 96–97
Moravek, Frantisek, 144
Morrell, Ed, 170, 194
Morrell, Norma Toronto, 11, 67–68, 194
Moses, 223–24
Moulton, Asael, 92, 110–17, 123, 124
Munich Diktat (Munich Pact), 92
Murdock, Franklin J., 86
music
    Heber J. Grant's love for, 58
    missionary work through, 53, 54
Mutual Improvement Association General Board, 130

N

Nauvoo, Illinois, 3–5
Nauvoo Temple, 3–5
Nazis
    crimes of, 141–47
    methods of, 125
    missionaries arrested by, 109–17, 119–20
    occupy Czechoslovakia, 99–104
Nedela, Dr., 55
newsletters, 61–62, 75–77. *See also* magazine and newspaper articles
Nosek, Václav, 171–72

O

oncological hospital, 207
opera, 36–37

P

Pansky Club, 55, 56
Payne, Rulon S., 109–17, 119–23
peanut butter, 162
photos, illegal, 50–52
Pinecrest, 32
Pioneer Day, 61
Pioneers, 159–60
Poland, invasion of, 121, 124
Potter, Mr., 52, 111–14
Prague Spring, 220–21
pranks, 16, 158
prayer, 76–77
preaching, 66–67
press, 60–61
priesthood, 206
priesthood blessings, 65, 202, 218
public meetings, 42–50, 88, 209
public relations, 60–61

R

rationing, 157–58, 161–62, 185
reactivation of Church members, 130
Red Cross, 130
Rees, Alfred, 85, 86
Relief Society, 38–39, 167
Relief Society handbook, 63–64
Roosevelt, Franklin D., 122
Roubíček, Josef, 92, 197
Russian soldiers, 135–36
Russon, John, 197

S

same-sex attraction, 74–75
Schuschnigg, Kurt von, 83–84
secret police, 113, 173–75
seminary, 128–29
Seventh-day Adventists, 180
Sharp, Harlow, 32
Sharp, John, 30–31
Sharp, Sally Luella Ferrin, 30–31, 40
Slánský, Rudolf, 188–89
Smith, Jesse Evans, 106–7
Smith, Joseph Fielding, 105–8, 120–22, 124
Šnederfler, Jiří, 179, 220–21, 222–23
soap, 151
Sokol Slet, 87, 209–11
"Some Socio-psychological Aspects of the Czecho-Slovakian Crisis of 1938–39" (Toronto), 128–29
Sonne, Alma, 178
Spartakiada, 209–11
spirituality
- of missionaries, 69–70
- and success in missionary work, 65–67

Star: The Czechoslovakian Mission Newsletter, 75–77
Světozor magazine, 60
Switzerland, following WWII, 134

T

Taggart, Spencer, 81
talks, advice for giving, 78–79
Talmage, James E., 63
Taranto, Giuseppe, 1–3. *See also* Toronto, Joseph
technology, in missionary work, 66
temple marriage, 64–65
Terezín concentration camp, 141–42
Tingey, Dale, 77–78, 168, 219–20
tongues, gift of, 6
Toronto, Alan, 11
Toronto, Albert, 6–9, 11, 12, 13–14, 23–24
Toronto, Allen, 114, 130
Toronto, Carma, 160–61, 193
Toronto, Carol, 100–102, 155–56
Toronto, David, 156–57, 192
Toronto, Joseph, 3–6, 9. *See also* Taranto, Giuseppe
Toronto, Joseph (Wally's brother), 11, 23–25
Toronto, Judy, 155
Toronto, Marion
- adjusts to Czechoslovakia, 39
- birth of, 33
- develops feelings for Vern Miller, 164–65
- dyes eyelashes, 163–64
- evacuated from Czechoslovakia, 88
- followed by secret police, 175
- life of, in Czechoslovakia, 162–63
- on life under Communist regime, 222–23

Toronto, Marion (*continued*)
and Martha's mental breakdown, 192
sneaks out of hotel room, 127–28
Toronto, Martha Sharp
background of, 29–30
and birth of Carol Toronto, 100–102
and birth of Robert Toronto, 40
called back to Czechoslovak Mission, 131–32
called to preside over Czechoslovak Mission, 33–35
celebrates Christmas in Czechoslovakia, 40
courtship and marriage of, 32–33
education of, 31–32
evacuated from Czechoslovakia, 88, 92–93, 118, 120–21
and expulsion of missionaries from Czechoslovakia, 181, 184–86
and extension for Czechoslovak Mission, 106
family of, 30–31
financial concerns of, 39
health problems of, 39–40
interests of, 196
learns Czech language, 35–36
makes cake with rotten egg, 162
and missionaries arrested by Gestapo, 110, 115, 117
and missionaries called to Czechoslovak Mission, 147–48
as mission mother, 37–39, 152, 167, 193, 207
as interim mission president, 218–19
as mother, 160–61
and Nazi occupation of Czechoslovakia, 102–3
Toronto, Martha Sharp (*continued*)
readjusts to life in United States, 130–31
and Relief Society, 38–39
returns to Czechoslovakia, 97, 151–52
returns to United States, 127–28
separation of Wally and, 148–50
suffers mental breakdown, 191–93
visits Czechoslovakia, 198–207, 209
and Wally's bird imitations, 36–37
Toronto, Norma, 11, 67–68, 194
Toronto, Robert "Bob" Sharp
birth of, 40
evacuated from Czechoslovakia, 88
and expulsion of missionaries from Czechoslovakia, 186
life of, in Czechoslovakia, 155–60
and Martha's mental breakdown, 193
and Nazi occupation of Czechoslovakia, 102–3
sneaks out of hotel room, 127–28
Toronto, Ruth, 11
Toronto, Wallace "Wally" Felt
adolescence of, 15–16
birth of, 1, 11
callings held by, 196–97
childhood of, 11–15
courage of, 68
courtship and marriage of, 32–33
death of, 217–18, 220–21, 224
education of, 128–30
events surrounding life of, x–xi
expelled from Czechoslovakia, 187–88

Toronto, Wallace "Wally" Felt (*continued*)
as father, 156–57, 164–65
financial concerns of, 23–24, 39
last visit of, to Czechoslovakia, 209–15
missionaries' respect for, 77–78
as mission president, 41–43
as Moses of Czechoslovakia, 223–24
occupations of, 128–29, 193–94
personality of, 67–68
released as mission president, 124–25
returns to Czechoslovakia, 92–93, 132–36
returns to United States, 127–28, 193–94
sense of humor of, 16, 36–37, 53, 114
transferred to Czechoslovakia, 20
visits Czechoslovakia, 198–207, 209
trolley tracks, greased, 16
"Truth Must Prevail," 147

V

Veněčková, Frieda, 93
Vesela, Marie, 197–98, 201
Vojkůvka, Gad, 67, 181–82, 205, 210, 223
Vojkůvka, Otakar Karel, 107, 222
Vojkůvka, Valerie, 107
Vrba, Ceněk, 205, 207, 220

W

Wallace, George B., 2
Ward, Brother, 72
Warriner, Doreen, 122
weddings, 64–65
Welch, Charles, 12
welfare supplies, 140–41, 195
Whipperman, Donald, 148
Widtsoe, John A., 20, 21–22, 188
Williams, Brother, 72–73
Winton, Nicholas, 122–23
Wondra, Johann, 68, 222
Wood, Evelyn, 121
Wood, M. Douglas, 86
World War II
aftermath of, 132–35, 136, 138–39, 146–47, 151–52
Church members endure hardships of, 141–42
evacuation of children during, 122–23
events leading to, 81–85
German invasion of Poland, 121, 124
German takeover of Czechoslovakia, 99–104
impact of, on missionary work, 86
and interment of American fliers in Czechoslovakia, 139
Joseph Fielding Smith's prophecy regarding, 121–22
last baptisms in Czechoslovakia before, 107–8
missionaries evacuated due to, 87–89, 91, 117–22, 123–24
political situation in Czechoslovakia during, 94–97

World War II (*continued*)
and razing of Lidice and Ležáky, 142–47
return to Czechoslovakia during, 92–93

Y

Young, Brigham, 2, 3, 5, 9, 60
young adults, 167–68, 179

ABOUT THE AUTHOR

Mary Jane Woodger, EdD, is a professor of Church history and doctrine at Brigham Young University. Born and raised in American Fork and Salt Lake City, Utah, Mary Jane has always had a great love for teaching. After obtaining a bachelor's degree in home economics education, she taught home economics and American history in Salt Lake City. She then completed her master of education degree at Utah State University, and received from Brigham Young University a doctor of education degree in educational leadership, with a minor in Church history and doctrine.

Since then, Dr. Woodger has written and published over a dozen books, including three books about the life and teachings of David O. McKay, as well as a book on the timely subject of self-esteem. She has also authored numerous articles on doctrinal, historical, and educational subjects. These articles have appeared in various academic journals, as well as the *Journal of Book of Mormon Studies*, the *Church News*, the *Ensign*, and the *Religious Educator*. Awards Dr. Woodger has received include the Best Article of the Year Award from the Utah Historical Society, the Brigham Young University Faculty Women's Association Teaching Award, the Harvey B. Black and Susan Easton Black Outstanding Publication Award, and the Alice Louise Reynolds Women-in-Scholarship Honor. Dr. Woodger's current research interests include twentieth-century Church history, Latter-day Saint women's history, and Church education.